MANAGING GLOBALIZATION
IN THE AGE OF
INTERDEPENDENCE

George C. Lodge

Johannesburg • Oxford
San Diego • Sydney • Toronto

Cover Design: Paul Bond
Interior Design, Page Composition: Lee Ann Hubbard
Figures: Susan Odelson, Norine Spears, Judy Whalen
Editor: JoAnn Padgett
Production Editor: Dawn Kilgore
Editorial Assistants: Kathleen Deming, Susan Rachmeler

Published by Pfeiffer & Company
8517 Production Avenue
San Diego, CA 92121-2280, United States of America

Editorial Offices: (619) 578-5900, FAX (619) 578-2042
Orders: (USA) (606) 647-3030, FAX (606) 647-3034

Printed in the United States of America.

Printing 1 2 3 4 5 6 7 8 9 10

Library of Congress Cataloging-in Publication Data

Lodge, George C.
    Managing globalization in the age of interdependence
/ George Lodge.
      p.   cm. — (Warren Bennis executive briefing series)
    Includes index.
    ISBN 0-89384-271-0 (hard : alk. paper)
    1. International economic relations.   2. International business
enterprises—Management.   I. Title.   II. Series.
HF1359.L63 1995
658' .049—dc20   95-17969
                                            CIP

Dedication

For N.K.L.

Contents

EDITOR'S PREFACE   VI

AUTHOR'S PREFACE   VII

FOREWORD   VIII

INTRODUCTION   XI

1: THE PHENOMENON OF GLOBALIZATION   1

World Trade and Investment Trends   2
    Foreign Direct Investment   4
Convergence and Conflict   10
    The Supply Side   11
    The Demand Side   17
    Globalization and the Environment   18
    The Wealth Gap   23
    The Migrants   25
    Culture Clash   26
    Who Decides? What Are the Criteria?   28
Summary   29

2: THE COLLAPSE OF THE OLD PARADIGM   31

The Old World Order   32
The Paradigm Concept   33
Breakdown   36
    The IMF and Global Money   36
    The World Bank   41
    The General Agreement on Tariffs and
       Trade (GATT)   46
    The Asian Paradigm   48
Looking Backward   49
Looking Forward   51
    A New World Economic Organization   52
    New Initiatives Taking Shape   55
    The Montreal Protocol   57
Summary   59

3: GLOBAL LEADERSHIP   61

A Leadership Imperative   62

American Recovery   64
    The Trade Impact   64
    Lessons From the Japanese Economic
        National Strategy   65
    American Paradigm Shifts   69
    The Winning Asian Paradigm   70
The Role of Business   74
    Serving Community Needs   75
Sources of Authority   77
Toward Corporate Reponsibility   81
Summary   83

4: THE BASIS FOR GLOBAL CONSENSUS   85

Ideology Defined and Examined   86
Capitalism or What?   89
    Individualism Versus Communitarianism   91
Capitalism   94
Socialism   95
Communism   96
The Historical Roots   96
The Moral Bases   98
    The Protestant Ethic   99
    The Catholic Ethic   100
Communitarianism   103
The Chinese System   105
The Future   108
Summary   109

5: WORLD IDEOLOGY: VARIATIONS ON A
COMMUNITARIAN THEME   111

Communitarianism   113
Rights and Duties of Membership   117
Community Need   118
Active Planning State   120
Holism-Interdependence   120
Conclusion   123

NOTES   125

INDEX   127

Editor's Preface

How do you conduct business profitably and ethically in a world that is borderless, but bounded on all sides by economic, technological, and ecological forces beyond the control of the individuals they affect most? This is the question George Lodge wrestles with in *Managing Globalization in the Age of Interdependence.*

Lodge examines globalization, the increasing interdependence of the earth's people, in terms of the opportunities it offers and imperatives it commands. Globalization impacts trade in goods and services, the movement of labor, the spread of information, and capital flows. Trade is managed by governments and by businesses; open markets in a world of free trade do not exist.

This new reality of globalization means a nation's economic and political autonomy will depend on its ability to compete successfully in the world economy. International trade and foreign investment are critical, but social tensions, culture clashes, and ecological pressures must be reckoned with as well.

Political disintegration and change have eroded the power of old economic institutions that once stabilized the world. Cultural disintegration has dissolved powerful social bonds. Lodge's point hits hard: some 100 million workers leave their countries annually, seeking jobs. The wages paid these migrants, almost 10% of the total value of world trade in services, is earned outside their home country yet flows back to these countries; migrant money comes home, even if migrants can't.

As globalization forces convergence around the most competitive practices and the most powerful technologies, it also forces increased awareness that the planet's fragile environment, a "commons which we share together," is in terrible jeopardy.

Citizens must think about globalization and how to manage the tensions it creates. Choices must be made. New leaders who can make them must emerge.

The leaders could be the most powerful, making decisions based on wisdom or whimsy, and the world would have to live with the consequences. However, Lodge promotes a more sensible alternative, "collective leadership," a shared consensus among the world's people. The challenge of globalization is the creation of collective leadership and of new institutions to manage these international tensions.

Like Marjorie Kelly, publisher of *Business Ethics,* Lodge sees the potential for "workplaces that are healthy for employees, of corporate citizens who are powerful yet responsive, and of a corporate community that is a humane presence on the earth."

Warren Bennis
Santa Monica, California, 1995

Author's Preface

I am most grateful to Warren Bennis, Bill Pfeiffer, and Dick Roe for having invited me to write this book. Even though I have been teaching master's candidates and executives at Harvard Business School about aspects of globalization for 30 years, it never would have occurred to me to tackle the whole thing in a short book.

The concept of globalization is so broad, deep, amorphous and mysterious that academics like me tend to approach it in pieces, making use of existing specializations such as economics, political science, or sociology to approach the subjects it covers. After all, there is no expert in globalization nor probably will there ever be unless he or she is a special emissary from the divine.

And yet, as I discovered writing this book, approaching globalization as a whole, picking and choosing academic specializations as they are useful, has been worthwhile, at least for me. It has forced a recognition of the interconnectedness of things; a realization that the old connections that held the world together and gave it a certain direction have gone; and provided a glimpse of what the new connections might be.

I owe a special debt of gratitude to many at Harvard Business School who over the years and with this project have generously supported me: Dean John H. McArthur; Senior Associate Dean and Director of Research, F. Warren McFarlan; and Professor W. Earl Sasser, Jr., chairman of the Advanced Management Program. My thanks go also to many friends and colleagues on the Harvard Faculty who have kindly read all or parts of this book: Sharon Daloz Parks, Jack S. High, Thomas K. McCraw, Forest L. Reinhardt, Bruce R. Scott, Lynn Sharp Paine, Debora Spar, and Richard Vietor. Michael I. Stevenson of Baker Library collected much useful data, as did Research Associate Robert Hochman, who also provided valuable editorial advice. My assistant, Lois Smith, and the staff of Harvard's Word Processing Center were, as always, indispensable to the preparation of the manuscript.

In addition, Michael E. Ebert of International Business-Government Counsellors, Inc., and Edward M. Graham of the Institute for International Economics, shared their knowledge of global economic phenomena; and Michael S. Teitelbaum of the Sloane Foundation provided useful data regarding global migration. I am deeply grateful also to JoAnn Padgett for her imaginative and careful editing.

Finally, my deepest thanks go to my wife, Nancy Kunhardt Lodge, for her love and patience.

While these people deserve credit for what is good and true in this book, I alone am responsible for errors.

George C. Lodge
Boston, Massachusetts, June 1995

Foreword

"Globalization" has become one of today's buzz words, but that doesn't make the phenomenon any less real. Nor does the apparent declining public interest in world affairs take away any of its impact. The globalization of communications, media, finance, trade and politics has become a fact of life, changing the daily lives of citizens in myriad ways—whether they know it, or like it, or not. And many will not.

Though globalization has already transformed the way we do business, our thinking about how it relates to national and international interests has not progressed very far. None of this is surprising. Globalization is hard to get your head around. The scale and speed of measureless instantaneous worldwide economic transactions is dizzying and beyond the reach of governments—the value of internationally traded goods alone approached an estimated $3.8 trillion in 1993; rocketing from $309 billion in 1950. Principally driven by international trade and investment through the actions of some 300 giant multinational corporations—not governments—globalization has greatly complicated relations between and among nations.

Thus, long before the fall of the Berlin Wall, globalization had begun to forge a new international reality. Whatever the post-Cold War paradigm will be, it must take into account the pervasive effects of globalization. Governments often neither know nor understand what is happening and policy making becomes even more problematic. What, then should decision makers do?

In this succinct, vivid, and helpful text, George Lodge helps us all get a grip on what globalization is and what it portends—not just for the bottom line but also for the common good. Lodge provides a wealth of empirical information on the effects of globalization across a wide spectrum of national and international life. He also offers some thought-provoking suggestions about how business and government might work together to make the most out of today's globalized environment.

Globalization, growth, and regionalization are helpful to develop or rejuvenate economies. Indeed, over the long term, increasing global integration through trade and investment will vastly improve the well-being of developing and industrial countries alike—helping to mitigate hostilities, build confidence, and peacefully channel competition. But this process also entails difficult adjustments in both developed and less developed countries. Not everyone is finding a niche in the world economy—many have fallen between the cracks, if not into chasms of chaos.

Beyond the leading industrial nations, integrative economic processes are still in their infancy. Building up economic interrelationships will not be a sufficient deterrent to disintegration and conflict for the foreseeable future. Yet there is little willingness on the part of many publics to invest in domestic and international efforts—whether social programs, development aid, relief operations, or peacekeeping—beyond those that pay them direct economic dividends.

In an age when many if not most problems—socioeconomic, environmental, or military—must be solved multilaterally or not at all—how is it possible to build political space for international cooperation and institution-building? Lodge rejects the notion that globalization has unleashed forces too vast, too fast, and too profit driven for national decision makers to harness in ways that serve the needs and goals of national and international communities. He believes that Asian societies show the way by employing close government and business partnerships, channeling markets toward meeting national needs.

Contrary to the "Clash of Civilizations" theory, Lodge sees a gradual process of convergence between East and West, with the West moving away from a traditional, "laissez faire" premise toward a more "communitarian" model where "the needs of the community are becoming increasingly distinct from, and more important than, what individual consumers may desire."

The future lies, Lodge believes, in forging a new consensus on how to better manage trade and growth for the public good and in constructing new institutions—advocating even a World Economic Organization, not just a World Trade Organization—that better reflect the interconnectedness of trade, investment, and monetary policies. A thriving, confident United States will be indispensable to that effort; only such an America would be willing and able to do the job.

Considering all the hype, one might expect any book about globalization to include generous slices of "globaloney." George Lodge's fast-moving, tightly argued brief not only informs but also convinces the reader that globalization is not baloney, but serious food for thought. This is the tantalizing first course of what will be a long and lively discussion.

Morton I. Abramowitz, President
Carnegie Endowment for International Peace

Introduction

Globalization is a fact and a process. The fact is that the world's people and nations are more interdependent than ever before and becoming more so. The measures of interdependence are global flows of such things as trade, investment, and capital, and the related degradation of the ecosystem on which all life depends, a degradation that constantly reminds us that we are passengers on a spaceship, or, more ominously, a lifeboat.

The process of globalization is both technological and human. Technologically, new systems of global information and communication foster and link the agents of globalization—multinational corporations, sometimes with governments as their partners. On the human side, globalization is pulled by exploding consumer desires, especially in the rapidly growing countries of Asia, and pushed by ingenious corporate managers, who themselves are driven by a variety of urges—to serve their communities or their shareholders, to gain wealth and power, or simply to exercise their skills and talents.

Globalization is a promise of efficiency in spreading the good things of life to those who lack them. It is also a menace to those who are left behind, excluded from its benefits. It means convergence and integration; it also means conflict and disintegration. It is upsetting old ways, and challenging cultures, religions, and systems of belief. It accentuates global diversity. Imagine the world to be a global village of 1,000 inhabitants. Today, 564 of them would be Asian, 210 Europeans, 86 Africans, 80 South Americans, and 60 North Americans. By the year

This book asks whether there is some overarching value system within which a consensus seems possible. And it explores what that system might be.

2020, Africans will outnumber Europeans 185 to 107, and Asians, with 577 people, will continue to be the clear majority.

The people in our village will have very different ways of thinking about ultimate reality and the community: There will be 300 Christians, 175 Moslems, 128 Hindus, 55 Buddhists, 47 Animists, 4 Jews, about 210 "other," and 210 who will profess to have no religion at all. Fortune has discriminated among our people: 60 control half of the income, 500 are hungry, and 600 live in shanty towns.[1]

Whether globalization is a positive force in the world will depend upon how it is controlled. Thus, although it appears to be an economic and technological phenomenon, it is also a political one. Twenty years ago Harvard Sociologist Daniel Bell wrote:

> The decisive social change taking place in our time—because of the interdependence of men and the aggregative character of economic actions, the rise of externalities and social costs, and the need to control the effects of technical change—is the subordination of the economic function to the political order. The autonomy of the economic order (and the power of the men who run it) is coming to an end..."[2]

In a sense, he was right. But in assuming that a "political order" would have the will and the capacity to control "the economic order," he may have underestimated the power and importance of multinational corporations and overestimated humanity's capacity to create political institutions that serve the appropriate purposes of globalization.

Economic and technological engines are running at full speed; however, the political mechanisms to control them are either nonexistent or in trouble. Indeed, even as economic integration proceeds apace, it is accompanied by political disintegration. The old order of the Cold

War, which in its day provided a form of stability, has dissolved. One associated consequence has been strife in Russia and Eastern Europe; tribal clashes in Somalia, Angola, South Africa and other parts of Africa; and uncertainty in the relationships among the West Japan, and China, between the two Koreas, and among other Asian countries.

At the same time, multinational corporations and their technological infrastructure span the world, merging, acquiring, cooperating, and competing with dizzying speed. National governments vie for their favors but increasingly cannot control them. And such transnational apparatus as exists are inadequate to the task.

At the end of World War II, the world, led by the United States, readied itself for globalization by forming the United Nations and its sister institutions, the International Monetary Fund, the World Bank, and the General Agreement on Tariffs and Trade (which became the World Trade Organization in 1995). There was even talk of a world government. Then the Cold War set in and the world divided—the "free" part against the "evil empire." The Cold War paralyzed globalization, replacing it with regionalization exemplified by NATO, the European Community, the Atlantic Alliance, and other pacts, initiated and led by the United States.

Now, the Cold War is over. The UN has burst into new life and we hope it will succeed in its role as a global caretaker. Yet the governance of globalization remains weak and confused. And the capacity of the United States to lead, as it once did, is in question.

There is no consensus about the purposes that globalization serves and the direction it should take. It proceeds, therefore, in limbo; as it intensifies, it highlights conflicts about its effects and priorities. These conflicts arise from different systems for interpreting values. This book asks whether there is some overarching value system within which a consensus seems possible. And it explores what that system might be. In so doing it defines the problems accompanying globalization and attempts to clarify the choices to solve those problems.

It is not, however, about solutions so much as it is about a way of thinking.

The literature on globalization, of which there is a great deal, shares a common trait: it takes a specialized approach. There are books and papers on globalization as an economic factor, as a trade phenomenon, as the creation of multinational corporations, or the manifestation of this or that technology. There are works by political scientists, economists and experts of all kinds. But I have been unable to find any attempt to view globalization holistically, drawing together all of its elements, seeking to find the interactions among them, and thus to portray it in all of its dimensions.

I believe such an approach is necessary, especially for the managers of the chief agents of globalization, multinational corporations. They must realize the full reach of their activities in order to understand their impact and manage them accordingly.

I hope also that this book will help all those who are involved in the management of globalization—in business, government, universities, and elsewhere—to inspect the assumptions that they hold about it. Beyond this, it will also help them to inspect their assumptions about their own values, and perhaps, if need be, to renovate them in the light of globalization.

We proceed now to

- ♦ Analyze the phenomenon of globalization and the convergence and the conflicts it is causing

- ♦ Examine and appraise the transnational governmental institutions available to manage it

- ♦ Explore the sources of initiative and leadership for managing it in the future

- ♦ Consider the basis for a global consensus within an ideological framework

In spite of many variations and differences, an ideological framework can be composed so that globalization may serve the cause of humanity. This framework, which 20 years ago I named communitarianism, has an existential aspect and a normative one: It is happening. It is being forced by global pressures. It is inevitable. But it is by no means necessarily good; it is no utopia; and it will take different forms in different places. Some will be more authoritarian, some less so; some more austere, some more liberal. Whether the world gets the best or the worst of communitarianism depends upon how these choices are made by its political leaders and business managers.

What I argue is that these choices all lie within a communitarian framework; it provides the language all will use. The purpose of the book is to reveal the choices and to help managers make the best of them.

OVERVIEW

- ♦ The Trend Toward Globalization
- ♦ World Trade and Investment Trends
- ♦ Convergence and Conflict:
  Supply and Demand
  Spread of Technology
  Human Resource Management
  Economy, Trade, and the Environment
  The Wealth Gap
  Migration and Culture Clash

THE PHENOMENON OF GLOBALIZATION

1

Globalization is the process whereby the world's people are becoming increasingly interconnected in all facets of their lives—cultural, economic, political, technological, and environmental.

A major impetus to globalization is the ever-increasing flow of information, money, and goods through multinational corporations (MNCs). "Transnationals often rely on specialized production using lower-price labor from one region, cheap materials from another, markets in a third, and financing from a fourth."[1]

All of this activity threatens the world's fragile ecosystem and adds to the confusion surrounding the political disintegration that has followed the end of the Cold War.

Because there are winners and

Globalize: to extend to other or all parts of the globe; make worldwide

Reuters/Bettmann

losers, there is a need to manage the tensions that globalization creates. Old paradigms do not address the reality of globalization. And while its results are desirable for many, for others it means a world of unwelcome surprises.

WORLD TRADE AND INVESTMENT TRENDS

The current rate of accelerated world trade shows almost yearly increases since 1950, when it stood at $308 billion; in 1993, internationally traded goods were valued at $3.8 trillion.[2]

Growth is the result of the following factors:

♦ Expanded commercial opportunities and intensified global competition

♦ Liberalized trade laws

♦ Reduced transportation and communication costs

♦ Advocacy of free trade by the United States and other industrial countries

♦ A shift among developing countries from inward-looking, protectionist strategies to the promotion of exports and open economies

♦ The growth of multinational corporations with widely dispersed administration, manufacturing, and distribution

The 1990-91 Gulf War was financed by foreigners, mostly Saudis, Germans, and Japanese. The Pentagon estimates the cost at $38 billion; foreign contributions totaled $52 billion, so the U.S. could make a profit if it collected all pledges. [3]

One measure of globalization is the flow of capital, which tripled during the 1980s and continues to grow in the 1990s. Take, for example, borrowing and lending. In 1980, cross-border lending by international banks was

$324 billion. By 1991 it was $7.5 trillion; and during that time the volume of transactions in equities also grew at a compound rate of 28% a year from $120 billion to $1.4 trillion a year.

Exchange rates are symbols of interdependency. The daily turnover in foreign exchange is estimated at about a trillion dollars. Technology makes transactions instantaneous and contributes to the illusory nature of sovereignty. As Mexico learned in December, 1994, billions of dollars can leave a national economy within hours if exchange rates get out of line."

The most common ways to do this are to

♦ Purchase devalued currency on the open market or raise interest rates through the central bank or regulatory institution

♦ Increase exports

♦ Reduce government expenditures

These are apt to be politically difficult actions because they are recessionary and painful in the short-run.

In July 1992, the German Bundesbank raised interest rates to control inflation and to attract foreign borrowing to finance reunification with East Germany. But the effects were inevitably global. The mark became more desirable as its value went up relative to other currencies, such as the British pound.

Under the ERM, Britain was obliged to bring the pound back in line by raising its value, which meant raising interest rates. With an ailing economy and 10 percent unemployment, Britain was unwilling to comply. Traders descended and sold pounds in anticipation of a

> ## The Meaning of Interdependency
>
> **To further European integration, in the early 1990s the 12 member nations of the European Community were striving for monetary union and ultimately a single currency. Economic integration required stable currencies tied to one another through what was called the Exchange Rate Mechanism (ERM). The Deutsche mark, Europe's strongest currency, was the benchmark against which other currencies were rated.**

Around 800 A.D., Charlemagne established the first European unified monetary system with a common currency.[4]

Reuters/Bettmann

devaluation. In September of that year, Britain was forced to abandon the ERM. Other countries soon followed suit.

At the same time, across the Atlantic, the Federal Reserve Board in Washington, D.C., had to respond to the Bundesbank's decision by keeping U.S. interest rates high enough to prevent money from flowing out to Germany and to keep it flowing in to fund America's huge debts. Thus, the Federal Reserve Bank was unable to oblige the Bush administration, which wanted lower interest rates to end the U.S. recession before November's election day. It is too much to say that the Bundesbank decision in July 1992 elected Bill Clinton, but it certainly helped. That is the meaning of interdependency.

Prior to the October 1991 reunification of East and West Germany, the average West German had an annual income of $20,440 and East Germans less than $5,000.[8]

FOREIGN DIRECT INVESTMENT

If the principal driver of globalization is international trade and investment, the vehicles are multinational corporations. Global corporations create and deploy foreign direct investment (FDI). There are about 35,000 with 170,000 foreign affiliates. But power is concentrated in the top 300, which account for 25 percent of the world's productive assets. The top 100 hold $3.1 trillion of worldwide assets and account for about 50 percent of all cross-border FDI.[5]

Japanese investment abroad is the fastest growing, but still it is less than one-third that of either the United States or Europe.[6] The U.S. Office of Technology Assessment reported that, since the late 1960s, U.S.-based companies have dropped off the list of the world's 500 largest firms at the rate of six firms per year or about 150 firms. They have been replaced by Japanese firms.[7]

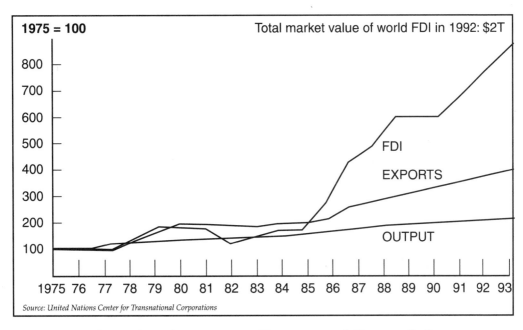

Foreign Direct Investment, Exports, and Output Index

Since 1985, world output has been growing slowly. Trade, as measured by exports, has been growing somewhat more. The most dramatic growth has occurred in foreign direct investment At the beginning of 1992, the total market value of foreign investment worldwide was around $2 trillion.[11]

Japanese companies are the dominant investors in Asia, American companies in Latin America, and Western European companies in Eastern and central Europe, as well as much of Africa.[9]

Many governments regard foreign investment with understandable ambivalence. With foreign ownership of national assets there is an inevitable loss of control and sovereignty.

> *However, if they are going to pay their debts, generate investment, create jobs, and secure the standard of living their people expect, governments must not only accept multinationals; they must court them.[10]*

Of an estimated 35,000 multinationals, just under half are from four countries: United States, Japan, Germany, Switzerland.[12]

The 25 Largest Nonfinancial Multinationals Ranked by Foreign Assets*

Rank	Industry	Country	Foreign assets $bn	Total assets $bn	Foreign sales $bn	% of total sales
1 Royal Dutch/Shell	Oil	Britain/Holland	n.a.	106.3	56.0†	49
2 Ford Motor	Cars and trucks	United States	55.2	173.7	47.3	48
3 General Motors	Cars and trucks	United States	52.6	180.2	37.3	31
4 Exxon	Oil	United States	51.6	87.7	90.5	86
5 IBM	Computers	United States	45.7	87.6	41.9	61
6 British Petroleum	Oil	Britain	39.7	59.3	46.6	79
7 Nestlé	Food	Switzerland	n.a.	27.9	33.0	98
8 Unilever	Food	Britain/Holland	n.a.	24.8	16.7†	42
9 Asea Brown Boveri	Electrical	Switzerland/Sweden	n.a.	30.2	22.7‡	85
10 Phillips Electronics	Electronics	Holland	n.a.	30.6	28.6‡	93
11 Alcatel Alsthom	Telecoms	France	n.a.	38.2	17.7	67
12 Mobil	Oil	United States	22.3	41.7	44.3	77
13 Fiat	Cars and trucks	Italy	19.5	66.3	15.8	33
14 Siemens	Electrical	Germany	n.a.	50.1	15.1‡	40
15 Hanson	Diversified	Britain	n.a.	27.7	5.6	46
16 Volkswagon	Cars and trucks	Germany	n.a.	41.9	27.5‡	65
17 Elf Aquitaine	Oil	France	17.0	42.6	12.2	38
18 Mitsubishi	Trading	Japan	16.7	73.8	41.2	32
19 General Electric	Diversified	United States	16.5	153.9	8.3	14
20 Mitsui	Trading	Japan	15.0	60.8	43.6	32
21 Matsushita Electric Industrial	Electronics	Japan	n.a.	59.1	16.6	40
22 News Corp.	Publishing	Australia	14.6	20.7	5.3	78
23 Ferruzzi/Montedison	Diversified	Italy	13.5	30.8	9.1	59
24 Bayer	Chemicals	Germany	n.a.	25.4	21.8	84
25 Roche Holding	Drugs	Switzerland	n.a.	17.9	6.8‡	96

Source: United Nations

*where not available, foreign assests have been estimated for ranking † outside Europe ‡ including export sales

Increasingly, trade and investment are connected; you can't have one without the other. Intrafirm trade—for example, Ford Europe selling to Ford U.S.—in the early '90s accounted for up to 40 percent of all U.S. trade.[13]
It is argued that direct investment is a prerequisite to exports, especially of technologically sophisticated products and services. Links to customers for such products and services can only be created through a foreign subsidiary. In Japan, low U.S. investment has contributed to relatively low penetration by U.S. exports.[14]

Rich and poor countries are competing to attract or retain foreign investment; it has become an increasingly significant share of a nation's total investment.

The bulk of foreign investment stems from and is funneled into large industrial countries. Between 1986 and 1990, investments from the United States, Japan, West Germany, France, and Britain increased from $67 billion to $162 billion, an annual growth rate of 26 percent. A United Nations study showed a trend away from foreign direct investment in labor-intensive manufacturing toward more capital-intensive industries, with technology-intensive businesses attracting an increasing portion.[15]

Global Impact of Foreign Investment

When a nation accepts foreign investment, it necessarily loses some control over its resources, as Canada discovered in the 1970s. Americans owned more than half of Canadian manufacturing industries and an even larger amount of its natural resources.[16] Decisions about plant closings, products, and sales were made at headquarters in the U.S. Dividend outflows impacted the nation's balance of payments and Canada was forced to borrow more from abroad. This resulted in higher interest rates at home and additional interest payments abroad.

In 1973, Canada sought liberation from foreigners by establishing the Foreign Investment Review Agency to screen and restrain foreign investment and promote domestic investors. Five years later, the government enacted the National Energy Plan to reduce foreign ownership of the oil industry to 50 percent. But the costs of such autonomy became politically unbearable. Foreign investment, the lifeblood of their economy, declined; unemployment soared; Canada's standard of living declined; and its foreign borrowing increased. It was hooked. It did not have the political will to assert its independence at the expense of its standard of living. Globalization had arrived.

Canada had to change the sign on the office door of the Foreign Investment Review Agency to read Investment Canada. Like a Siamese twin joined at the wallet, Canada was tied to the United States; the bond was secured in 1988 by the U.S.-Canada Free Trade Agreement and tightened further in 1993 with the North American Free Trade Agreement (NAFTA).

If Canada lacked the political will to change its development strategy, Mexico by the late 1980s apparently did not. Burdened in the early 1980s by more than $90 billion of foreign debt that it could not service, Mexico was forced to depart from its revolutionary aversion to foreign investment and, instead, to welcome it. In effect, Mexico went Canadian. Americans and other foreigners seized the chance to benefit from Mexico's low-cost labor.

The political reaction was severe, but Mexico's one-party political system gave greater

Reuters/Bettmann

Mexican President Salinas and U.S. President Bush meet in Agualeguas, Mexico, for talks in November 1990.

authority to the central government than did Canada's pluralistic democracy. Mexico was becoming a major competitor in the world economy. To make sure that it did not slip back into its old, inward-looking, protectionist ways, President Carlos Salinas de Gortari initiated NAFTA. The United States and Canada went along.

Mexico's reforms, however, illustrated the pain of globalization. The economic changes required by world competition, especially in agriculture, threatened the nation's traditional political structures. The Chiapas Indians fought to protect their *ejidos* (small, collective farms that were part of the promise of the Mexican Revolution) against modern farms, and Luis Colosio, the ruling party's chosen presidential candidate, was assassinated by the enemies of reform. The changes also threatened Mexico's cherished sovereignty.

After the assassination, the dollar value of the peso fell rapidly, eroding the high yield of Mexican bonds in which U.S. mutual funds had invested billions. Within hours, fund managers were on the telephone pressuring the Mexican government to continue the reforms, promising to pour in an additional $17 billion if the government did "the right thing."

But, as 1994 came to a close, the peso's value again plummeted, down 45 percent in two months, as foreign investors—mainly from the U.S.—withdrew their money. Mexico's continuing trade deficits had created anxiety about the country's global competitiveness, and thus about its ability to earn the dollars required to pay its debts. Financial panic was narrowly averted when, on January 31, 1995, President Clinton hastily put together a rescue package of loans and loan guarantees totalling nearly $50 billion.

Crucial to the success of Clinton's plan was the International Monetary Fund, which provided $17.8 billion, the largest loan it had ever made. The purpose of the plan was to build international investor confidence in the Mexican economy so that the reforms begun a

NAFTA provides for the eventual elimination of trade barriers separating Canada, Mexico, and the United States. In so doing, it opens the Mexican and Canadian economies to unprecedented competition, especially from the United States, forcing changes that are politically unsettling.

The new reality of globalization is that a nation's standard of living as well as its independence depend upon its capacity to compete successfully in the world economy.

By 1986, only 1% of Japan's assets were owned by foreign-controlled firms compared to 9% in the United States, 14% in Britain, and 17% in West Germany.

decade earlier could take effect and produce the economic growth required to keep Mexico a peaceful neighbor and to slow the illegal migration of Mexicans into the United States.

If Canada and Mexico have adopted strategies of welcoming foreign investment as well as foreign debt, Japan has done nearly the opposite. Japan's strategy includes high rates of savings and investment; allocation of resources to high-tech sectors that promise high returns; first-rate education and training; and capital markets and government policies that encourage firms to think long-term rather than short-term.

Japan typifies the Asian model in many respects. Its economy is externally focused, aimed at gaining market share in the world economy through exports. Most importantly it is oriented toward strengthening producers rather than encouraging consumers.[17]

Japan's approach to foreign investment has been highly selective, taking only what it needed and wanted. Furthermore it has a system of corporate organization, governmental policies, and a political structure that allowed it to implement the policies it designed.

CONVERGENCE AND CONFLICT

The new reality of globalization is that a nation's standard of living as well as its independence depend upon its capacity to compete successfully in the world economy. Globalization is forcing convergence around the most competitive practices.

On the supply side are such issues as education, training, human resource management, technological innovation, productivity, and the roles and relations of business and government. On the demand side the issues relate to making and marketing the goods and services that people want to buy.

Convergence does not come easily; it is fraught with conflict that results from

- ♦ Destruction of old and often cherished ways
- ♦ Tensions between environmentalists and trade specialists and economists
- ♦ Gaps between rich and poor
- ♦ Impact of migration and culture clash

THE SUPPLY SIDE

Technology

> *"Instant information lubricates world trade. You could telegraph overseas in 1866, but you couldn't fax images."*[19]

Convergence is both forced and facilitated by global information systems, television, faxes, fiber optics, and the like. Daniel Boorstin, the distinguished historian, described our age as one driven by

> *"the Republic of Technology (whose) supreme law... is convergence, the tendency for everything to become more like everything else."*[18]

One could argue that the break-up of the Soviet Union and its convergence with the rest of the world was inevitable once Radio Free Europe's messages from the outside world began to be communicated by satellite freed from jamming.

Education

Yet while competitiveness fosters convergence, it also breeds conflict. As technology becomes more complicated and essential, the necessity of rigorous and effective education to manage it becomes more obvious, again meaning convergence.

The global Internet has moved 8,000 white collar jobs in software design and manufacturing from the United States to Bangalore, India, where there are highly educated people who speak English and work for far lower wages than their American counterparts. Thus, it is technology combined with education and wage levels, not NAFTA, that is driving jobs out of the U.S.

Human Resource Management

By 1970, it was clear that America's labor relations system couldn't compete with those of Japan, Germany, and Scandinavia. Characterized by adversarial bargaining between unions and management, the American system led to excessively rigid, legalistic, and hostile relations between managers and employees. Management's goal of maximizing shareholder return in direct opposition to the union's goal of maximizing returns to workers resulted in poor quality, soaring costs, employee alienation, and reduced motivation, productivity, and efficiency. American industries such as steel and autos were losing market share to foreign competitors with more consensual systems. Convergence was inevitable despite the obstacles, and, fundamental changes in human resource management occurred.

In the American automobile industry the roles and relationships between the United Automobile Workers (UAW) and management have changed dramatically. At the New United Motor Manufacturing, Inc. (NUMMI), the car factory owned jointly by Toyota and General Motors, "workers" are "team members" and the managers' job is to support the team. There is a commitment to employment security, extensive training, constant consultation, and worker control and involvement in plant decisions.

Mission Statement: Through teamwork, build the highest quality vehicles at the lowest possible cost to benefit our customers, team members, community and shareholders.

The Intersection of Government and Business

In spite of successful collaborations in many areas—such as aircraft, weapons, agriculture, shipbuilding, housing and real estate—Americans have been ideologically averse to government involvement in their lives, especially in the world of commerce, the domain of "private enterprise." The theory was that firms competed against other firms in open markets in a world characterized by free trade with government staying on the sidelines.

The Japanese and other cultures have shown that this view of the world was not only unrealistic but also a handicap. There, consortias of firms cooperating with one another and with the government have emerged to become fierce competitors.

Industry-government consortia and cooperative efforts have helped Japan gain leadership in many high-tech sectors, including machine tools, semiconductors, computers, flat panel displays, and telecommunications. More such initiatives are on the way in superconductivity, ceramics, and software technology. The United States has been forced to follow with Sematech, a consortium of 14 companies, to regain leadership in semiconductors, and in 1994 with the flat panel display initiative to try to repatriate that technology lost in the early 1980s.

Conflict

The changes forced by global competition do not come easily. Union and management attitudes in the West have been cemented by years of adversarial tradition. Companies and governments, accustomed to cautious and often hostile relationships, find it difficult to replace suspicion with trust and respect.

Nationalism provokes tensions, as the so-called Triad—Europe, Japan, and the United States—and rising stars in Latin America, such as Brazil and Chile, and in Asia, like China, attempt to mobilize their resources for

Meiji Restoration: The time in Japan's history (1867—1868) when the Tokugawa Shogunate came to an end and power was nominally restored to an emperor, Meiji. In reality, power was held by the emperor's advisors in an authoritarian government that transformed Japan from a feudal to a modern industrial nation.

global commerce. In juxtaposition to national or regional competition, multinational corporations spread around the world and seek efficiency regardless of national or regional boundaries. They join with one another, they compete, they cooperate.

And multinationals are not all the same. Their purposes differ and here, too, there is tension. For some, American firms in particular, the highest goal is often satisfying shareholders with little regard for the company's employees and the community at home. For others, Japanese companies for example, their purpose is to promote the welfare of their employees and their nation over the long run, an aim not dissimilar from that of their government. So a cooperative relationship is relatively easy as indeed it has been since the Meiji restoration. Not only have Japanese companies succeeded in their purpose beyond the expectations of virtually all Westerners fifty years ago, but they have grown rich doing so. It should suffice here to note several varieties of business-government conflict.

Global Versus Local Interest

First, there is the tension between the global interest of the multinational and the national or regional interest of corporate home base. For example, Philips in the Netherlands, which between 1988 and 1990 received the lion's share of the $1.2 billion European Currency Units (about $1.5 billion) the government provided to the Dutch manufacturing sector. The Dutch government's expectation was that Philips would use the money to expand its Dutch operations and provide Dutch workers with good jobs at high wages. Philips, on the other hand, felt obliged to increase its foreign commitments in the United States, Asia, and elsewhere to help retain global competitiveness.

Similarly, in the United States tax incentives to foster research and development are supposed to benefit

American taxpayers, but when "saved" money is spent abroad, the only American beneficiaries are corporate shareholders, not employees or the public at large.

Merits and Demerits of FDI

Second, there are concerns that foreign direct investment may not be all good. The European Community put quotas on Japanese automobiles assembled in Japanese-owned plants in Europe. Some European governments have performance requirements that affect the operation of multinationals in their jurisdictions.

The United States through its Committee on Foreign Investment in the United States (CFIUS) has imposed mild restraints in the name of national defense but refuses to identify "good" as opposed to "bad" foreign investment. Nevertheless, the Office of Technology Assessment suggested that the United States should want multinationals "to conduct business here and interact with local firms in ways that generate and retain wealth and quality jobs within its borders." It added:

> The connection between the location of technology leadership, both product and process, and the health of national economies and living standards is becoming ever more apparent to governments...The United States cannot remain competitive unless MNCs that sell and conduct business in America also contribute to its research and technology base, employment, manufacturing capabilities, and capital resources.

Some MNCs, especially Japanese ones, it bemoaned, tended "to retain high value-added R&D and production functions at home, and to export sophisticated parts and components to their foreign subsidiaries."[20]

The European Currency Unit (ECU) is an intangible monetary unit held by member countries of the European Union as part of their international reserves. Its value is based on a basket of members' national currencies.

Defining Roles

Third, there are the conflicts among multinationals and their home governments about what are "fair" and "proper" conceptions of the roles and relationships of business and government. This conflict is revealed in the continuing debate about such matters as government subsidies and targeting, business cooperation in consortia, supplier relationships, capital markets, and, most of all, industrial policy. It is in these areas that the United States government as well as its companies accuse Japanese and Europeans of "cheating."

There is concern in the United States that competition from firms based in Europe, Japan, and other Asian countries will "threaten the survival of key U.S.-based multinationals in a range of (high-tech) industries." These foreign firms often benefit from capital markets that produce relatively low-cost, patient capital, which allows managers to think long-term about market share instead of forcing them to be preoccupied with short-term returns to shareholders.[21] They also benefit from government subsidies, incentives, and other programs that target selected export industries for promotion. It is said, "arguments about free trade and protectionism have nothing to do with the major global issues facing" high-tech industries whose competitiveness depends on company collaboration for research, government partnerships, industry and national strategies, and multilateral sectoral agreements on common rules.[22]

In spite of these conflicts, globalization seems to push on, glacier-like, flattening the obstacles in its path. So powerful is the self-reinforcing cycle of globalization—convergence leading to innovation transfer, leading to both integration and more convergence, leading to an even faster transfer, leading to further convergence and integration—that, once truly started, it cannot help but defeat the varied resistances of protectionism in all its forms.[23]

THE DEMAND SIDE

Markets and consumer desires also force convergence—and conflict. Theodore Levitt saw it coming a decade ago when he wrote of "the sweeping gale of globalization" pushing markets toward "global commonality" with corporations selling

> standardized products in the same way everywhere—autos, steel, chemicals, petroleum, cement, agricultural commodities and equipment, industrial and commercial construction, banking and insurance services, computers, semiconductors, transport, electronic instruments, pharmaceuticals, and telecommunications, to mention some of the obvious....Everywhere everything gets more and more like everything else as the world's preference structure is relentlessly homogenized....Global competition spells the end of domestic territoriality, no matter how diminutive the territory may be....Different cultural preferences, national tastes and standards, and business institutions are vestiges of the past.[24]

Cultural Conflict

Here, too, convergence has meant conflict. The entertainment industry, America's second largest exporter just behind the aerospace industry, nets a U.S. trade surplus of about $8 billion, and sells so-called "packaged cultural products."[25] Indeed, the spreading of "culture" appears to be America's leading comparative advantage.

Tokyo Disneyland opened in 1983. It has had more than 15 million visitors a year with an economic ripple effect that Mitsubishi Research Institute estimated to be about $6.3 billion, approximately the value of Japan's annual camera exports. Ten years later, in a former

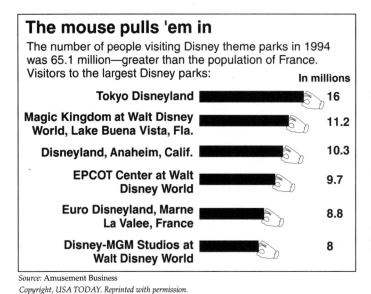

The mouse pulls 'em in

The number of people visiting Disney theme parks in 1994 was 65.1 million—greater than the population of France. Visitors to the largest Disney parks:

In millions

Tokyo Disneyland	16
Magic Kingdom at Walt Disney World, Lake Buena Vista, Fla.	11.2
Disneyland, Anaheim, Calif.	10.3
EPCOT Center at Walt Disney World	9.7
Euro Disneyland, Marne La Valee, France	8.8
Disney-MGM Studios at Walt Disney World	8

Source: Amusement Business

Copyright, USA TODAY. Reprinted with permission.

sugar-beet field twenty miles east of Paris, the $5 billion Euro Disneyland opened. Continental intellectuals attacked the transplantation of Disney's fantasyland as an assault on native culture, a "cultural Chernobyl."

A 1991 survey revealed that the most popular motion picture in Japan—foreign or domestic—was *Terminator 2.* It earned five times its nearest Japanese rival and twice the nearest American film, which was *Home Alone.*[26]

MTV is a worldwide rock-and-roll network with hundreds of millions of viewers. Technology has decontrolled culture. Although a lot of American television, cinema, and music has redeeming qualities, critics contend that it increasingly offers the illusion of escape while preaching rebellion against parents, civil authority, and hard work and extolling lust, greed, and violence.

Convergence around such consumer desires worries those with more traditional values. For them, market forces are by no means benign; globalization can be a menace that engulfs virtue.

GLOBALIZATION AND THE ENVIRONMENT

Perhaps the greatest impulse to globalization is mankind's increased awareness of the importance of earth's life-support system—the air we breathe, the water we drink, the earth upon which we depend for food, the ozone layer that surrounds and protects us—all these things are in jeopardy. The earth is a commons that we share together, but there is a growing consensus that it is threatened by the depletion of stratospheric ozone, global warming, increased waste disposal, deforestation, desertification, water depletion, and the extinction of animal species, including perhaps humans.

This consensus, however, runs smack into another, which is also a principal driver of globalization—the belief that increasing the gross national product of a country and the world is good, and that consequently so are trade and investment, the more the better. For 20 years, Brazil's annual rates of real GNP growth averaged an impressive 7 or 8 percent. This growth, however, was accompanied by substantial deterioration of its environment, especially in the forests of the Amazon.

Jeremy Warford, an environmental economist with the World Bank, writes:

> Growth built on resource depletion is clearly very different from that obtained from productive efforts and may be quite unsustainable.... Unless net capital formation is larger than natural resource depreciation, the economy's assets decline as resources are extracted and degraded: this appears to be exactly what is happening in many of the poorer natural resource-based economies.[27]

Warford commented on trade:

> Trade liberalization to encourage exports is held to be a good thing by many experts. It could, however, result in a country shifting cultivation from Crop A to Crop B to serve an export market, earn foreign exchange and repay its foreign debt. All good things, but the long-term effects on vegetative cover could be disastrous.[28]

One problem with the environment is that it is everywhere, yet the institutions to manage it—governments—

are local. Even within their jurisdictions, governments need to make trade-offs in the name of environmental integrity that would try King Solomon. And these trade-offs depend on where you sit, how you make your living, and what your choices are. If you are starving in that Amazon forest and cut down a tree and sell it, thereby getting something to eat, you would be impatient with a government that told you that your actions were endangering the world's biosphere.

The Role of International Agencies

A number of international governmental agencies have entered the trade-off debate, but not without a good deal of controversy. Two such agencies are the World Bank and the World Trade Organization, formerly known as the General Agreement on Tariffs and Trade (GATT).

The World Bank. The World Bank's mission is to lend money to developing countries to help alleviate poverty. In the 1990s, it became the center of two debates. The first, which we shall consider in Chapter 2, was whether the Bank's policies, focused on increasing per capita GNP, were in fact alleviating poverty. The second, our concern here, was whether its policies were good for the environment.

World Bank environmentalists, such as Jeremy Warford, challenged a number of the basic tenets of the Bank's reigning professionals, the economists. Free trade, the environmentalists said, was not an unmitigated good. The free market was frequently an unreliable device to secure community needs. Government nonintervention was not necessarily a virtue. National income accounting was misleading.

On this last point, Bank ecologist Robert Goodland noted that "the Valdez oil spill clean-up increased GNP; driving to work instead of using a bicycle increases GNP; turning up the furnace instead of putting on an

The G-7 nations (Canada, France, Germany, Italy, Japan, the United Kingdom, the United States) produce 45% of the world's greenhouse gases. Industrial nations, with 25% of the population, consume 70% of its resources.[29]

extra blanket increases GNP."[30] Cost-benefit analysis, a favorite measuring device of economists, attached quantitative values to what environmentalists perceived to be immeasurable environmental goods.

The environmentalists' criticism was especially bothersome, because it included the nations that controlled Bank policies, its owners.

"You ask me what the Bank should do?" said Goodland. "Reparations are being demanded from the rich world for the damage it has done the poor world. This is what the LDCs (less developed countries) are asking for and our clients are the LDCs, yet the Bank does not fully seem to share such views."[31]

Herman Daly, when he was an environmental economist at the Bank, argued that in a very short time the world had passed through an historical turning point. The human economy, he said, had moved from an era in which human capital was the limiting factor in economic development to one in which "remaining natural capital has become the limiting factor." The transformation has been impelled by the change from a world relatively empty of human beings to one that is relatively full.

Not surprisingly, the economists regard the ecologists with some disdain, although they grudgingly respect the latter's capacity to mobilize public opinion. The economists believe that if you "get the prices right" and do not interfere with the market mechanism and free trade, new technology and substitutes will come along that will go a long way toward achieving sustainable development. As nonrenewable resources, like oil, are used up, their prices will rise and their use will diminish, and as the prices rise, the incentives for finding substitutes, especially through improved technology, increase. The trouble is, they say, that governments intervene for political reasons to prevent the sequence.

World Trade Organization. A similar debate is underway between environmentalists and trade experts.

©Twilly Cannon/Greenpeace

©Morgan/Greenpeace

A good way to understand it is to examine a 1992 GATT judgment on an American dolphin protection law, the Marine Mammal Protection Act (MMPA).

In 1988, the United States Congress amended the MMPA to ban imports of tuna fish caught by countries that used fishing methods fatal to dolphins, and that killed dolphins at a greater rate than did U.S. commercial fishermen. The ban was aimed at purse-seine nets, especially those used by Mexican fishermen in the eastern Pacific Ocean, where yellowfin tuna liked to swim beneath dolphins. The dolphins become ensnared in the nets and cannot break free and rise to the surface for air, thus they drown.

In 1988, the Bush administration, eager not to irritate Mexico at a time when the NAFTA was being negotiated, opposed the ban. When the White House evaded enforcing the law, Earth Island Institute, an environmental group that had lobbied Congress to pass the 1988 amendment, filed a lawsuit against the government. In 1991, a federal court told the Department of Commerce to enforce the law. The department imposed an embargo on tuna coming from Mexico and several other nations. Mexico complained to GATT that the United States was violating free trade principles.

A GATT arbitration panel concluded that Mexico was right: the MMPA was incompatible with GATT precepts for two reasons: first, the application of environmental regulations outside of a nation's jurisdiction would violate the other nation's sovereignty, and second, using trade regulations to alter another nation's processes of production would be "eco-colonialism," i.e., the use of commercial muscle to impose green values of one country on to another.[32]

Environmentalists were enraged. The Sierra Club wrote:

> Meeting in a closed room in Geneva last June, three unelected trade experts…conspired to kill Flipper….Because of the extraordinary breadth of the GATT decisions, however, victims of free trade are not limited to finny mammals….Out go international bans on drift netting, whaling, and seal-clubbing….And if you want to protect the ozone layer, make sure you're acting in your own airspace.[33]

The panel's rulings were subsequently shelved and the disputants attempted a negotiated settlement. The 1994 GATT agreements focused on relationships between trade and the environment, and those relationships will surely preoccupy the new WTO.

THE WEALTH GAP

Globalization has clearly enriched the rich in the industrial worlds of Asia, Europe, and North America, but at the same time it has widened the gap between rich and poor both within and among countries. In the United States, the educated, the skilled, and those who hold shares in the stock market have done well. Others have seen a decline in their standard of living as measured by real hourly wages. The same is or will be true in Europe. East Asian countries have managed the most equitable distribution of incomes in the world, but there are signs that their wage gap is growing also.

Whatever its benign effects on the Northern hemisphere, globalization has done little for much of the Southern hemisphere, where the World Bank reports, one billion people lived in "acute poverty and suffered grossly inadequate access to the resources—education, health services, infrastructure, land, and credit—required to give them a chance for a better life."[34]

According to the United Nations, in the last 30 years the countries where the richest 20 percent of the world's people live increased their share of gross world product from 70 to 83 percent. Those countries are now 60 times better off than those where the poorest fifth of the world's people live. The gap between the two has doubled in 30 years.[35]

Poverty and Globalization

There are many causes of Third World poverty. Two relate to globalization. First, was the huge outflow of funds from the poor world to the rich during the 1980s to service the bank loans that resulted from the increases in oil prices during the 1970s. These increases produced a flood of so-called petrodollars from the oil producers that had to be invested, and the poor countries of Latin America and Africa offered the bank's best rates. In general, however, the funds enriched the few at the expense of the many in the borrowing countries, Brazil and Mexico, for example.

The second cause was a nationalistic response to globalization in which the rich world has increasingly denied its markets to poor world products. While extolling the virtues of "free trade," the United Nations estimates that 20 out of the 24 industrial countries that comprise the Organization for Economic Cooperation and Development were more protectionist in 1991 than they were a decade before. (The four who were not—Japan, Australia, New Zealand, and Turkey—were the most protectionist in 1980.) The other 20, led by the United States, have been erecting new trade barriers to augment their old ones. By the end of 1990, GATT members had put 284 arrangements in place to obstruct the sale of cheap products from developing countries.[36]

Many of these will be eliminated by the new WTO (World Trade Organization) established in 1995.

THE MIGRANTS

Among the effects of Third World poverty is migration. People do not flow as freely as money or goods. That, indeed, is why many are in poverty. Nevertheless, in 1993 there were an estimated 100 million migrants and the number was increasing, causing anger and resentment in Europe and the United States, especially in California with its shared border with Mexico.

Reuters/Bettmann

It would be nice to suppose that development would reduce migrant flows, but a World Bank study shows that, in the short-run at least, the restructuring caused by development tends to increase migration.

Money sent home—"official remittances"—from these migrants was approximately $66 billion in 1989, second in value only to trade in crude oil. This constituted a whopping 8.5 percent of the total value of world trade in services.

Migrants are of many sorts:

♦ Settlers who move on a permanent basis, legally or illegally

♦ Temporary contract migrants, such as Mexican farm workers in the United States and European "guest workers"

♦ Short-term skilled workers and personnel with technical skills

♦ Students

♦ Refugees, whose numbers have soared from two million in 1972 to 19 million in 1993

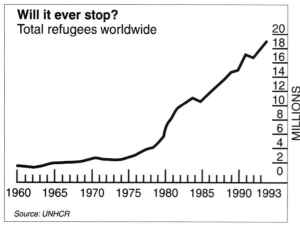

Will it ever stop?
Total refugees worldwide

Source: UNHCR

The forces that push migration are not purely economic; they are political, tribal, and familial as well. Of the 80 million migrants in 1989, for example, 35 million were *within* sub-Saharan Africa alone.[37] Aside from the impulse to survive, the forces that attract migrants to a new country include movies, television, and access to new forms of transportation.

CULTURE CLASH

One final—and related—form of conflict attending the convergence impelled by globalization is that of civilizations. Samuel P. Huntington of Harvard identified eight major civilizations: Western, Confucian, Japanese, Islamic, Hindu, Slavic-Orthodox, Latin America, and "possibly" African. He offered six reasons why conflicts among these civilizations will occur. [38]

1. Their differences are "real" and "basic." They include differences about relationships between God and man, individual and community, citizen and state, parents and children, husbands and wives, as well as different notions of rights and duties, liberty and authority, freedom and order, equality and hierarchy.

2. Globalization is making the world smaller. Interactions among different civilizations will increase. "North African immigration to France generates hostility among Frenchmen and at the same time increases receptivity to immigration by 'good' European Catholic Poles."

3. Modernization—technology, change, MTV and

the like—weakens traditional feelings of identity and undercuts the nation state as a source of identity. "Fundamentalist" religion often moves in to fill the identity gap. The revival of religion, he notes, "is one of the dominant social facts of life in the late Twentieth Century."

4. The dominance of the United States and the West, acceptable during the Cold War, has become less so, especially inasmuch as the West's economic strength relative to Asia is not what it used to be. So there is a search for indigenous civilization—"Asianization in Japan, the end of the Nehru legacy and the 'Hinduization' of India, the failure of Western ideas of socialism and nationalism and, hence, the 're-Islamization' of the Middle East...."

5. Cultural characteristics are not easily sloughed off or compromised. Ethnicity and religion "discriminate sharply and exclusively among people....A person can be half-French and half-Arab..., (but) it is more difficult to be half-Catholic and half-Muslim."

6. Regional economic blocs in Europe, North America, and possibly in Asia will tend to reinforce civilization-consciousness. They may, however, obstruct regionalism. Japan, for example, does not enter easily into an East Asian trading bloc in which Chinese/Confucian culture is dominant. And one of the most important forces of globalization in the future will surely be China and the Chinese throughout the world.

Although ingenious organizations have sprung up to deploy the new technology and to manage the flows of money, goods, and services, the whole lacks coherence and direction; the pieces are endangered by illegitimacy. There may be economic integration, but there is political

Everything is related to everything else: the flows of trade and investment impacting the differing roles and relationships among government and business, in turn constrained by the necessity of ecological integrity and shaped by different value systems.

disintegration. Tribal, ethnic, and religious tension and violence abound.

WHO DECIDES? WHAT ARE THE CRITERIA?

Globalization is like the child's kaleidoscope. With every shake of the tube old patterns give way to new ones, which appear accidental, unplanned, and unpredictable. The new designs result from the countless separate actions of innumerable players.

There is order in the kaleidoscope of globalization, a pattern to the little chips of glass. Everything is related to everything else: the flows of trade and investment impacting the differing roles and relationships among government and business, in turn constrained by the necessity of ecological integrity and shaped by different value systems. The world is indeed a system, comprehensible only if it is perceived as such. No single discipline or group of experts are competent to explain it.

There is no overarching framework. The rules by which the global game is played are far from clear. Winners jealously guard their power and losers resent their losses. Trade-offs must be made—are being made—but who decides, using what criteria?

There would seem to be two choices. Whoever has the power decides, wisely or whimsically. This would be a world of progressive illegitimacy and deepening conflict—one vast gambling casino.

The more sensible alternative requires what Fred Bergsten, director of the Institute for International Economics, has called "collective leadership," acting on a shared consensus among the world's people.

SUMMARY

The old systems of governance, centered on the nation-state, are inadequate, and new transnational paraphernalia is weakened by conflicting purposes and priorities.

For forty years following World War II collective leadership was orchestrated by the United States and the Soviet Union. Each had a set of purposes, which derived largely from mutual hostility. Today, those purposes are irrelevant or decayed.

Within the framework of the Cold War, institutions evolved, which, however imperfectly, provided ways of dealing with global tensions, a framework with rules, within which multinational corporations could proceed with some confidence.

The challenge globalization puts to us is the resurrection of collective leadership and the construction of new institutions to manage global tensions.

OVERVIEW

♦ Old World Order

♦ Paradigm Shifts

♦ Convergence/Divergence

♦ Integration/Disintegration

♦ New World Order

THE COLLAPSE OF
THE OLD PARADIGM

2

The management of globalization and its tensions requires a global consensus about purposes and direction. On the foundations of such a consensus it is possible to design and construct institutions—national and international governmental organizations as well as corporations—that can cope with the issues described in Chapter 1. To be stable, the consensus must be perceived as legitimate, or in keeping with some system of values.

In the fifty years or so since the end of World War II there has been such a consensus. Its central purpose, shared by virtually everyone, was a negative one—to avoid nuclear war. A second purpose was to restrain the aggressive tendencies of those who ruled what was the Soviet Union. The United States had wealth, power, and sufficient moral authority to lead the so-called "free world" in the fulfillment of this second purpose. And the

Cold War was a "holy" one because of the brutality of successive Soviet regimes. It acquired additional legitimacy for Americans, if not for others, from the ideology of individualism, so deeply ingrained in the American consciousness, and so counter to Soviet totalitarianism.

Individualism is defined here as a set of beliefs, closely associated with laissez-faire capitalism and classical economics, springing from the philosophy of John Locke and the economics of Adam Smith and David Ricardo. The ideology regards the individual as separate from and more important than the community, and holds that property rights are the basis of civil society, derived from nature, God's promise, which it is the role of the state to preserve, and protect.

Individualism sees unfettered competition to satisfy consumer desires in the marketplace as the best way to control the uses of property. It regards the least government as the best. And, finally, following the thought of Sir Isaac Newton, it perceives in scientific specialization the route to an understanding of reality: if we study the pieces, we will somehow know the whole. Individualism was thus a coherent social philosophy aimed at creating a just and prosperous community. It should be emphasized that although this ideology was *practiced* by few of America's Cold War allies (even the United States had over the years been forced away from it), all were prepared to at least sing the appropriate hymns to gain the benefits flowing from U.S. leadership.

THE OLD WORLD ORDER

In 1989 the Cold War ended. Ironically, at the same time the ideology of individualism was withering because it could not justify or support the actions being taken by corporations and governments to compete in the world economy, to make the world a just place, or to achieve environmental integrity.

Thus the old paradigm for ordering the world and legitimizing global institutions was shattered. With it went the consensus that sustained the institutions that most of the world has relied on to manage globalization: the World Bank, the International Monetary Fund (IMF), the General Agreement on Tariffs and Trade (GATT) and more. Whatever the ostensible purpose of these organizations has been, their underlying mission was to contain communism and to promote property rights, free trade, free markets, limited governmental intervention, and scientific specialization. They demonstrated their zeal for this mission in the form of ever-more specialized and narrow economic thinking as well as faith in technology to deal, for example, with environmental questions and dilemmas.

These institutions are important for managing the tensions of globalization, but they are weakening and will weaken further unless their missions are redefined to conform to a new consensus. That consensus depends on a new paradigm. (At the same time the end of the Cold War has freed the United Nations from the paralysis imposed by the Soviet veto. Its efforts to bring peace in Bosnia, Somalia, Cambodia, and elsewhere would have been unthinkable a decade ago. But to reach its potential it, too, needs a new consensus.)

One of the most striking features of a paradigm is the extent to which it insulates and preserves the status quo.

The rest of this chapter will be devoted to some thoughts on why and how the old paradigm died and will suggest some elements of the new one that might take its place.

THE PARADIGM CONCEPT

A paradigm is a way of looking at things. The paradigm concept is borrowed from *The Structure of Scientific*

Revolutions, a classic work by Thomas S. Kuhn that examines the history of science. By "paradigm" he meant

♦ A collection of ideas within the confines of which scientific inquiry takes place

♦ An assumed definition of legitimate problems and methods

♦ An accepted practice and viewpoint from which the student prepares for membership in the scientific community

♦ Criteria for choosing problems to attack

♦ Rules and standards of scientific practice.

He looked at such major scientific transformations as those associated with Copernicus, Newton, Lavoisier, and Einstein. Each of these required "the community's rejection of one time-honored theory in favor of one incompatible with it." One of the most striking features of a paradigm is the extent to which it insulates and preserves the status quo and so prevents major changes —conceptual or phenomenal. It does this largely by controlling the criteria for choosing problems to be solved:

> To a great extent these are the only problems
> that the community will admit as scientific or
> encourage its members to undertake. Other
> problems...are rejected as metaphysical, as the
> concern of another discipline, or sometimes as
> just too problematic to be worth the time.[1]

Thus, a paradigm can prevent us from perceiving and attacking important problems that make us prisoners of our particular viewpoints. It is only when anomalies confront the old model that new theories emerge. New theories are preceded by a time of dramatic professional insecurity as those loyal to the old paradigm repeatedly fail to make them work.

To illustrate a paradigm shift, Kuhn used the example of the Ptolemaic versus Copernican view of the world. For Ptolemy the earth was the center of the universe and the solar system moved around it. In the Second Century AD, the Vatican endorsed this conception.

In 1513, Copernicus announced that the earth rotated on its axis and orbited around the sun once a year. The Church condemned Copernicus and he died an apostate. In 1633, Galileo confirmed the Copernican view. He was summoned to Rome, declared a heretic, and threatened with torture. In his eighties and a bit old for the rack, he disavowed his belief in a revolving earth. However, as he left the Inquisitorial chamber he was heard to mutter, "E pur si muovo" ("Nevertheless, it does move.") His recantation was therefore dismissed and he died blind and in disgrace.[2]

Old paradigms die hard, but eventually the anomalies become too great. If you use the Ptolemaic system, the calendar doesn't come out right, and of course neither do the astrologers' calculations based on the calendar. In the Sixteenth Century practical people like calendar makers and astrologers would no longer pay the price of the old ways, also the Vatican had lost some of its lustre; the paradigm changed.

Stock Montage

Nicholaus Copernicus, Polish astronomer, 1473-1543

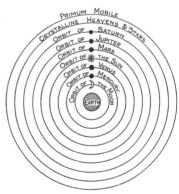

Stock Montage

A model of the Ptolemic System

When the anomalies become strong enough, a crisis occurs that causes a shift in paradigms.

Perestroika was a paradigm shift. The anomalies of the communist system became so great and so costly that there had to be a change; the old paradigm was destroyed, things changed. So far there has been massive experimentation, with the people of Russia and Eastern Europe groping for a new but undiscovered paradigm.

How much crisis does it take to replace an outworn paradigm with a new one? It depends upon how good we are at recognizing what is struggling to be born.

BREAKDOWN

In July 1944, shortly after D-Day, representatives of the countries who were winning World War II—most importantly Britain and the United States—gathered at a resort hotel in Bretton Woods, New Hampshire, to stabilize the international economy and national currencies.

UPI/Bettmann

Bretton Woods Conference

THE IMF AND GLOBAL MONEY

The International Monetary Fund (IMF) was established to negotiate and maintain stable exchange rates among the world's currencies. Before the war, many countries deliberately lowered the value of their currencies in order to cheapen and, thus, promote their exports, which disadvantaged those who chose to maintain so-called strong currencies.

A system of fixed exchange rates was adopted. The value of each currency was set in terms of dollars, and the dollar was tied to gold at $35 an ounce.

A country's central bank had the job of preserving agreed-upon exchange rates. If a currency strayed from the prescribed rate—generally, if it fell below that rate—the central bank was bound to intervene and purchase that currency on the open market, borrowing dollars from the IMF if necessary to do so. If the country's difficulties persisted, the IMF would examine the underlying economic situation and specify conditions to be met before the country was allowed to borrow more.

The fixed exchange rate system resulted in the proliferation of dollars around the world. The dollar was, after all, as good as gold, and the world wanted them to buy U.S. goods and services. The system depended on the willingness of the United States to redeem unwanted dollars for gold. This was not a problem at the end of World War II because the United States held about 70 percent of the world's mined gold in its vaults at Fort Knox, Kentucky, and between 1946 and 1960, the United States exported $58 billion more than it imported from other countries.[3]

But the world was changing. By 1958, for the first time, dollars held by foreigners exceeded the value of U.S. gold stocks. Central banks began to cash them in. The next year, the United States lost 10 percent of its gold. During the 1960s, Japan and Germany made spectacular comebacks. In 1964 the United States suffered the first of thirty years of trade deficits with Japan. In 1971, the high value of the dollar and other countries' growing competitiveness in automobiles, steel, and high-tech products caused the United States to suffer its first overall trade deficit—the excess of imports of goods and services over exports—since 1893. Then a mere $2 billion, by 1994 the U.S. trade deficit ballooned to more than $130 billion, about half of which was with Japan. The current account deficit (which in addition to trade includes, among other things, outflows of interest payments on what the U.S. had borrowed from foreigners) was running at close to $150 billion. This, of course, had to be balanced by borrowing from—or selling assets to—foreigners on the capital account. At the same time, America's standard of living as measured by real hourly wages had been declining steadily since 1973.

In 1971, to stop the flow of gold out of Fort Knox and to lower U.S export prices, President Richard Nixon abandoned the Bretton Woods system and announced that the United States would no longer exchange dollars for gold. The gold window closed and the value of the dollar became whatever anyone would pay for it. In a word, it floated and its value declined. In turn, the yen and deutsche mark increased in value; however, the German and Japanese economic systems were highly competitive and these countries' exports continued to grow in spite of the rise in their currencies.

In summary, the United States emerged from World War II all powerful and committed to the establishment of a new world order. It took its economic supremacy for

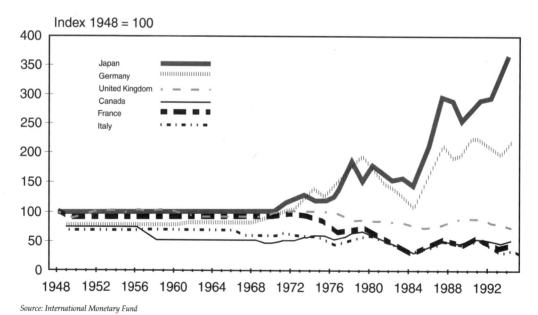

Index 1948 = 100

Japan
Germany
United Kingdom
Canada
France
Italy

Source: International Monetary Fund

Nominal Exchange Rate in Terms of the Dollar

The collapse of the Bretton Woods accords brought diverging "floating" exchange rates. The dollar, for example, which in the 1960s was worth 360 yen, bought less than 90 yen in 1995.

granted and regarded its central purpose as being to lead a coalition of nations against the forces of evil. In this context, the rise to world economic dominance of Japan and its East Asian neighbors was consistent with U.S. interests.

An outworn paradigm, the laissez-faire notion that competition in the world was among firms not among national systems.

However, twenty years of decline in the global market share of large U.S. industrial and banking enterprises accelerated in the 1980s. This was especially true in high-tech sectors where in thirty years the U.S. share of worldwide sales of electrical equipment, for example, declined from 71 percent to 11 percent.[4] Yet, the United States refused to perceive the nature and the power of the economic strategies of the world's most competitive countries. Consequently, it refused to change its own outworn paradigm, the laissez-faire notion that competition in the world was among firms not among national systems. Ironically, Japan had become dependent on a nation that was sustaining an uncompetitive system with borrowed money—indeed, much of it borrowed from Japan.

The IMF's Role Change

Although the world seems to recognize the need for stable exchange rates to facilitate the expansion of international trade, the IMF, which was created to assure them, no longer performs that role. After 1971, the IMF became a lender of last resort. Its conditions for borrowing became a doctrine concerning the prerequisites for economic development in the world economy. Since the IMF is controlled by the wealthy countries who regard themselves as already "developed," this doctrine became their gift to the poor world; a gift that had for many the look of a Trojan horse.

IMF conditions, which invariably hurt a nation's poor more than its rich, have caused animosity among debtor countries, who feel unrepresented on the IMF

When a country's economy deteriorates and its ability to earn foreign exchange in the world's competitive markets declines, it often seeks help from commercial bankers. When the commercial bankers are no longer willing to lend, the indebted country—the United Kingdom, in the '70s; Mexico in the '80s and '90s; Russia in the '90s—goes to the IMF for help.

The IMF conditions its loans on such internal changes as cutting government spending, lowering subsidies, increasing user fees for public services, cutting tariffs, devaluing the currency, and welcoming foreign investment; changes that, in the short run, often mean economic austerity and recession. Since commercial banks agree not to lend money until the IMF conditions are met, these conditions are not a choice but an imposition. However sensible, many of these conditions constitute among the most severe invasions of national sovereignty in history.

governing boards. Voting power in the IMF is based on the financial endowments of each member government—one dollar, one vote. (United Nations voting is based on one nation, one vote.) Many also question whether the IMF's formula works for all cases. Opponents argue that it takes a strictly macro-economic approach to problems that, in many countries, are structural. The IMF is accused of wearing ideological blinders about the role of government and markets, and of refusing to include the strategic model of East Asian development in its prescriptions. While its remedies can be effective, they are often regarded as crude and unproductive.

To cite an example, a few years ago Zambia held its first democratic elections and put Frederick Chiluba in the presidency. He followed the IMF's prescribed "reforms," as described by *The Economist*:

> For the first time in thirty years, state hospitals and clinics have started charging fees. Patients now have to pay for their own drugs. Tariffs for electricity and water, no longer fixed by the government, have spiralled. Subsidies for fuel and mealie meal, the staple food, have gone. True, the shelves of city stores are now lined with imported goods. But, since public-sector wages were frozen in July, people can barely afford basic necessities let alone luxuries.

lized, Zambia's fragile industries had
...ing with imports. Swamped by a del-
...econdhand clothes from
...es, more than three quar-
...factories have closed in the
...inflation above 200 percent
...erest rates at 140 percent,
...and farmers have been

Shortly after Zambia did the IMF's
bidding, Lonrho, a British multinational
and a major factor in Zambian agriculture
announced it was pulling out of maize,
wheat, soya, and cotton. The closure of its
cotton operations alone cost 10,000 jobs.
The government reckoned that another
40,000 jobs were lost over two more years
of "reform."[6]

Countries like Zambia lack the economic institutions and the political infrastructure to become successful entrants
into the competitive world being created
by globalization. The macroeconomic
norms imposed by the IMF presume the
existence of capabilities that simply are not present. A
better approach is needed to help such countries develop the governmental and business structures they lack.

Reuters/Bettmann

*Frederick Chiluba, first democratically
elected president of Zambia, 1991*

THE WORLD BANK

The IMF's companion in lending to developing countries
is the World Bank. It also was created at Bretton Woods,
and opened its doors for business in 1946 with $12 bil-
lion in capital. In 1993 the World Bank was the world's
single largest lender to the amount of $23.7 billion.[7]

The Bank's purpose is to help developing countries
increase their standard of living as measured by per
capita gross national product. With subscribed capital of

some $140 billion and 6,000 employees, the Bank has financed a wide variety of projects in many fields, including infrastructure, agriculture, energy, transportation, and industrial development.[8]

Its emphasis on reducing poverty is clear in the opening paragraph of a recent World Bank Annual Report. After noting that more than a billion people—about one-third of the total population in developing countries—live in poverty, and that poverty in many places increased in the 1980s, the report stated that the Bank's strategy was "designed to make sure that the poor gain from growth...."[9] Its charter, however, states that its "decisions to lend must be based on economic considerations alone," and a Bank statement on "Governance and Development" emphasized that the Bank was "guided solely by its concern for economic development and not by any political agenda."[10] Here, of course, is the rub. Is it possible for the Bank to make sure that growth is consistent with "development" and that the poor gain from it without having a "political agenda?" Obviously not.

In the early 1980s, the bank emphasized so-called "structural adjustment" loans. This policy reflected the growing concern of the Bank's owners with the ability of developing countries to earn the dollars required to pay off their foreign debts. These loans, therefore, were designed to increase a nation's ability to compete in the world economy. They encouraged and facilitated policy changes to open markets, free trade, reduce subsidies, deregulate, privatize, and minimize the role of government so as to remove "policy distortions" and promote fairly straightforward laissez-faire economics.

Critics of the Bank, many of whom were Bank members themselves, argued that this approach to development invariably made matters worse; that it did not take into account the experience of Japan and the other Asian "miracle" economies; and that it reflected a bias toward Anglo-American individualistic ideology.

All Bank loans are made to developing country *governments*. Such loans, the critics argue, tend to strengthen existing political and economic regimes, which are themselves often the chief obstacle to greater distribution of income and power. They enrich the rich with little trickling down to the poor; and the rich often invest their gains outside the country. There might be "growth," but certainly not "development." This criticism did not matter during the Cold War because everyone knew that what was really at stake was the containment of communism. That having been achieved, however, the Bank had to face a new reality in the 1990s.

The Bank's reliance on market forces caused some to point to the thoughts of a leading scholar of development, Mahbub ul Haq: "Those who have the money can make the market bend to their own will. When we start from a position of gross inequalities, the so-called market mechanism mocks poverty, or simply ignores it, since the poor hardly have any purchasing power to influence market decisions."[11]

As an example, Brazil's annual rates of growth in real gross national product (GNP) averaged an impressive 7 or 8 percent for twenty years. The country was among the largest beneficiaries of both World Bank and other bank funds, receiving well over $100 billion. But, by the Bank's own measure, it also had the most extreme inequality in the distribution of income of any country in the world with nearly 40 percent of the population living in poverty. At the same time, the growth of GNP had been accompanied by substantial environmental deterioration. Properly defined, development should result in the more equitable sharing of power and wealth, in higher levels of education, and in greater opportunities for fulfillment.

Indeed, looking at the development of the Asian

East Asian countries were following a development strategy characterized by extensive government intervention, often intimate relations between government and business, and less than full respect for free markets and free trade.

countries this is what occurred. But those countries followed economic strategies that were not at all what the
Bank recommended. They protected home markets;
their governments allocated resources to targeted sectors
in order to make those sectors able to acquire market
share in the world economy; savings were forced to
build funds for investment; foreign investment—and
local democracy—was managed by clever bureaucrats to
serve the national interest as defined by strong leaders
and backed by a national consensus.

It was not until 1993—and then only at the urging
of the Japanese government—that World Bank economists reluctantly acknowledged that the East Asian
countries—Korea, Japan, Taiwan, Indonesia, Malaysia,
Thailand, and China—were following a development
strategy quite different from the one advocated by the
Bank, one characterized by extensive government intervention, often intimate relations between government
and business, and less than full respect for free markets
and free trade.[12]

The World Bank is an extremely important institution for the future of the world. Its studies of global
development are the best available; its headquarters and
network of field offices are staffed by exceptionally competent individuals; its purpose of closing the gap
between the world's rich and poor is of the highest
importance. However, it must face the new reality of
global development. That reality has some built-in
truths:

1. Many "nations" are not nations at all. They are
   the vestigial remains of colonialism, an accident
   of history, or the preserve of some illicit collection
   of oligarchs. To finance such political units is to
   strengthen the obstacles to development, not to
   encourage it. What was once acceptable in order
   to contain communism is clearly not justifiable
   today.

2. Development in many African and Latin American countries requires the permanent reallocation of power from those who have it to those who do not. This process is only superficially "economic." It is overwhelmingly political, social, and psychological. It requires radical change. It raises critical and controversial questions: Who is changing whom? At what speed and for what purpose? Whose interests are being served?

   The most significant lesson to be learned from East Asia is that what counts most is a consensus among members of the community about what development means and how it is to be achieved.

   It is generally assumed that democracy is the best way to answer these questions, but too often democracy is a hypocritical facade behind which the powerful work what amounts to a dictatorship. Sometimes the radical change essential for development may require some tainting of democratic purity.

   Over the years neither Korea nor Singapore would have won any world prizes for democracy, yet their peoples have prospered. Mexicans say that President Carlos Salinas de Gortari was not really elected president of Mexico in 1988; the election was marred by "a broken computer." Nevertheless, these same Mexicans assert that he was the best choice.

3. The most significant lesson to be learned from East Asia is that what counts most is a consensus among members of the community about what development means and how it is to be achieved. Such consensus requires widespread sharing of gains as well as pains, a willingness to sacrifice for the long run, a respected and powerful government that can plan coherently for the nation's

Successful development requires investment in people. From 1970 to 1989, Korea increased its spending on education at the primary level by 355%, whereas Kenya increased such investment by only 38%.[13]

future, and first-rate education for all. These elements of consensus do not necessarily flow from traditional conceptions of "capitalism," nor are they necessarily the result of laissez-faire economics or Western-style parliaments.

4. Finally, all foreign assistance is interventionary and is, therefore, political—whatever the World Bank's charter says. So is the withdrawal or refusal of such assistance by those who are in a position to provide it.

These four truths suggest the need to divide nations and so-called nations into categories according to their political readiness for development as properly defined, and then to insure that economic infusions come in a form that fosters that development. That may be a loan to government or it may be a grant to a grassroots organization with no connection to the government. It may be a subsidy or guarantee to a multinational corporation whose purposes clearly include the satisfaction of the community needs of the host country.

It would be a tragedy for the world if the World Bank were to become obsolete because of its inability to make a paradigm shift. The Bank's focus on poverty is important. Two-thirds of the world's people live in countries with per capita incomes less than 20 percent of that of the United States. None of us can be happy with such a condition, nor can we feel secure.[14]

THE GENERAL AGREEMENTS ON TARIFFS AND TRADE (GATT)

Created in 1948 to eliminate trade barriers and expand the world economy, the GATT concluded its eighth round of negotiations in 1994, and in January 1995, transformed itself into a new institution, the World Trade Organization.

The GATT divided the world into those who were

"favored," among whom trade was supposed to be free, and those who were not favored, against whom the favored were pitted. Like the IMF and the World Bank, it was part of the Cold War apparatus to strengthen the anti-communist coalition.

In reality, trade is nowhere free; it is managed by governments and corporations through a variety of devices including

♦ Subsidies for such export industries as steel, computers, and aerospace

♦ Cartels, such as oil, diamonds, coffee, and other commodities

♦ Intercorporate understandings such as intimate relations with suppliers and cooperative arrangements among competitors

♦ Protection of critical industries at home, such as telecommunications

♦ Environmental restrictions that often affect trade, as in the case of Mexican tuna

The GATT contained no provisions to deal with international investment or competition issues such as those associated with cartels or the Japanese *keiretsu* (corporate conglomerates which prefer to buy from one another rather than from outsiders). The important barriers to trade in the '90s and beyond are not tariffs but so-called non-tariff barriers. Often, these are built into the political, economic, and social system of a country.

GATT was based on an idea originated by David Ricardo in 1817 that trade was among firms and that all would benefit if the market were kept free and open with limited government intervention. Firms were supposed to benefit from the comparative advantage of the country in which they operated—typically natural resources, although it might also be cheap labor. Portugal, said Ricardo, endowed with sunshine, was supposed to make grapes and press them into wine; Britain was supposed to raise sheep and convert the wool into textiles. In the best of all possible worlds, Britain would export wool and Portugal wine.

Textiles was, of course, the high-value, high-wage, high-profit industry of the time—sort of like computers today. So Ricardo's conception worked well for Britain, and he was, after all, British. As my colleague, Professor Bruce Scott has pointed out, what the East Asians have shown is that a country can do very well despite a lack of natural resources if government and business act together to *create* a comparative advantage through intelligent planning and a willingness to save and invest for the long run. They have used a different paradigm.

THE ASIAN PARADIGM

After World War II when General MacArthur and his occupation task force descended on Japan to assist with its revival, the economic advisors who followed Ricardo recommended that Japan concentrate on small-scale, labor-intensive industries to take advantage of its low-cost, populous work force. Japan, of course, did the opposite, reasoning that if it followed the Western economic model, it would never achieve its goals of growth through exports of high-value-added products.

Myohei Shinohara, an architect of Japan's postwar development, wrote that during Japan's miracle growth period, the Ministry of International Trade and Industry (MITI) applied two consistent criteria in selecting particular industry sectors for promotion and protection: income elasticity and comparative technical progress.

"MITI's industrial policies were expected to foster the industries in which demand growth and technical progress were comparatively high."[15]

Neither Ricardo nor GATT had anticipated such an approach. GATT Director General Peter Sutherland remarked that "the trading system that provided one of the pillars of postwar reconstruction and recovery is falling behind the realities of trade and investment in the 1990s."[16]

Since the United States was unwilling to adopt an industrial policy of its own, it retaliated against Japan and other nations that targeted and subsidized industrial sectors by enacting a series of ever-harsher laws aimed at punishing them. They have been used unilaterally against a wide variety of countries to protect or promote such American industries as steel, computers, and semiconductors. Many countries have pressed to weaken these U.S. trade laws in the new WTO agreement, which substantially lowers world tariffs; establishes international rules governing patents, copyrights, and trademarks; sets limits—albeit generous ones—on government subsidies; and provides a much stiffer framework for defining and enforcing "fairness" in trade.

An erosion of national sovereignty, consistent with the realities of globalization, seems inevitable. The WTO's dispute-resolution panels have wide-ranging authority to investigate and rule on trade laws and practices.

The WTO has sweeping new powers to interpret and enforce its rules, and unlike its predecessor, each of its 117 member nations has one vote with no vetoes allowed. An erosion of national sovereignty, consistent with the realities of globalization, seems inevitable. The WTO's dispute-resolution panels have authority to investigate and rule on trade laws and practices.

> **The WTO could become the centerpiece of an evolving globally managed economy.**

That is threatening to traditionalists; hopeful to realists.

LOOKING BACKWARD

For half a century the United States organized the collective leadership that guided global institutions and defined their missions. It had the power, the will, and the resources, financial and otherwise, to do so. European allies were prepared to help, and Japan happily acquiesced in return for access to U.S. markets.

By the mid-1990s, all that had changed. The power of the U.S. depended on foreign lenders. Its will was uncertain. Its resources, human and financial, were deteriorating because of bad schools, uncompetitive industries, capital markets that focused business purpose on short-run returns to shareholders instead of long-run market share, adversarial labor relations, consumer-oriented government policies, a huge government deficit, adversarial and often shortsighted relations between business and government, and a lack of any long-run economic strategy.

World leaders, especially old ones who remembered the good old days of World War II and the Cold War, yearned for the United States to continue its global role.

"What we want really is no sudden unscrambling of the balance which is prevailing today," said Lee Kuan Yew, the founder of today's Singapore, noting apprehensively that a power vacuum in Asia could be filled in coming decades by Japan, China, a reunited Korea, Russia, Indonesia, Vietnam, or India. Americans have "the technology and the markets that have allowed us to grow, and they have a certain generosity of spirit."[17] Unlike other nations, the United States "did try to live up to its principles." The key imponderable, he said, was the U.S. economy. Those principles, purposes, and policies that the U.S. sustained derived from a world situation that had changed.

One fourth of U.S. business loans are from foreign sources.[18]

Reuters/Bettmann

Lee Kuan Yew, Prime Minister
Singapore 1959-1990

LOOKING FORWARD

Today the United States lacks an enemy, and there are four instead of two centers of world power: Japan, China, Europe, and the United States. Asian centers are growing fast; Western ones are floundering. Japan's difficulties in the early 1990s were but a pause in its continuing ascendancy. And the Asians are employing principles scarcely understood and generally suspect in the West.

> *If the United States is to continue to organize collective leadership, as many seem to want, it must strengthen itself and replace the old Cold War paradigm with a new one.*

Perhaps most important, the United States must recognize that, although it is no longer number one, its importance to the world is not lessened. However, its traditional ideological paradigm of individualism is flawed and it must consider other paradigms. In doing so the United States can develop a truly profound relationship with the Asian power centers of Japan and China. Thus, far from being dead, ideology today is at the very center of the globalization process.

The people of the United States, their government, and their great corporations will play an important role in the creation of the new paradigm and the associated strategies. To do so, however, America must regain its confidence; revive its ability to compete in the world economy, especially in those high-tech sectors that will shape the future; and recover a sense of moral purpose. We will address this in the next chapters.

We face a world of convergence, divergence, integration, and disintegration. The old structures are in trouble; they were created to implement old strategies that were designed for an old reality. They

There are four instead of two centers of world power: Japan, China, Europe, and the United States.

Trade, investment, and monetary and exchange rates cannot be separated. Their interconnectedness requires coordinated management at a global level.

are large, powerful, and important, but they lack direction. Their mission is unclear and uncertain. They drift, their inertia powered by outworn assumptions and massive bureaucracies. Their renovation requires new strategies, which in turn require a new paradigm.

Let us close this analysis of the breakdown of the old institutions of multilateralism with a look at new forms that are taking shape and some thoughts as to what the future may bring.

A New World Economic Organization

This review of global institutions reveals their key deficiency: Trade, investment, and monetary and exchange rates cannot be separated. Their interconnectedness requires coordinated management at a global level.

Regional coordination, exemplified by the European Community (EC), is a good beginning but ultimately such coordination needs to be global to be effective. Fred Bergsten has suggested an "informal steering group" of representatives from the United States, Europe, and Japan to work quietly behind the scenes to "strengthen and foster" the IMF, the World Bank, and the new WTO and, perhaps, to combine them into what he has dubbed a World Economic Organization (WEO).

Let us speculate about the sorts of things a new WEO might do to manage global tensions, and then go on to examine some small but significant business and government initiatives to handle those same tensions.

WEO could view development as the political process that it is and would use the full range of potential engines of change to foster development. High on this agenda would be multinational corporations specifically organized and dedicated to development purposes. In addition, a reformed World Bank and IMF would depart from their Western orientation and draw on the experience of Asia to permit a wider range of appropriate development policies for governments.

WEO would be a great leap forward in global understanding and would be a first step in the direction of cooperation and conciliation around some kind of global consensus. It would also allow for integrated negotiation and deal-making where matters could be properly addressed as interconnected parts of a whole rather than as separate pieces. For example, migration policies could be coordinated with investment flows and special incentives could stimulate corporations to emphasize job creation and skill development.

Representation and Strategic Thrust

WEO membership might be the same as that of the World Trade Organization, including representation from regional organizations, such as the European Union, the North American Free Trade Agreement, and the Asia Pacific Economic Cooperation forum, and augmented by representatives of the leading multinational corporations.

Every member nation would draft an economic strategy statement to be deposited with the WEO. The statement would include the member's

- ◆ Goals regarding inflation, unemployment, interest rates, and the like
- ◆ Policies regarding trade, investment, industrial targeting, and the environment
- ◆ International agreements and understandings
- ◆ Estimation of their strategy's impact on the world

These statements would help WEO

- ◆ Design special programs and incentives to

encourage the expansion of multinational corporation activity in developing countries

♦ Do global environmental planning covering such matters as technological solutions to environmental problems as well as what new problems technology may cause

♦ Design the most efficient programs to assist poor countries

♦ Manage effectiveness of global trade while taking into account particular problems and needs of individual countries/members

Authority

Because of the interconnectedness of trade and investment, the WEO would attempt to facilitate both trade and foreign direct investment. It would address such questions as: Who gets the benefits of foreign investments? Where do they flow? What are the consequences? At the very least, the WEO would move the world toward some shared understanding of these issues and possibly toward a greater consensus about what is "fair." While openness would be the rule, the WEO would determine justifiable exceptions; several obviously come to mind: national security, control of the national community, the consistency of the national system—jobs, training, education, incomes, etc.

To encourage foreign direct investment, the WEO would provide dispute-settling services comparable to those in the WTO and NAFTA agreements. Disputes brought by one of the parties—governments or private investors—would be submitted to binding arbitration under the rules of the World Bank's International Centre for Settlement of Investment Disputes (ICSID) or the United Nations Commission on International Trade Law. Under either set of rules, the arbitrators would be empowered to protect the rights of the disputants. They could, for example, order that an award be made to an offended investor, including monetary damages and/or restitutions of property plus interest.

NEW INITIATIVES TAKING SHAPE

While the world waits for improvements in its official global paraphernalia, energetic and creative individuals in government, interest groups, and corporations are quietly assembling global arrangements to deal with crises and tensions. For the most part, they work outside of legislatures and parliaments and are screened from the glare of the media in order to find common interests, shape a consensus, and persuade those with power to change.

The International Capital Adequacy Agreement

Throughout the decades of the '60s and '70s, Eurodollars were completely unregulated. This meant that banks in Europe, including the branches of U.S. banks, could conduct their business in dollars with fewer constraints than banks located in the United States. U.S. bank lending soared, while their capital levels, that is the stakes of the bank's owners, declined. Thus, the buffer that banks held to protect them against bad loans wore thin.

Paul Volcker, chairman of the Federal Reserve Board, and Gerald Corrigan, president of the Federal Reserve Bank of New York, were determined to find a way to improve the safety of the U.S. banking system by increasing the amount of capital that banks must hold. This required an agreement among the international banks of Japan and Europe to adhere to the same standards. Otherwise, the foreign banks would

Paul Volcker, chairman of the Federal Reserve Board

While no formal international currency exists, there *is* supranational money, which is beyond the reach of any government regulation or safeguards. It is called Eurodollars or Eurocurrencies. These are dollars—or yen or Deutsche marks—which are held in countries other than their home country throughout the world—*not just Europe*. They are called "Euro" because it was in Europe that they were first spawned. About 80% of the Eurocurrency market, which by 1986 had grown to $3.6 trillion—up from $110 billion in 1970—is in dollars.[19] These huge quantities of funds are among the principle sources of capital for multinational corporations.

have a competitive advantage as they could lend more using a lower capital base.

In July 1986, Volcker suggested a joint U.S.-U.K. agreement on capital adequacy to the Governor of the Bank of England, Robert Leigh-Pemberton; details were worked out by October.

Japanese banks had generally operated with much lower capital requirements than those of Europe and the United States. Long and intense negotiations were required to meet the unique characteristics of Japanese banking, but by August 1987 an agreement had been reached. Soon thereafter central bank governors from the so-called "Group of Ten" members also approved.

In July 1988, the world's international banks and their corresponding governments agreed to adopt a common set of rules governing how much capital the banks were required to hold in order to ensure their solvency and liquidity. This was important for several reasons. First, because the world was awash in stateless money— Eurocurrency—that a number of major banks were lending to developing countries and the loans were turning sour, threatening the banking system of the United States as well as other countries. Second, because disparities among nations in capital requirements affected the ability of banks to compete.

A small group of exceptionally competent persons at the highest levels of the Japanese, American, and British governments, operating in privacy if not secrecy, responded to a global issue that had all the makings of an oncoming crisis that was beyond the control of national governments. They proceeded incrementally, working closely with the private sector, gaining agreement and making adjustments as they went along—first with Britain, then with Japan and finally with the remaining countries of the Group of Ten.

The initiative's success makes one wonder about the virtues of democratic openness when it comes to managing global tensions. It is possible that a measure of secrecy is required to secure global agreement on sensitive matters.[20]

THE MONTREAL PROTOCOL

Secrecy, however, is unlikely to characterize the management of tensions growing from environmental degradation where the glare of media attention—instigated and intensified by environmental activists—seems likely to be an important, perhaps essential spur to action.

Global networks of environmentalists are exposing an expanding array of problems. In response, new initiatives in world diplomacy are proliferating, agreements in which the leaders of multinational corporations are as important as government officials—sometimes more so. Problems include the destruction of forests, unprecedented extinction of animals and plant species, desertification, soil erosion, and pollution of the oceans, the atmosphere, and the Antarctic continent.

It is hoped that the Montreal Protocol to protect the earth's ozone shield will be a forerunner of many global accords growing out of the far-sighted initiative of corporate leaders, working together with national governments and international agencies such as the United Nations and the GATT.

It began as a governmental effort with industry cooperation from DuPont and sixteen other chemical companies from the United States, Europe, Japan and South Korea, to reduce the use of ozone-depleting chemicals, especially chlorofluorocarbons (CFCs) and halons. These chemicals were widely used for refrigeration, air

The Group of Ten was actually 12: Belgium, Canada, France, Germany, Italy, Japan, Luxembourg, Netherlands, Sweden, Switzerland, United Kingdom, and the United States.

Species extinction occurred at the rate of approximately 1 per year over the last 300 years; today's rate is at least 1,000 times as great.[22]

conditioning, aerosol sprays, and cleaning electronic parts. The industry raced to find substitutes, with firms cooperating in joint research efforts. By 1991, sixty-two countries had ratified agreements to ban all CFC emissions by 1999. New trade measures would require countries to ban imports of all products containing CFCs.[21]

Other environmental agreements, designed and undertaken by governments, have been less successful. The Basle Convention on the Control of Transboundary Movements of Hazardous Wastes, designed to prevent rich countries from dumping their poisons in the poor ones, was ratified in 1992 by only twenty national governments. At this writing, the biggest exporters, including the United States, Japan, and most of the European countries, had refused to sign.

Somewhat more successful was the Convention on International Trade in Endangered Species of Wild Fauna and Flora (CITES), which by 1993 had more than 120 signatories. The convention outlawed trade in many animals and their body parts: elephants, rhinoceroses, whales, turtles, bears, seals, bats, and migratory birds, among others.

Agreements such as these put a crimp in world trade and tend to subvert the principles of GATT as well as to curtail growth as traditionally measured. Trade experts and economists in general insist that trade and the environment are separate issues, but a growing body of opinion holds otherwise.

SUMMARY

The Cold War U.S.-U.S.S.R. power base has been replaced by four centers of world power: China, Japan, Europe, and the United States.

Globalization will be accompanied by an inevitable erosion of national sovereignty.

If the U.S. is going to organize collective leadership, it must strengthen itself and replace the old Cold War ideological paradigm of individualism.

Old paradigms preserve the status quo and thwart major changes.

Old institutions must be reshaped or replaced with ones based on a new paradigm.

Trade, investment, and monetary and exchange rates cannot be separated; their coordination must be global to be effective.

Asian centers are growing fast while Western ones are floundering; the Asians operate according to the notion that competition is among national systems, not among firms.

Asian development strategies are characterized by extensive government intervention, often intimate relations between government and business, and less than full respect for free markets and free trade.

A World Economic Organization would be a first step toward creating some kind of global consensus.

People are not waiting for a new institution to emerge but are dealing with issues out of a sense of need.

OVERVIEW

- ◆ The Leadership Imperative
- ◆ The Road to American Recovery and Leadership
- ◆ Competitive National Strategies
- ◆ The Role of Business and Management
- ◆ The Community's Needs
- ◆ Corporate Responsibility

GLOBAL LEADERSHIP

3

The leadership to manage the tensions of globalization will be rooted in economic power and moral purpose. During the Cold War, the United States had enough of both, and the "free world" followed along. In spite of a substantially weaker economy and a more ambiguous moral purpose, if any country is to lead the world into the twenty-first century, it seems that it must be the United States—and that means both its government and its multinational enterprises. America can do so, however, only in partnership with Europe, Japan, China, and other rapidly growing Asian countries. But America's leadership potential is ebbing, so there is no time to waste.

A Leadership Imperative

At present, world economic power is shared by the United States, Europe, and Japan. As soon as Germany has managed its enormously expensive reunification of east and west, it will supercharge Europe. Japan will emerge from its economic restructuring of the mid-1990s stronger and more competitive than ever. Within the next 10 or 15 years, Japan's GNP is expected to surpass that of the United States.[1] Confidence in German and Japanese recovery and growth is based on the following:

1. These nations understand the concept of a national economic strategy.

2. They know what it takes to win.

3. They have the political, economic, and social structures in place to provide the consensus necessary to make their strategies work.

China, too, is on its way to becoming a leading—if not the dominant—world economic power with a population of 1.2 billion and a sustained growth rate of more than 10 percent a year. Its strategy, however, remains uncertain, and its political structures are strained and fragile. Taiwan, South Korea, Singapore, and Hong Kong could overtake America's GNP per head within the next quarter-century, and Indonesia, Malaysia, and Thailand are close behind.

How will the collective leadership the world needs arise from these centers of power? In the short run, preoccupation with its internal development and the defense of its borders will leave China with little time or inclination to worry about the world. And, since the end of World War II, Japan has shied away from converting its awesome economic power into political influence, which might be bad for business and inflame latent fears of Japanese imperialism among its Asian neighbors, especially China and Korea. Germany has increased its international leadership to aid European integration and East Germany's economic development, but memories of Germany's grim past are obstacles to a larger role. Which brings us to the United States.

America's version of "human rights" is by no means universal; its internationally marketed "culture" is objectionable to many; its disintegration at home is not reassuring. Furthermore, its generosity is sorely limited by a huge national deficit; and many Americans think they've done enough for the world. Nevertheless, the United States seems destined to continue, at least for a while, to bear an inescapable responsibility for organizing the collective leadership the world needs.

This task requires a clear recognition of U.S. national interest: isolation is not a choice. Additionally it requires the design and implementation of a national economic strategy to regain American competitiveness (especially in the high-tech, high value-added, high-wage, high-income industries of the future).

A weak America cannot lead: It needs strength to be magnanimous and the confidence to know and secure its vital interests. Only then can it negotiate the instruments of global order with others.

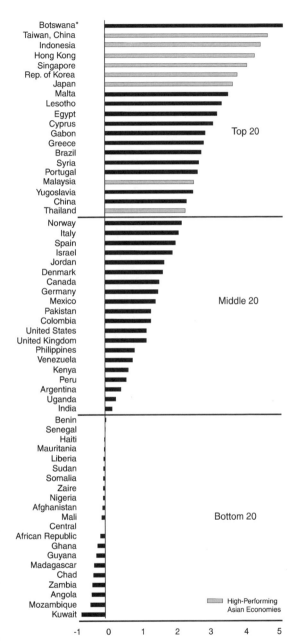

The oddity of Botswana's first-place ranking is explained by lots of diamonds and only a million people.

Source: *The World Bank*, The East Asian Miracle, Economic Growth and Public Policy, NY: *Oxford University Press, Inc. 1993, p. 3*

Change in GDP Per Capita, 1960-85

AMERICAN RECOVERY

The recovery of American economic strength and moral purpose are related in two ways. First, both require an ideological transition from individualism, briefly described in Chapter 2, to communitarianism, which I shall get to later when we consider the ideology or belief system that may serve as the basis for global convergence and cooperation.

And secondly, it is hard for America to feel good about itself and to provide the means for individual fulfillment and self-respect if it is not maximizing its competitive resources, both human and material.

American competitiveness has been eroding for more than two decades. National competitiveness is the ability of a nation to earn a rising standard of living for its people through the production of goods and services that meet the test of international markets.

According to the U.S. government's Competitiveness Policy Council:

> The average real wage is lower today than 20 years ago. Aggregate productivity has grown by only one percent annually for over a decade. We are running the world's largest trade deficits. Much of the economic growth of the 1980s was financed by borrowing from our future, both at home and from the rest of the world.[2]

THE TRADE IMPACT

Thirty years ago share of trade (imports/exports) was relatively unimportant to the United States, but since then trade's share in the economy has risen two and a half times. Today exports and imports of goods and services account for nearly one-quarter of total gross domestic product. In fact, the United States is now as

dependent on trade as the European Community and Japan.[3] And the prolonged inability of the United States to export more than it imports has resulted in trade deficits that have had to be paid for with foreign investment and debt, resulting in a loss of control by the United States of its economic resources. This loss has been deepened by the borrowing required to fund the federal government's budget deficits. At the end of 1994, the U.S. was by far the world's largest debtor with external liabilities of $750 billion. This was a major factor in the precipitous decline in the value of the dollar in the last year. As of March 1995, a dollar could buy only 85 yen, compared to 360 in the 1960s.[4]

LESSONS FROM THE JAPANESE ECONOMIC NATIONAL STRATEGY

Japan is certainly America's most important economic challenger in international trade, especially in high-tech sectors.

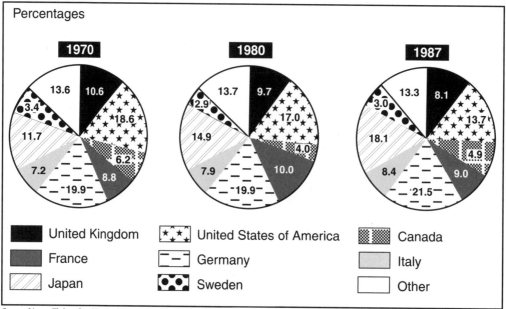

Percentages

Source: Liesner, Thelma, One Hundred Years of Economic Statistics, A New Edition of Economic Statistics 1900-1983, Revised and Expanded to 1987, London: The Economist Publications Ltd., c. 1989, p. 319. ©1989 The Economist Newspaper Group, Inc. Reprinted with permission. Further reproduction prohibited.

Exports: Market Shares of 8 Countries

Japan and other Asian challengers have demonstrated what it takes to manage a national economy competitively in the world today:

1. A high rate of personal domestic savings and investment in export industries that results in high productivity gains and fosters high employment, high wages, and a rising standard of living

2. An emphasis on education and training that produces modern production skills and talents and the discipline and hard work to follow through with these initiatives

3. A plan to move up the technology ladder through credit allocation and targeted acquisition of market share in future-oriented sectors affording big profits and opportunities

4. A synergy between corporate governance and financial markets that focuses on the long-run health of a company and that perceives corporate purpose in terms of acquisition of market share for the good of the company as a whole and for the communities of which it is a part

Implicit in these prerequisites for a successful economic strategy is a producer—rather than a consumer—orientation: Asian success has not been built on a buy-now-pay-later approach.

5. A trade policy that serves national strategic priorities and promotes the competitiveness of chosen sectors without protecting noncompetitiveness.

6. Government policies and industry organization that achieves all of the foregoing and encourages cooperation and collaboration among firms and industries to develop new technologies and commercially successful products.

7. Human resource management policies that link all employees to the company and its success: long-term employment, participatory decision-making, relatively small differences in wages between the top and the bottom, and a general willingness to share pains and gains. Implicit in these prerequisites for a successful economic strategy is a producer—rather than a consumer—orientation: tax, regulatory, and other policies that encourage efficient and competitive corporate endeavor rather than personal consumption; Asian success has not been built on a buy-now-pay-later approach.[5]

And what producers make is important; some industries are more important to national welfare than others. "What a country makes—the structure of its economy—matters," says Clyde Prestowitz, president of the Economic Strategy Institute. This runs counter to the conventional wisdom in the United States attributed to a

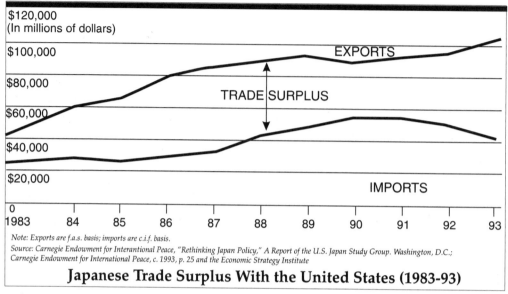

Note: Exports are f.a.s. basis; imports are c.i.f. basis.

Source: Carnegie Endowment for Interarntional Peace, "Rethinking Japan Policy," A Report of the U.S. Japan Study Group. Washington, D.C.; Carnegie Endowment for International Peace, c. 1993, p. 25 and the Economic Strategy Institute

Japanese Trade Surplus With the United States (1983-93)

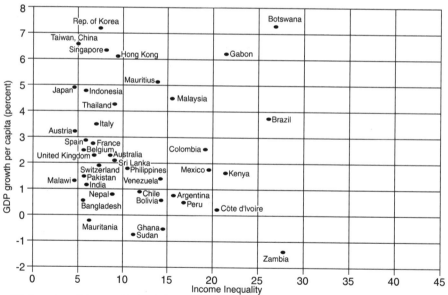

Note: Income inequality is measured by the ratio of the income shares of the richest 20 percent and the poorest 20 percent of the population.
Source: The World Bank, The East Asia Miracle, Economic Growth and Public Policy, NY: Oxford University Press, 1993, p. 31

Income Inequality and Growth of GDP, 1965-89

The East Asian high-growth countries have the world's most equitable distribution of income, an important factor in their ability to generate and maintain widespread consensus for often stringent if not austere economic policies. Although Botswana holds the title for the highest growth rate in the world (attributable to the discovery of diamonds), it is also distinguished by the worst income distribution.

former presidential economic adviser: "Potato chips, computer chips, what's the difference? A hundred dollars of one or a hundred dollars of the other is still a hundred dollars."6 These different perceptions reflect different conceptions of economic reality: They exemplify two different paradigms. Winners see the world as Prestowitz does; losers stick with the old conception.

The Asian model gives government the important role of targeting for special support those technologies and industries that are crucial to the nation's future strength. The United States has always supported industries vital to the country's national security—aerospace, agriculture, and weapons—but only recently has it conceded that it is proper to support other selected industries for the country's *economic* security.

Japan has shown that a partnership between government and business works better than an adversarial relationship.

AMERICAN PARADIGM SHIFTS

The United States has demonstrated this in its space and military activities, but these were justified by the Cold War. Antitrust restrictions and a managerial mind-set predisposed against it have slowed cooperation among firms and industries for joint research in the United States. Relations between suppliers and customers that are intimate in Japan have tended to be distant and hostile in the United States. American firms are further handicapped by the short-term expectations of Wall Street and pressures for profit maximization at the expense of market share.7

In his inaugural address, President Clinton addressed the need for change:

The Asian model gives government the important role of targeting for special support those technologies and industries that are crucial to the nation's future strength.

U.S. annual production of potato chips totaled 1.7 billion pounds worth $4.5 billion; manufacturers' shipments of computer chips were valued at over $5.5 billion. The importance of the latter lie in their long-term contribution to high-tech capabilities with high profits and good wages.

Communications and commerce are global, investment is mobile, technology is almost magical, and ambition for a better life is now universal. We earn our livelihood in America today in peaceful competition with people all over the world. Profound and powerful forces are shaping and remaking our world. The urgent question of our time is whether we make change our friend and not our enemy.

Laura Tyson, Clinton's chief economic advisor, reinforced the message when she said, "We can no longer afford to ignore the efforts of Japan and Europe to promote their own high-technology producers....

The policies and institutions that served the nation well when we were the world's unquestioned technological leader require overhaul now that Japan and Europe have emerged as our economic equals."[8]

The Clinton administration formulated a technology policy to achieve these purposes and the United States is starting to move in the direction of the Asian model, but change is slow. It threatens profound and cherished elements of the American heritage. Indeed it subverts capitalism itself, whose "deepest assumption," says the author, James Fallows, is that "governments can never outguess the market about where money should go. All that governments can—and should—do is make sure the necessary signals flow. Signals come in the form of prices; therefore the paramount goal is to 'get prices right.' After that everything should work on its own."[9]

THE WINNING ASIAN PARADIGM

On dozens of occasions, publications such as *The Economist, Business Week,* and *The Wall Street Journal* have confidently predicted the collapse of the Japanese system. It was, after all, a violation of their paradigm of free markets, free enterprise, the limited state, and laissez faire. When the system went on from strength to strength, Western thinkers took one of two different tacks. Some twisted the Japanese system around so as to make it appear legitimate by Western standards, an exceptionally complicated bit of intellectualizing reminiscent of the medieval astronomers' attempts to make Ptolemy's view of the heavens come out right. Naysayers continued to predict the worst, certain that eventually Japan would see the error of its ways. Christopher Wood, financial editor of *The Economist,* characterized the Japanese financial system in 1992 as "bordering on feudal...distorted...inefficient...weird." It must become more like the West—Britain, for example— "for its own good." "Japan's managed economy can only delay the impact of market prices, not prevent it."[10] This was a classic reaction by the practitioner of one paradigm to the practitioner of another.

The Asians, being in the winning paradigm, are forcing those in the other—the losers—to change, but it does not come easily. The Asian paradigm has four premises that subvert the capitalist

1. A country can create its comparative advantage with a strategy aimed at global competitiveness; it does not have to rely on nature's endowment and the invisible hand of marketplace competition, firm versus firm.

2. It is the job of government to design a competitive economic strategy. Marketplace competition is an extremely useful tool but it is not an end in itself.

3. The purpose of business is to preserve and promote the long-run health of the enterprise for the good of the community as a whole. Relationships between managers and managed should be harmonious and consensual because both ultimately

Leading U.S. Trade Deficit & Surplus Items with Japan

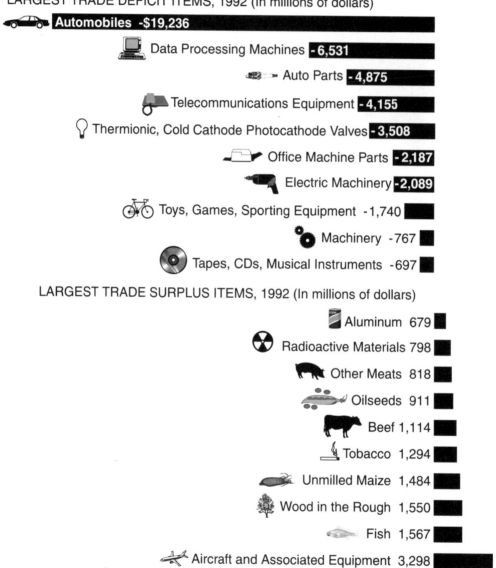

LARGEST TRADE DEFICIT ITEMS, 1992 (In millions of dollars)

Automobiles -$19,236

Data Processing Machines - 6,531

Auto Parts - 4,875

Telecommunications Equipment - 4,155

Thermionic, Cold Cathode Photocathode Valves - 3,508

Office Machine Parts - 2,187

Electric Machinery -2,089

Toys, Games, Sporting Equipment -1,740

Machinery -767

Tapes, CDs, Musical Instruments -697

LARGEST TRADE SURPLUS ITEMS, 1992 (In millions of dollars)

Aluminum 679

Radioactive Materials 798

Other Meats 818

Oilseeds 911

Beef 1,114

Tobacco 1,294

Unmilled Maize 1,484

Wood in the Rough 1,550

Fish 1,567

Aircraft and Associated Equipment 3,298

Source: Carnegie Endowment for International Peace, "Rethinking Japan Policy," A Report of the U.S. Japan Study Group, Washington, D.C.: Carnegie Endowment for International Peace, c. 1993, p. 22. Based on data from the Economic Strategy Institute.

The United States looks like a less-developed country, importing high-value, high-tech products and exporting raw materials and minerals.

have the same interest in the prosperity of the firm. Shareholders benefit along with everyone else.

4. The members of any community have rights and duties, which the community—not individuals— must determine in accordance with the nation's strategy. To be effective, these determinations have to be regarded as fair and equitable.

The Asian model of government intervention differs significantly from that of discredited European socialism and the "welfare state" because it is outward-looking and focused above all on global competitiveness in the world economy. Labor relations, social policies—indeed all else—are fixed to that end.

Japan and other Asian nations are forcing the United States to question cherished beliefs and to change its ways; this, after fifty years during which the United States waged a cold war, in part, to defend those very beliefs. And change it must if the United States is going to regain its economic strength, mend divisions at home, and be able to play its role in managing the tensions of globalization.

A move in the direction of the Asian competitive strategy requires a radical shift in the way Americans perceive the role of government, the purpose of business, and the relationship between the two. Because the shift is unpopular, there is a tendency to regard the foreigners who are forcing it as the enemy. Yet it is nonsensical in the extreme to regard Japan, for example, on whom the United States depends for credit and, increasingly, technology, as an enemy.

The United States must—and has begun to— change its system in order to make more effective use of its resources and to strengthen its economy. This is important not only for Americans' standard of living, but also as a prerequisite for America's leadership role for organizing the consensus required to manage the ten-

The main creators and controllers of the global flows of money, investment, goods, services, and technology are not governments but instead some 300 giant multinational corporations.

sions of globalization. Only a strong and confident America can work with others to design and assemble the transnational governmental institutions discussed in Chapter 2. Over time, these institutions will assume increasing power as the processes of globalization undermine the integrity of the nation-state.

THE ROLE OF BUSINESS

The main creators and controllers of the global flows of money, investment, goods, services, and technology are not governments but instead some 300 giant multinational corporations. While these corporations are enriching many, their blessings are neither universal, nor unmixed.

Changing structures of international business and investment may exacerbate the gap between the world's haves and have-nots notes Paul Kennedy in his book, *Preparing for the Twenty-First Century.*

> "The internationalization of manufacturing and finance erodes a people's capacity to control its own affairs...The real logic of the borderless world is that nobody is in control—except, perhaps, the managers of multinational corporations, whose responsibility is to their shareholders, who, one might argue, have become the new sovereigns, investing in whatever company gives the highest returns....The people of the earth seem to be discovering that their lives are ever more affected by forces which are, in the full meaning of word, irresponsible."[11]

Communities worldwide bid against one another to offer corporations the most appealing concessions in order to secure jobs and incomes, often unmindful of the possible effects on the community and its needs. Furthermore, the bargain is often struck by elites who are not subject to any adverse consequences. Japan's corporations have built

With globalization, the relevant community for an increasing variety of needs is the world.

national loyalty into their purposes; other nations, including America, often do not. This difference has political, social, and economic effects. A nationalistic corporation helps its nation, perhaps at the expense of other nations. It designs its global operations to maximize the benefits at home, such as high-paying jobs, skill development, and future technological gains. By contrast, a non-nationalistic corporation designs its operations strictly for the benefit of the corporation, unmindful of the effects on the home country. It being unclear which procedure is more competitive, both approaches will continue to flourish with important effects on different communities.

SERVING COMMUNITY NEEDS

The future requires new and improved ways of assuring that businesses, especially the giant multinationals, act responsibly: that they serve the needs of the community.

But what is "the community?" Is it the neighborhood, city, nation, a region of nations (the European Community or NAFTA), or the world? Most important, who decides which community is the relevant community? Obviously when it comes to ozone depletion or global warming or exchange rates or trade policies, the relevant community is the world. When it comes to jobs, health, housing, incomes, toxic dumping, and the like, the relevant community is more local. With globalization, the relevant community for an increasing variety of needs is the world.

The community can determine community needs by acting through its local, state, federal, regional, or global government, or the decision can be left to competition among private companies to satisfy marketplace demands. Communitarian societies prefer the former; individualistic ones the latter.

There are four ways to align business activities with the needs of the community.

1. The virtues of marketplace competition are that it both defines and fulfills community needs. Drawbacks occur if consumer desires are an unreliable or unacceptable measure of community needs.

2. Regulations are used when competition does not work to meet the community's needs as defined by the community—needs for clean air, safe food, and so on.

3. Because regulation is cumbersome, it often devolves into a partnership or cooperative relationship between government and business to fulfill community needs as defined either by government or by government and business together.

4. Finally, there is the corporate charter—the birth certificate the community gives the corporation through which it may stipulate what it does. Socialist ownership of the means of production is a failed example of the charter form of control. The Tennessee Valley Authority and COMSAT in the United States and Telecom in France are more successful varieties.

An efficient community picks the most appropriate combination of these four methods to control business. The Soviet Union collapsed to a great extent because it precluded itself for ideological reasons from using any but the charter route. Japan has made good use of all four; it prefers partnership but employs competition—not as an end but as a means to achieving predetermined community needs such as export competitiveness. In its early years the United States employed both the charter and partnership routes. In the Nineteenth and early Twentieth Centuries it preferred marketplace competition, enforced through its unique set of antitrust laws and augmented by regulation. Over the years it has drifted back toward partnership in order to meet such community needs as clean air, space exploration, advanced military technology, and, of late, international competition. This transition is part of what was referred to in Chapter 2 as the "withering of individualism."

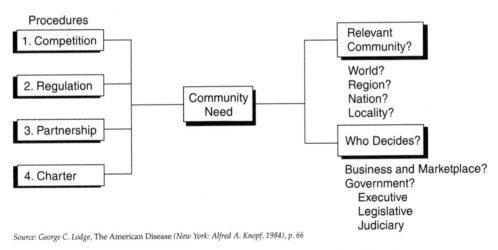

Source: George C. Lodge, The American Disease (New York: Alfred A. Knopf, 1984), p. 66

Aligning Business With Community Needs

SOURCES OF AUTHORITY

Related to these four control procedures are four possible sources of authority for business managers. These sources in tandem with the control procedures dictate a community's conception of the purpose of business—its legitimacy and its responsibility. The four sources of authority are as follows:

1. Equity holders—the owners or shareholders, who it is believed derive authority from property rights.

2. Debt holders—banks and the like—which in some countries, like Germany and Japan, are also owners.

3. The managed, which is very much the case in Japan and Germany, as well as in some American companies hard pressed by international competition such as NUMMI—General Motors (GM) and its Toyota plant in Fremont, California, and also its Saturn plant in the Midwest.

4. The community itself acting through its own government.

It is important to distinguish theory from practice. Theoretically, management's purpose in the United States is to satisfy shareholders, but increasingly that purpose is unachievable unless at least equal weight is

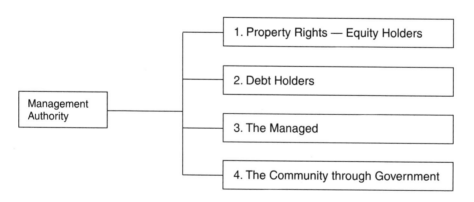

Source: George C. Lodge, The American Disease *(New York: Alfred A. Knopf, 1984), p. 71*

Sources of Management Authority

given to the long-run interests of the managed and the community.

General Motors and other American automobile companies exemplify the transformation occurring in the sources of management authority in the United States, which in turn is part of the transition from individualism to communitarianism in the country. Pre-1973 management authority at General Motors came primarily from the shareholders. Management's task was to maximize shareholder return over the short run. Managers hired and fired workers as needed to compete in the marketplace. On the other hand, the mission of the United Automobile Workers was to maximize returns to its membership. Thus, two warring camps were established at GM: managers and workers, connected by a rigid, legalistic, and adversarial contract. It was the final flowering of the old paradigm and it became a disaster. When Japanese and German companies showed the world a quite different model of authority and purpose, Americans had to change in order to survive.

NUMMI, mentioned earlier, is an example of such change. Similar changes have occurred at Ford under the heading of "employee involvement," and at Chrysler where union representatives sit on the board of directors. In all three companies, the right to manage increasingly comes from the managed. Shareholders are still important, but priorities have changed as a matter of survival.

Conflict among different sources of authority, as in the United States, causes

The right to manage increasingly comes from the managed.

Mitsui was founded in 1671 as a merchant house at a time when society was controlled by the local shogun and his samurai bureaucracy. The population was ranked in the following order: samurai, peasants, artisans, and merchants.

When the Meiji modernization transformed Japan in 1868, Mitsui's purpose remained to serve the interests of government. The industrialization of Japan was in no sense marked by a flourishing of individualism. Indeed, it was carried out "for the sake of tradition itself, because in the Japanese context tradition had divine meaning and was symbolized in the Emperor." The modernization was necessary to protect Japan from foreign predators and to preserve its "innate superiority to any other nation."[12]

uncertainty. In Japan and Germany, the sources of authority are better integrated and more focused on long-run corporate health, which gives managers' greater confidence about their purpose.

An executive of Mitsui, Japan's giant *soga shosha* (trading company with sales of $120 billion in 1986, one of the largest companies in the world) described Mitsui's purpose as follows, emphasizing the order:

1. To contribute to Japanese society, to serve the greater glory of Japan

2. To realize profit for the company so as to promote the welfare and happiness of its employees

3. To foster and strengthen the spirit of Mitsui for the future, as that spirit is set forth in the company motto *"Ten, Chi, Jen"* (heaven, earth, and human beings)

The satisfaction of shareholders, he said, is but a means to these ends. Clearly, the sources of authority are the managed and the community.

Ranking of Corporate Objectives: U.S. and Japan

	United States	Japan
Return on investment	8.1	4.1 (2)
Share price increase	3.8	0.1
Market share	2.4	4.8 (1)
Improve product portfolio	1.5	2.3
Rationalization of production and distribution	1.5	2.4
Increase equity ratio	1.3	2.0
Ratio of new products	0.7	3.5 (3)
Improve company image	0.2	0.7
Improve working conditions	0.1	0.3

Source: Adapted from Economic Planning Agency, Japanese Government, "Economic Survey of Japan 1980/1981" (Tokyo: Japan Times, 1982), p. 196, as used in Kaisha: The Japanese Corporation by James C. Abegglen and George Stalk, Jr. Copyright ©1985 by Basic Books, Inc. Reprinted by permission of Basic Books, a division of HarperCollins Publishers, Inc.

291 Japanese companies and 227 U.S. companies ranked factors from 1, least importance, to 10, most importance

TOWARD CORPORATE RESPONSIBILITY

The first responsibility of the multinational corporations is to its employees and to its home country.

We can now envisage a way in which the social arrangements upon which corporate responsibility depends can be designed and built. We can perceive a framework of controls, rooted in the notion of community need, in which business purpose and management authority come increasingly from affected communities.

The first responsibility of the multinational corporations is to its employees and to its home country. Without strong competitive economies, the United States and other industrialized countries cannot manage the tensions of globalization. If they do not manage globalization, even their own multinationals will suffer. In the United States, this requires a far more intimate relationship between government and business than exists. Government must see business competitiveness as essential to the national interest, and business must make satisfaction of community needs at home a high priority.

The multinational's second responsibility is to other communities that its activities affect. Multinational managers must realize that the needs of those communities are not necessarily defined by the sum of consumer desires.

The largest investors in China over the last two years have been Asian multinationals coming from Taiwan and Hong Kong. These corporations are run by ethnic Chinese, and a large share of their investments has gone to reform woefully inefficient state enterprises. This is in keeping with China's perception of its needs. The Asians have also invested heavily in extremely underdeveloped and highly bureaucratic sectors of the Chinese economy such as real estate and retail, again partly because it is in these sectors that China's need are most pronounced. Unlike their Western counterparts, these firms have engaged in little haggling over fine points of property rights and contract. They have endeavored to find a reliable and legitimate definition of community need and to serve it efficiently and profitably.[13]

In many developing countries the community need has not been well defined and local governments often cannot be relied on to do so. Here is where our proposed World Economic Organization (WEO) can help, setting forth the needs that multinational corporations should be encouraged to meet and serve.

In addition, the WEO itself might charter corporations to meet special needs in such areas as communications, education, technology transfer, health services, agriculture, and food processing. Thus, such corporations would have a global charter and purpose to serve global needs in the most efficient and profitable way. There is not enough money to meet those needs in any other way.

These suggestions, thoughtful executives will perceive, are not designed to curb or damage multinationals, but rather to expand, encourage, and assist them by providing a more reliable context within which they can become more certain about their role, more confident about their purposes, and more effective in contributing to the collective leadership the world needs.

SUMMARY

Appropriate interrelated political, economic, and social structures are essential to provide the consensus necessary to make a national economic strategy work.

A successful economic strategy depends on a producer orientation and policies that encourage efficient and competitive corporate endeavor versus personal consumption.

The relationship between business and government should be a partnership.

Business must serve community needs.

The authority to manage is increasingly derived from the managed.

OVERVIEW

♦ 20th Century Value Systems

    Capitalism

    Socialism

    Communism

♦ New Global Institutions

♦ A Basis for Global Consensus

THE BASIS FOR GLOBAL CONSENSUS

4

Changes confront the world that are unprecedented, profound, and complex. There is convergence in much that is occurring: Different communities with different political and economic systems are being forced to adapt to one another. There is also conflict. To comprehend the dimensions of the changes requires nothing less than what Paul Kennedy has called "the reeducation of humankind."[1] To direct them toward peace and justice means the creation of totally new global institutions of planning and cooperation.

Before we explore the ideas that can provide the basis for a global consensus within which changes may be managed, we would do well to untangle the economic value systems the world has used in the Twentieth Century—capitalism, socialism, and communism—

analyze what the words mean, what has become of them, and ultimately to reject them as inadequate.

IDEOLOGY DEFINED AND EXAMINED

Every community has a framework of ideas or an ideology for defining values and for giving them institutional vitality. Ideologies are bridges for carrying such universally accepted values as survival, justice, economy (more benefits than costs), fulfillment, and self-respect into the real world in order to give them meaning in government, business, universities, and the community as a whole. Ideology constitutes the body of assumptions about values that communities use to shape their activities. Without an ideology there is no community.

An ideology must fit the real world. As the world changes, so will the ideology. Ideology is not and cannot be dogma, though many would like to make it so.

An ideology can be conveniently divided into the following five components:

1. The relationship between the human being and the community, the individuals within it, and the group; and the means to individual fulfillment and self-respect

2. The institutional guarantees and manifestations of that relationship, e.g., property rights

3. The most appropriate means of controlling the production of goods and services

4. The role of the state

5. The prevailing perception of reality and of nature, concerning, for example, the role of science and the functions of education

Ideology has to do with how communities think about these five things. Ideologies in the world can be seen as mixtures and variations of two ideal types: individualism and communitarianism. To exemplify these two types, consider the fifth component listed—the prevailing thinking about reality, nature, and science. Individualism gives authority to the expert, the specialist, the one with the most initials beside her name. It presumes that one can understand reality by looking at the pieces and that the whole will take care of itself. To understand Humpty Dumpty, you count the molecules at the bottom of the wall. Communitarians, on the other hand, know that wholes do not take care of themselves and that we live and work within wholes, within wholes within a fragile biosphere, a big blue bubble that just might pop. Somehow, in spite of the power—and value—of the specialists, a way must be found to discern and analyze systems, whether they be political, economic, social, ecological, or all of these combined and more.

Ideology is controversial for several reasons. The ideology of one community is not that of another. Institutions lose legitimacy when they depart from prevailing ideologies to cope with the real world: to seize opportunities and to deal with threats. They are in limbo either until they return to the ideology or until ideology changes to support and justify their actions. There is an ideological schizophrenia: the new practice brings forth a new ideology to justify itself, but loyalty to the old ways discourages its articulation. This Legitimacy Gap is illustrated on page 89. As the legitimacy gap widens, two conflicting pressures converge on managers: one seeks to force errant institutions back into conformity with the old ideology; the other argues for a more powerful expression of the new one as being the only means of legitimizing what is occurring.

We have also seen how the definition of "community" can change and strain old ideologies. The multinational corporation operating in many communities is

Ideology: A Bridge Between Values and the Real World

Values	Traditional Ideology		New Ideology	Real World
Survival	1. Individualism		1. Communitar-ianism	Geography
Justice	Equality (opportunity)		Equality of (result)	Demography
Economy			or Hierarchy	Economic
	Contract		Consensus	performance
Fulfillment				
	2. Property rights		2. Rights and	Technology
Self-respect		Int. Grps.	duties of membership	Scientific insights:
Etc.				Newton
	3. Competition to satisfy consumer desires		3. Community need	Einstein Ecologists, et al.
				Traditional institutions
	4. Limited state ←		4. Active, planning state	vs. New: e.g., OPEC, Japan
	5. Scientific specialization		5. Holism	Traditional behavior patterns

Source: George C. Lodge, The American Disease *(New York: Alfred A. Knopf, 1984).*

sustained by no single ideology. The "real world" once bounded by national or regional borders, has in many ways become global, which means that ideologies that historically served national communities now must serve the world community. But, since each national ideology differs, the process is fraught with controversy.

This chapter will suggest in broad terms what a world ideology might look like with the hope of making this controversy at least manageable. This is not an

The Legitimacy Gap

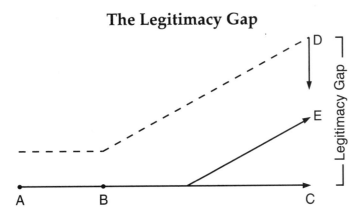

Source: George C. Lodge, The American Disease *(New York: Alfred A. Knopf, 1984).*

During time period AB, institutional practice conforms to the pre-vailing ideology; after that it departs because changes in the real world invite or compel the institutions to behave differently. By time C, institutional practice is very different from what the ideology presumed. There is a gap, DC, which may be called a "legitimacy gap."

attempt to spell out what *should* be, but rather to sketch the overarching ideology that seems to best fit what is happening and what seems likely to happen in the years ahead: a framework with many variations given the differences among the communities of the world, but one that also could provide a basis for global consensus.

CAPITALISM OR WHAT?

Socialism and communism are dead. Capitalism reigns supreme. Such conventional thinking is dangerously misleading. In fact, all three isms are meaningless, replaced by mixtures of the three that differ radically among national and regional communities. The mixtures have one thing in common: They share a communitarian, as opposed to an

The appropriate language of communication and cooperation among national systems is communitarian, not individualistic.

individualistic, ideology, even though particular nations' versions of communitarianism differ widely.

This is important because it means that the appropriate language of communication and cooperation among national systema is communitarian, not individualistic. And the choices about what kind of national system is best are choices within a communitarian ideological framework, not an individualistic one.

Since "capitalism" is generally associated with an individualistic ideology and "socialism" with one that is communitarian, the assertion that capitalism has conquered socialism is apt to lead many to the erroneous supposition that individualism has conquered communitarianism. Persisting in such an error distorts one's view of the world and hinders effective action.

Take, for example, the countries of Eastern Europe. The coming of *glasnost* and *perestroika* amid the wreckage of socialism and communism caused Eastern leaders to junk the old ways with a vengeance and to seek to introduce what they regarded as the "purest" form of "capitalism"—free trade, free markets, free enterprise, property rights, the limited state, adversarial contractual relations between managers and the managed, and other elements of individualism. However, it was not long before these leaders realized that their cultural traditions, politics, and global strategic objectives required steps that were communitarian in nature:

♦ Workers needed a stake in the enterprise.

♦ Property rights had to be constrained for environmental reasons and to ensure an equitable distribution of income.

♦ Government had to plan and think about the long-term needs of the community.

So while "socialism" or, more precisely, the traditional socialist form of communitarianism was not the answer, neither was "capitalism" as individualism. The choices which all nations have are choices within a communitarian framework.

As we have seen, global forces such as commercial competition and the requirements of ecological survival are pushing national systems in the direction of ideological convergence—differences among the various forms of communitarianism appear to be diminishing. The analysis of this convergence reveals points of conflict.

INDIVIDUALISM VERSUS COMMUNITARIANISM

Property rights

I: A sacred right derived from God, or "nature."

C: One of a number of rights defined and bestowed on members of the community by the community, generally acting through government.

The definition and relative weight given to property versus other rights (income, health, shelter, etc.) varies among systems, but the individualistic notion is dead or dying. The privatization happening worldwide is neither the result of ideology nor individualism but rather a judgment about efficiency in reaching certain community needs.

Society

I: Life is a lonely, competitive struggle. You get what you deserve and duties are the result of your upbringing, religion ("the Protestant ethic"), and conscience, not of community dictates.

C: The community bestows membership rights (education, income, health, housing) and duties (to work hard, be good parents, and so on).

Everyone is for such values as "fulfillment" and "self-respect," but according to individualism, they are achieved individualistically. For the communitarian, their achievement depends on participation in a carefully designed group or community.

Community Needs

I: These are best defined through market-place competition to satisfy consumer desires; the more competition, the better. Cooperation among competitors is naturally suspect.

C: Marketplace competition is only one of the ways to align business and community needs. Definition of those needs is the proper task of government, augmented as appropriate by the market; cooperation among competitors as well as with government is often essential to their fulfillment.

Relationships

I: The contract is the appropriate mechanism for tying individuals together, whether as employers and employees, suppliers and customers, or husbands and wives; lawyers are essential to interpret contracts. Government's role is to enforce contracts and protect property, meaning one's body and estate.

C: Relationships are organized around the notion of consensus, employing a minimum of legal paraphernalia. And government's role is to define and assure the good of the community.

The individualistic idea flourishes mainly in the United Kingdom and the United States, but there are many signs that even there its earthly manifestations are eroding: for example, marital (contractual) breakdown, labor relations at GM (NUMMI), and healthcare (the universal recognition of governmental responsibility to assure adequate healthcare and in the United States the rise of health maintenance organizations (HMOs) replacing the old, individualistic doctor-patient relationship).

It is useful to separate two sets of ideological conflict: those between individualism and communitarianism, and those among varieties of communitarianism. The first set includes disputes over such matters as property rights, patent protection, and the role of government; differences concerning antitrust laws and cartels; and disputes about industrial policy, government subsidies, "free markets," and "free trade."

The second category includes such conflicts as definition of community need and designation of the relevant community. If every Chinese family had two cars, the pollution might well stifle the world. Also, included in the second category are disputes about human and other rights that impact competition among countries. Cheap labor in Mexico costs jobs in Detroit. Healthcare dilemmas also fit here. How healthy is healthy enough? When should one let the old die? If one smokes, should the community pay for one's cancer treatments?

Traditional American ideology exemplifies individualism. Its ideas first came to America in the Eighteenth Century, having been set down in Seventeenth Century England as natural laws by John Locke, among others. These ideas found fertile soil in the vast, underpopulated American wilderness and served the country well for over a hundred years.

Individualism is the epitome of the American dream, but in many ways its dreamlike characteristics have hidden the fact that the United States was and increasingly is a communitarian country from the days of the Puritan theocracy in New England to the developmental state of Alexander Hamilton, the New Deal of FDR, industrial mobilization for World War II, the military-industrial complex during the Cold War, and the budding national economic strategy of President Clinton. America's communitarian drift has been driven most recently by the need to respond to Japanese competition and the requirements of environmental integrity. Even as the ideas of individualism have been buffeted and eroded by communitarian practices, particularly in times of crisis, they continue to be remarkably

Stock Montage

John Locke, English philosopher, 1632-1704

resilient, as 1995 Republican rhetoric revealed. "They are," says Samuel Huntington, "at the very core of {our} national identity. Americans cannot abandon them without ceasing to be Americans in the most meaningful sense of the word—without, in short, becoming un-American."[2] This is why the transition requires a good deal of crisis, and realistic leadership that can interpret the crisis accurately to make it useful instead of wasteful.

Historically, capitalism has been more or less synonymous with individualism. Socialism and communism represent different historical variations of communitarianism. The death of socialism and communism does not leave capitalism; it leaves something quite different which is poorly defined and varies widely. The variations are obscured by the use of the word capitalism. To better understand the distance between the reality of today's economic systems and "capitalism," "socialism," and "communism," let us briefly review and define these notions.

CAPITALISM

"Capitalism" has come to describe all economic systems that are not socialist or communist; since there are not many of the latter left, it describes virtually all systems. But, since systems differ radically, the word has lost descriptive value.

The *Oxford English Dictionary* defines capitalism as "a system which favors the existence of capitalists," that is "one who has accumulated capital or has it available for employment in...enterprises." It follows that capitalism is a system that emphasizes individual property rights, and private ownership, and control of enterprises. The distribution of wealth is left to competition among self-interested individuals.

Capitalism derives legitimacy from Adam Smith's idea that competition among proprietors in an open marketplace will produce the good community, and from John Locke's notion that government is a necessary evil; ideas that both men regarded as consistent with the "natural order." This idea of a natural order is centered in certain religious convictions. (What is "natural" in Protestant England may not be so in Catholic Italy, Jewish Israel, Moslem Iraq, Confucian China, or Shinto Japan.)[3]

Alexander Hamilton, Frederich List, and the Japanese developed a different theory of economic development: a nationalistic, mercantilist nation-state focused not on the consumer but on the producer and the organizations that the producer manages. Their theory entails a very different view of markets, property, and government's role than

Historical Pictures Service, Chicago
Adam Smith, Scottish economist, 1723-1790

that espoused by Adam Smith and his followers. If the economy and the political surroundings envisaged by Smith define "capitalism," then what Hamilton and List advocated, and the Japanese, Koreans, Taiwanese, and others Asians have adopted is surely not capitalism. But then, of course, neither is it socialism.[4]

SOCIALISM

"Socialism" arose in England during the 1830s in protest to the perceived injustices of capitalism. Indeed, socialists coined the word "capitalism" in the early 1800s to embody all that they detested. Joseph Schumpeter defined socialism as "an institutional pattern in which control over means of production and over production itself is vested with a central authority—or...in which, as a matter of principle, the economic affairs of a society belong to the public and not to the private sector."[5] Others have defined it more broadly as "a movement of human liberation, in which the transformation of the economic system is only one element."[6] The Oxford dictionary says it is "a theory or a policy of social organization which aims at or advocates the ownership and control of the means of production, capital, land, property, etc., by the community as a whole, and their administration or distribution in the interests of all."

COMMUNISM

Indistinguishable in many respects from socialism, communism was first used in France around 1840 and taken up by Karl Marx in 1848 with his publication of *The Communist Manifesto*. The *Encyclopedia Britannica* calls it "a system of society in which property (is) owned by the community and in which wealth (is) shared by citizens according to their need." Schumpeter says that Marx preferred it to socialism because "socialism had by that time acquired a flavor of bourgeois respectability."[7] Thus, communism was conceived of as a radical subdivision of socialism equipped with a revolutionary action plan. With the rise of the Soviet Union in the middle of the Twentieth Century, the word became distorted to mean whatever system was imposed by political organizations calling themselves communist.

THE HISTORICAL ROOTS

Capitalism and socialism (including communism) are creatures of Nineteenth Century Europe. They acquired meaning mainly from their

The Bettmann Archive

Karl Marx, German political philosopher, 1818-1883

The Importance of Being Precise

The importance of precision in describing a nation's economic system was impressed upon me in 1959, when as a young assistant secretary of labor for international affairs I visited India and found myself on a radio program with Ashok Mehta, the distinguished leader of India's socialist party. The Cold War was at its most virulent and India at the time was an important battlefield, with the Soviet Union and the United States competing for influence in the country's trade unions and other ruling circles.

As we hurried to the radio station, I asked my embassy guide what I was supposed to discuss with Mr. Mehta. He said the subject was "the American economic system." Having majored in history and literature at Harvard College, I knew nothing of economics. We stopped by the embassy to get me some briefing material, which I perused in the car as we sped through Delhi's crowded streets. The American economic system, said the embassy's brief, was capitalist, characterized by staunch adherence to the principles of free trade, free markets, and private enterprise and based on respect for the individual and the virtues of self-reliance. The familiar echo of Ralph Waldo Emerson comforted me, so I proceeded confidently to the confrontation with Mr. Mehta.

Asked to describe the American economic system, I spoke with gusto, parroting the briefing sheet. Mr. Mehta, a kindly old man with a short beard and penetrating eyes, then proceeded to question me. Why had I not mentioned social security, minimum wage, the TVA, the vast U.S. agricultural subsidies, rural electrification, or unemployment insurance? Were these somehow un-American? Good point, I allowed. Do you know, he asked me, what percent of the gross national product is disposed of by government in the United States? I had only the vaguest notion of what he was talking about and no idea what the answer to the question might be. Twenty-one percent, he said, and then with a smile he asked me what percentage of India's gross national product was disposed of by government. I was on the ropes. Twelve percent, he told me, following up with: "Now you are the capitalist country. Right?" "Right," I said. "And we are the socialist country. Right?" I was silent.

"My point is this," he said. "You in the United States call yourselves capitalist not realizing that most everyone listening to this radio program identifies capitalism with the loan shark, the money lender, the imperialist, the racist, in short, with everything bad. For them socialism means only a system in which government cares about the welfare of the people. In fact, you are more socialist than we are. That's why I love America."

interaction. Their mutual antagonism defined them. By the late Twentieth Century they dissolved themselves by intermingling. Capitalist systems had adopted most of the aims of Socialism—if not the means—and "socialist" systems realized that to reach their lofty goals required many "capitalist" tools.

The excesses of Nineteenth Century capitalism gave birth to socialism, a movement dedicated above all to closing the gap between rich and poor, powerful and weak. The means socialism chose to attain its ends varied among its adherents, but all socialists placed constraints on private property rights. Most emphasized the government's role in meeting the needs of the community: to make incomes more equitable, to provide health care, and to assure safety in the workplace. Some advocated the abolition of private property in favor of government ownership, but all socialists wanted to change "the system," which they regarded as unjust.

Joseph Schumpeter was partially correct when he predicted that capitalism would destroy itself. He gave three reasons:

1. The bureaucracy of large corporations would undermine the entrepreneurial and technological innovation essential for capitalist success.

2. The diffusion of ownership would weaken the individualism essential to a capitalist institutional framework.

3. Capitalism encouraged a critical attitude and the creation of intellectuals who have "a vested interest in social unrest."[8]

THE MORAL BASES

Capitalism and socialism were rooted in quite different ideological formulations. Capitalism followed the tenets of individualism; Socialism was one of a number of reflections of communitarianism. Before we examine what a world ideology might look like (Chapter 5), we need to review the connections between ideology and some religious systems. Business and conceptions of its purpose are deeply rooted in theological and philosophical thought, such as that associated with Buddhism, Catholicism, Confucianism, Protestantism, Shintoism, Taoism, and other Asian traditions. What will be clear is that whatever basis in religion pure individualism or capitalism may have once had, it has dissipated, and the overwhelming majority of religious systems today are in general compatible only with a communitarian ideology.

THE PROTESTANT ETHIC

As John Locke and Adam Smith provided the political and economic justification for capitalism as individualism, Protestant Christianity provided the theological justification. Indeed, according to Max Weber, the teachings of Luther, Knox, Calvin, and especially the American Puritans provided the driving force behind capitalist achievement. Holding that success in the marketplace was a sign of God's blessing, Protestantism encouraged the continual accumulation of wealth. But that accumulation had to be accompanied by steadfast denial of the worldly pleasures that wealth could purchase, pleasures that would divert the individual from a Godly life. Thus was created the moral imperative for saving and investment, and constraint on consumption, which for Weber was the essence of the spirit of capitalism.[9]

Let us note that the Asian propensity to save and invest, especially noteworthy in Japan and China, is no less powerful than that of old-time Western Protestants. The motivation is entirely different: it stems from the requirements of national survival and long-run community need; and, in Chinese communities, the health of the family. So while the macroeconomic outcomes may be

The Protestant ethic is individualistic in nature while Asian familism and nationalism are communitarian.

similar, the Protestant ethic is individualistic in nature while Asian familism and nationalism are communitarian.

By the Twentieth Century, certainly by the end of it, the Protestant citadels of the West clearly had become liberated from the strictures of the old ethic. They were buy-now-pay-later societies, deeply in debt to the saving and investing Asians. Clearly, any redemptive value that the Protestant ethic might have had for the individual was also gone. It was no longer a serviceable functioning grail. Individualism and hedonism do not make a sustainable mixture.

THE CATHOLIC TRADITION

Roman Catholic doctrine has been ideologically communitarian, quite different from individualistic Protestantism. It has, therefore, been leery of capitalism, but it has sought a version of communitarianism that is also separate from socialism.

Pope Leo XIII's encyclical *Rerum Novarum* (1891) attacked socialism head on, asserting, as had Locke, that the right to property was a "natural" or a "sacred" right: "In seeking help for the masses this principle before all is considered basic, namely, that private ownership must be preserved inviolate." Against the socialist's communitarian call for equality of result, Leo said:

"Therefore, let it be laid down in the first place that in civil society the lowest cannot be made equal with the highest. Socialists, of course, agitate the contrary, but all struggling against nature is in vain."[10]

However, *Rerum Novarum* also criticized the *individualistic* contention that all human beings are created equal, an idea that resulted in neglect of "the weak and the helpless who could not...compete with others on equal terms."[11]

Leo, like those that followed him, was opposed as

much to individualistic capitalism as he was to socialist communitarianism. Capitalism tended to judge all in terms of profit and loss while socialism's utopian vision carried with it the inevitability of authoritarianism, not to mention atheism, free love and other sinful behaviors. He chose a middle way, but a way which ideologically speaking was unquestionably communitarian.

By mid-Twentieth Century, Catholic communitarianism had become reformed. In 1967, for example, Pope Paul VI's *Populorum Progressio* withdrew significantly from Leo's views on property. "Private property does not constitute for anyone an absolute or unconditional right. No one is justified in keeping for his exclusive use what he does not need, when others lack necessities."[12]

The Bettmann Archive

Pope Leo XIII, 1810-1903

Approximately one hundred years after *Rerum Novarum*, Pope John Paul II in *Centesimus Annus*, "The Hundredth Year," condemned both Socialism and Capitalism:

> Can it...be said that after the failure of communism capitalism is the victorious social system and that capitalism should be the goal of the countries now making efforts to rebuild their economy and society?....
>
> The answer is obviously complex. If by *capitalism* is meant an economic system which recognized the fundamental and positive role of business, the market, private property and the resulting responsibility for the means of production as well as free human creativity in the economic sector, then the answer is certainly in the affirmative even though it would perhaps be more appropriate to speak of a *business economy, market economy* or simply *free economy*. [Like Mehta, the Pope was aware of

the word's dangers.] But if by capitalism is meant a system in which freedom in the economic sector is not circumscribed within a strong juridical framework which places it at the service of human freedom in its totality and which sees it as a particular aspect of that freedom, the core of which is ethical and religious, then the reply is certainly negative....

Vast multitudes are still living in conditions of great material and moral poverty. The collapse of the communist system in so many countries certainly removes an obstacle to facing these problems in an appropriate and realistic way, but it is not enough to bring about their solution. Indeed, there is a risk that a radical capitalistic ideology could spread which refuses even to consider these problems in the *a priori* belief that any attempt to solve them is doomed to failure, and which blindly entrusts their solution to the free development of market forces."[13]

He concludes: "It is unacceptable to say that the defeat of so-called 'real socialism' leaves capitalism as the only model of economic organization.[14]

In writing as he did in May 1989, the Pope may have been warning Russia and Eastern Europe, so recently liberated from socialism, against a careless lurch to what they regarded as pure capitalism.

The 1993 encyclical of Pope John Paul II, *Veritatis Splendor*, "The Splendor of Truth," is perhaps the church's most forthright attack on individualism. Read in the context of globalization, its doctrinal vigor demonstrates the inevitable clash among belief systems touched upon in Chapter 1.

The encyclical is aimed at Western ethicists and behavioral scientists who accord to "the individual conscience...the status of a supreme tribunal of moral judgment which hands down categorical and infallible decisions about good and evil.... Such an outlook is quite congenial to an individualist ethic, wherein each individual is faced with his own truth, different from the trust of others."

Says the Pope, "these theories end up, if not with an outright denial of universal human values, at least with a relativistic conception of morality."

And this is a denial "that there exists, in divine revelation, a specific and determined moral content, universally valid and permanent." Naturally, it is also a denial of the "doctrinal competence...of the church" to define what that moral content is.[15]

COMMUNITARIANISM

Thus far in our examination of Capitalism and Socialism (including Communism), we have seen that the words have many meanings and embody certain theories about how economic and social systems *should* work. They contain analytical critiques of how these systems actually *have worked*. And inasmuch as they were mutually antagonistic, they defined each other.

UPI/Bettmann

Pope John Paul II, 1920-

Socialism is deeply rooted in Europe, and capitalism in both Europe and the United States. They are inseparable from the economic, religious, and philosophical theories peculiar to those regions. They were inspired and affected by Christianity, just as they in turn seem to have affected Christian thought. Despite the Socialists' rejection of religion, it seems that their moral goals and thus their legitimacy was based in Christian thinking. And capitalism was legitimized by Protestantism, filtered through the thoughts of Locke and Adam Smith among others. As the Twentieth Century ended, a synthesis of both found favor with the Vatican.

Capitalism, though not named until around 1800— and then defined as much or more by its opponents as its adherents—dated from the middle of the Seventeenth Century. Socialism came later as a protest against capitalism's injustices. Ideologically speaking, as noted earlier, capitalism conformed roughly to the tenets of individualism and socialism to one variation or another of communitarianism. By the end of the Twentieth Century, socialist concerns regarding egalitarian outcomes, i.e., affirmative action, and guaranteed rights of membership to such things as income, health, and shelter had become accepted principles throughout the industrial world. The dispersion of ownership in the capital markets and ecological imperatives had distorted and diluted the power and legitimacy of property rights.

It seems fair to conclude that events have passed the two words by, and whatever meaning the words may have had was peculiar to Western Civilization. It verges on the preposterous and certainly the parochial to call the economic systems of China, Japan, Taiwan, Korea, Singapore, and other Asian countries by the words "capitalist" and "socialist" that are as irrelevant to their Confucian, Taoist, Buddhist, and Shinto traditions as they are to their historic experience. Although the literature of capitalism and socialism was certainly familiar to Nineteenth and Twentieth Century Asian intellectuals, one must suspect that the development of Asian economic systems had little to do with the Western "isms."

Asian economic systems are communitarian—not individualistic—and each represents a quite different form of communitarianism. In both China and Taiwan, for example, what might be called "familism" exists alongside "statism," the purpose of business invariably being, as I have mentioned, the enrichment of the Chinese family. On the other hand, the purpose of business in Japan—Mitsui, for example—is to serve the greater glory of Japan as well as the welfare of all the corporate members.

Asian systems such as Japan's have familiar characteristics, making them formidable competitors against their Western rivals. As noted earlier, these include the following:

Cooperative relationships between business and government and between managers and managed that produce a high level of consensus behind national goals. Consensus depends upon fairness in sharing both economic pain and gain: Asian countries have the most equitable distribution of income in the world.

National goals give top priority to national competitiveness, that is to the nation's acquisition of market share in collection of producers of high value-added products. In this regard, the distinction between public sector and private sector is insignificant.

Economic policies serve these goals. They are producer—not consumer—oriented. They encourage investment and saving, not consumption. The motive is not individual salvation, it is community prosperity.

Thus, we can say that the world's most competitive economies are neither socialist nor capitalist. They have elements of both but they are significantly, perhaps radically, different. Pretending otherwise leads to confusion and misunderstanding.

THE CHINESE SYSTEM

S. Gordon Redding, dean of the Hong Kong University School of Business Administration, interviewed hundreds of Chinese business managers. He says that an understanding of Chinese business must begin with the Chinese people's belief system. And this belief system, or what Redding calls "the prevailing ideology of China for most of its recorded history" has been a set of ideas which go under the convenient label of Confucianism.[16]

Confucianism constrains "the expression of individual desires" and encourages group sharing of limited resources. The family and loyalty to the family are of supreme importance. The family functions as "a rational collective" to insure individuals against disaster.[17] This idea of the family carries over into the Chinese conception of the state which is quite different from the western idea. The Confucian state is

> ...Seen by its members as an enormous, but nevertheless united group, while the Western version is doctrinally at least an abstraction, a universal or absolute idea. Thus the Chinese state is in essence the super-family of Chinese people....
>
> The society is constructed of morally binding relationships connecting all. In this the self is not an enclosed world of private thoughts. The individual is instead a connection, and the whole of society is passed down from one binding relationship to the next, rather than by the Western mode of uniting loosely coupled and free individuals by their separate espousal of coordinating ideas and principles. For the Chinese, fulfillment comes from the very structure and dynamics of the relationships and emphasis on belonging.[18]

Inasmuch as the Chinese state has tended toward despotism, the family is the protector of the individual against the state. "The family is the first and last resort, and for most the only resort." Welfare has traditionally been a family responsibility and schooling enforced the rigor of duty to family as a way of stabilizing the state.

> An inevitable consequence of this is the rivalry of families as they seek to control and accumulate scarce resources in competition with each other. Individual achievement becomes an aspect of family achievement and the spirit of family enrichment at the expense of other families becomes a primary force described as 'magnified selfishness,' and opposed to a wider sense of community and societal responsibility.[19]

There are three important differences separating Confucianism from other religions: It contains no deity, only rules of conduct. It doesn't compete with other religions. And it has no large-scale institutional "church."[20]

> Its dominance came about because it provided the philosophical basis for the filial piety which supported the family structures and in turn the state itself.[21]

It also provided the Chinese with their conception of the purpose of business: the long-term enrichment and preservation of the family.

The teachings of Confucius have been repackaged in a variety of ways and, although Mao tried to set them aside, they have remained remarkably resilient. For most Chinese they are mixed with Taoism, a kind of nature religion, more sympathetic to individualistic concerns. There is in Taoism a strong streak of what Westerners might call civil disobedience, which combined with Confucianism produces a most non-Western approach to government. Government is to be respected but knowing how to circumvent its strictures is admired. Putting it crudely: Respect government but its rules are made to be bent.

The Chinese belief system produces family firms in which members and employees work extremely hard because their survival depends upon it. These firms often have far-flung family connections in the Pacific Basin and the United States, but their growth is limited by the extent of the family. It is a business system also, says Redding, that is anything but transparent, and it is difficult to change. He speaks of the

Stock Montage

Confucius, Chinese philosopher, 551-479 B.C.

> ...passivity induced by a system which places the individual in a powerfully maintained family order, itself inside a

*K*eiretsu, kaisha, and *chaebol* are terms that describe giant conglomerates of companies, tied together in numerous ways, including joint stock ownership, intimate supplier relationships, and cooperation for achieving numerous ends—research and development, financing, market access, and more.

powerfully maintained state order, itself seen as part of a natural cosmic order (Taoist and Buddhist traditions), and all dedicated to the maintenance of the status quo. When the only true authority is tradition, and when deviant behavior meets heavy sanctions from an early age, when deference to elders is automatic, and when dependence on those same elders is nonnegotiable, then all the ingredients are present for producing a social system characterized on the one hand by an impressive stability and on the other hand by a debilitating incapacity to adapt, innovate, and change.[22]

This brief look at traditional Chinese ideology helps us to understand why Chinese firms are quite different from the Japanese *keiretsu* and *kaisha,* the Korean *chaebol,* and the Western multinational.

We may also get an idea of some of the managerial challenges when the different organizational forms compete, cooperate, or collide.

THE FUTURE

Some paths to the future are already quite clear. We have already seen the United States, which is perhaps as ideologically distant from Japan as any nation can be, changing its ways in a Japanese-like direction in order to become more competitive. And the pressures for ecological integrity are causing all nations to bow to certain global constraints affecting property rights, the uses of property, the role of government, and, most importantly, our perception of reality.

To seek to interpret such a future within the parameters of "capitalism"—or "socialism"—is fruitless. What is worse, it is virtually sure to lead to error. Those words carry blinders that both restrict what we see and condition our interpretation of what we see.

SUMMARY

National systems—economic, social, and political—are being forced to converge by two global forces: intensifying competition among the different systems and pressures to preserve ecological integrity.

The systems that respond most efficiently to the preceding two forces will survive and prosper and tend to change less responsive systems.

As competition among nations becomes more intense, the nation-state itself is being forced to surrender sovereignty and power to a variety of international organizations and entities upon which it is increasingly dependent. These organizations include a melange of public and private entities ranging from multinational corporations, corporate alliances, business-government coalitions, purely governmental regional associations, trade blocs, and the United Nations and its specialized agencies.

Overview

♦ Communitarianism:

  Equality of Result or Hierarchy

  Consensus

♦ Rights and Duties of Membership

♦ Community Needs

♦ Active, Planning State

♦ Holism

WORLD IDEOLOGY: VARIATIONS ON A COMMUNITARIAN THEME

5

There will, of course, never be a single world ideology. There will be as many ideologies as there are communities, but a variety of pressures are pushing the nations of the world toward ideological homogeneity.

Referring to the foremost of these pressures, Harvard's Ezra Vogel wrote in 1987: "If East Asian nations continue to be more competitive than other industrial nations, the world trading system will become more communitarian, with increased integration of business firms around the world and more global management of competition."[1]

If this is so, managers everywhere can more realistically anticipate and manage the future if they know what communitarianism is, and what choices it offers.

Let me repeat my definition of an ideology: the framework of ideas a community uses to define and to implement values. Values, assumed to be noncontroversial, include such universal notions as survival, justice (a notion of good and bad with rewards and punishments), economy (more benefits than costs), self-fulfillment, and self-respect. Ideology is the bridge of ideas through which these values are given institutional vitality in a particular place at a particular time—that is in a particular reality, which I have called "the real world." Thus, ideology is what legitimizes institutions such as government, business, or the university. And it changes—generally with great difficulty—in order to adapt or adjust to changes in the surrounding "real world."

For example, in the 1980s and '90s, Japanese competition and the need for ecological integrity forced changes in the roles and relationships of government and business in the United States that constituted a departure from an individualistic ideology. These changes, although pragmatic, reflected, however implicitly, a communitarian ideology. Therefore, to find legitimacy, the evolving institutions had to look not to traditional individualism but to an ill-defined communitarianism.

The community is more than the sum of the individuals in it; it is organic, not atomistic. The community as a whole has special and urgent needs that go beyond the needs of its individual members.

A communitarian ideology, like its individualistic counterpart, has five elements:

1. Communitarianism (characterized by its equality of result or hierarchy) and consensus (either coerced or arrived at more or less voluntarily)

2. Rights and duties of membership

3. Community need

4. The active planning state

5. Holism

Although this ideology might appear new to some, it is not. If you substitute the notion of *hierarchy* in place of equality of result in item one above, this ideology resembles the dominant ideologies of Europe before the Eighteenth Century. Communitarian practices came to the United States with successive waves of European immigrants, and, laced with a dose of egalitarianism, manifested themselves in such institutions as America's New England town meeting and the farmers' cooperative movements of the Midwest. Today, however, the increasing need for and introduction of communitarian practices in the United States as well as in other countries makes explicit recognition of the ideological implications of those practices useful and necessary.

Since a form of communitarian ideology always has been dominant in Korea, Taiwan, and Japan, an understanding of that ideology also helps us to perceive the nature of Western competition with those countries. It is, for example, difficult to translate the word "individualism" into Japanese with any other meaning than selfishness and egocentricity. Ideology pervades even our languages.

1. COMMUNITARIANISM

The community is more than the sum of the individuals in it; it is organic, not atomistic. The community as a whole has special and urgent needs that go beyond the needs of its individual members. The values of survival, justice, self-respect, and so forth, depend on the recognition of those needs.

Individual fulfillment, therefore, depends on a place in the community, an identity with a whole, participation in an organic social process. If the community—the factory, the neighborhood, or the country—is well designed, its members will identify with it strongly and maximumize their capacities. If the community or its components are poorly designed, people will be alienated and frustrated.

Corporations and unions played leading roles in eroding the old ideology of individualism in the West and creating the need for something new. Invariably they were ideologically unmindful of what they did. Thus they tended to linger with the old forms and assumptions even after those were critically altered.

Communitarianism can be relatively autocratic and statist as in Singapore and South Korea or nonstatist as in Germany. Its form is shaped by history, whether it be traditions of feudalism or the vestiges of colonialism and precolonial Indian life as in Mexico.

a. Equality of Result or Hierarchy. The West also has experienced a shift away from the old notion of equality. It used to be equality of opportunity: an individualistic conception whereby blacks, whites, men, and women were equal, and each could advance according to individual abilities without facing discriminatory obstruction.

Both the United States and Europe were concerned that the old idea of equality was not insuring adequate or acceptable results. Too many were being left behind. Thus, governments intervened to impose guarantees and safeguards. Here, the good corporation or community was the one that adapted itself to inequalities in the surrounding environment, producing equality of result.

As managers of government and business contemplated the implementation of the idea of equality of result, a variety of issues came to the fore. How does one avoid mediocrity? How does one handle the appeals of countless groups for representation? Can a school system possibly survive with such an idea?

The examples of medieval Europe and modern Japan remind us that this slot in communitarian ideology has generally been filled not by equality but by the notion of hierarchy. That is, individual fulfillment and self-respect result from knowing and accepting one's place in a social structure. One's place may be fixed in a variety of ways, by God, by the king, or, as in modern Japan, meritocratically by a sequence of rigorous examinations from which an elite emerges—the *summa cum laudes* of the University of Tokyo. And in the United States the "back to basics" movement to reform the schools envisaged a hierarchy with the brightest students on top—a long way from the egalitarian "nobody fails" syndrome.

In a communitarian society, the relationships between individuals are governed not so much by contract as by consensus.

b. Consensus. In a communitarian society, the relationships between individuals are governed not so much by *contract* as by *consensus,* which may be imposed autocratically by fiat or arrived at through democratic and participative means. In Europe these arrangements are called industrial democracy, codetermination, workers' councils, and the like. They tend to replace the adversarial contractual relationship between managers and managed with a consensual one, which may proceed from the top down or from the bottom up. Japan's manager-managed relationships have generally been consensual, at first feudal in nature with a good deal of coercion, and adapting over time to changing needs and expectations. In the United States more consensual practices fall under several headings: organization development, employee involvement, workers' participation in management, and quality-of-work-life programs. Whatever the form, the result for managers tends to be the same: the right to manage is coming from the managed in democratic systems or from government in autocratic ones.

In many countries the transition from individualist to communitarian practices is impeded by the hegemony of individualist ideology. Trade unions are naturally loath to give up the power and legitimacy that once was theirs under the old notion of the adversarial, bargained contract. Managers, too, are nervous about moving away from the old bases of authority implicit in property rights and the contract. If improved productivity depends upon the transition, the issue is clear: How much crisis, how much recession before countries like the United Kingdom and the United States catch up with the Japanese and others who are more able to achieve consensus? The problem in the United Kingdom is complicated by class consciousness. The idea of worker participation in managerial decisions is deeply rooted in Germany's communitarian traditions and, thus, is likely to be a boon to the recovery of German competitiveness.

There are signs that this transition from contract to consensus is contributing to, if not causing, the weakening of trade unions in Western countries where the adversarial mission of a union is taken for granted. The membership of unions has been declining, their influence eroding, and their confidence waning with regard to role and mission. Artful managers are increasingly seeking means of "union avoidance," employing the techniques of consensualism. The question then arises: Is a strong trade-union movement good for the community and its corporations? If the answer is yes, then it is important to redefine the union's mission. Pragmatic innovation without ideological renovation is not sufficient. And for unions, as for managers, the relevant community is no longer the nation. To survive, they must go global.

In South Korea and Japan, as well as in Brazil and Mexico, consensus in the community as a whole is usually imposed by a ruling elite, with government playing a leading role in its design and enforcement. Where dissidents are not suppressed, they are co-opted by a process that Asian communities condone through the religious conviction that consensus is a moral virtue. In the West, religious beliefs have tended to assign at least as much virtue to adversarial and contractual notions such as due process and the right to strike.

2. Rights and Duties of Membership

For some years in the West, a set of social rights has been superseding property rights in political and social importance. These are rights to survival, income, pensions, health, and other entitlements associated with membership in the community or in some component of that community, such as a corporation. These rights are not legitimized through reference to individualist ideology. Rather, they are best understood in the context of communitarianism, as rights that public opinion holds to be consistent with a good community.

*D*uties are just as integral a part of communitarian ideology as rights.

   The problem in the West—one that European socialism and U.S. liberalism tend to ignore—is that emphasis on rights has not been accompanied by as clear a concern about duties. Duties are just as integral a part of communitarian ideology as rights: If the community assures rights, it must—and eventually will—require duties. In countries where communitarianism is relatively undiluted by individualism, such as Japan, duties are regarded as equally if not more important than rights.

> *Western ambivalence on this point is proving increasingly costly as government and business strain to pay the escalating costs of rights while duties remain elusive. It is one of a number of causes of the West's competitive deterioration in the world economy.*

As rights and duties of membership have become more important, the notion of property rights has diminished as a source of authority for managers. This is attributed to a number of actual developments in the real world context, including the dispersion of ownership among many thousands of shareholders who have little motivation or ability to actually own "their property," and the escalating demands of government that business conform to community needs in such matters as employment, environmental protection, and safety. Thus, in practice, the source of management authority in the West has moved away from shareholders and toward debt holders, the managed, and the community acting through government. In this area the West and the East appear to be converging. There is also convergence around the notion that the community has an obligation to assure certain human rights, as, for example, health. The relevant community for these rights is increasingly perceived as the world.

> *The needs of the community are becoming increasingly distinct from, and more important than, what individual consumers may desire.*

But there is also profound conflict: The devout Catholic rejects the woman's right to an abortion, others see it as a matter of a woman's choice, and some, burdened by overpopulation, see it as a duty. These differences in the definition of rights call for tolerance, but some religions tend to be intolerant of violations of what the Pope calls "sound doctrine."[2] This only reminds us that while there may be a growing recognition that the management of globalization will be within a communitarian framework, the differences to be reconciled within that framework are substantial. This is "the clash" to which we referred in Chapter 1.

3. COMMUNITY NEED

The needs of the community (focusing on a national one, for example) for clean air and water, safety, energy, jobs, competitive exports, and so forth are becoming increasingly distinct from, and more important than, what individual consumers may desire. As a consequence, the means of determining community need require explicit attention, especially when it is impossible for the community to meet all of its needs at once.

This concept is radically different from the individualist idea that the public interest emerges *naturally* from the lobbying of interest groups and from free and vigorous competition among numerous aggressive, individualistic, and preferably small companies attempting to satisfy consumer desires.

According to communitarian ideology, business purpose is fixed by community need as defined by the community, generally through government or with its participation. As mentioned in Chapter 3, once community need has been determined, business activity can be harmonized with it in four ways: prescribed or ordered marketplace competition, regulation of business by government, partnership between government and business, and the corporate charter through which government gives business its license to exist.

In the production and sale of shoes, for example, competition to satisfy consumer desires may be the most efficient way to assure that the community is properly shod. Other products—food and drugs, for example—would obviously require regulation. Either the partnership or charter route might be the best way to harmonize community needs with the energy industry, communications satellites, or banking.

A wise choice among the four requires a clear definition of community need in the first place, a reliable delineation of the relevant community, and an understanding of what makes a business function efficiently and effectively in different social settings.

It is important to note that although communitarians are not prepared to leave the *definition* of community need to the vagaries of the marketplace, they wisely allow the use of competition in the marketplace as a means of controlling and directing the activities of business toward the *implementation* of that need.

The role of the state in a communitarian society is to define community needs and to insure that they are implemented.

4. ACTIVE PLANNING STATE

The role of the state in a communitarian society is to define community needs and to insure that they are implemented. Inevitably, the state takes on important tasks of coordination, priority setting, and planning. It needs to be efficient and authoritative, capable of making the difficult and subtle trade-offs among, for example, environmental purity, energy supply, economic stability and growth, rights of membership, and global competition.

There are wide variations among the forms that the general notion of the active planning state may take. In some communitarian countries, government may be democratic and tolerant, while in others it is autocratic and brutal. Some may be relatively centralized (Japan and South Korea), and others comparatively federal (Brazil). Another critical variable among communitarian governments is their ability to produce a consensus to support and implement their "plan"; some use naked force, others more sophisticated devices. It is important to delineate as precisely as possible the particular institutional forms that have evolved within the general context of communitarian ideology in the several countries.

Once these matters concerning the planning state are clear, it then becomes possible to describe and analyze the tensions between that particular form and current institutional practice, and to consider how those tensions are likely to develop in the future.

The idea of scientific specialization is replaced in a communitarian ideology by a consciousness of the interrelatedness of all things.

5. HOLISM– INTERDEPENDENCE

Finally, the idea of scientific specialization is replaced in a communitarian ideology by a consciousness of the interrelatedness of all things. Earth is experiencing the lim-

its of growth; the fragility of our life-supporting biosphere dramatizes the ecological and philosophical truth
that everything is related to everything else. Harmony
between mankind and nature is no longer the romantic
plea of conservationists. It is an absolute rule of survival,
and thus it is of profound significance; its practical ram-
ifications subvert individualist ideology in many ways.

One variety of holism on a local level is the notion
that in order to understand any particular aspect of a
community, for example, its economic performance, it is
necessary to view the community as a system, perceiving the critical roles and relationships of business, labor,
governmental, and educational institutions. For the
holist there is no separation between what the economists refer to as "macro" and "micro." The motivation of
workers on the shop floor is inseparably tied to overall
policies and incentives having to do with savings,
investment, and employment.

Individualism blinds us to the holistic reality. A sad
example is the effort in the United States over the last
thirty years to invigorate disintegrated urban communities. There are two aspects that bear on this discussion.
First, the government's approach has been specialized.
The problem has been defined in terms of housing, welfare, economics, safety, education, jobs, health, and
more. Bureaucracies have attacked these problems sepa-
rately—and unsuccessfully.

Second, the remedy has often been perceived in
individualistic terms with an emphasis on economics: If
we "empower" individual entrepreneurs to bring economic activity to the ghettos, market forces will rehabil-
itate the community. This is a patently false assumption.

The examples of hundreds—perhaps thousands—
of successful community organizations tell us clearly
what works. A strong leader takes charge and defines the
"community" and its needs. The new community har-
vests public funds from wherever they are available, creates subsidized housing, secures police protection,

screens members for admission, establishes standards of rights and duties for all community members, enforces those standards vigorously, expelling those who do not obey, and imposes discipline. The community provides a wide range of social services, including preventive health care, drug counseling, and such educational assistance as tutoring, job training, and job placement.[3]

On the international level, the problems of Third-World debt requires an understanding of the world trading system, then analyzing what impedes debtor countries from competing in that system to earn the foreign exchange with which to pay their debts.

These examples of holism demonstrate the problem for specialists and specialized education. If understanding the real world depends upon holistic analysis, the traditional expert may well be at best tangential and at worst downright wrong.

Lest the reader conclude that communitarianism is just another word for big government, the welfare state, and an antibusiness bias in society, it is important to point out that Japan is unquestionably more coherently communitarian than Britain and yet suffers from none of these maladies. Japan's preference for little government involvement in enterprise ownership does not spring from an ideological reverence for property rights; it is a communitarian concern with efficiency. Perhaps ironically, the Asian communitarians seem to be substantially more probusiness than the more individualistic West, but, of course, their conception of the purpose of business is different: it is closely tied to community need. And, whereas, in periods of economic decline, communitarian impulses cause Western countries to emphasize rights more than duties, the reverse seems to be true in Japan and perhaps in Taiwan and South Korea.

It is important, therefore, to clear the head of old ideological shibboleths if one is going to be precise, and indeed one of the major purposes of ideological analysis is to allow more precision than is generally associated with words like capitalism, socialism, communism, left, right, liberal, and conservative.

CONCLUSION

> *The shape which communitarianism takes in different communities will be formed by crisis. The task of leadership is to prevent crisis from becoming catastrophe—to make maximum use of minimum crisis for maximum change. This requires early perception and definition of community needs, and the artful design of institutions and incentives to insure that they are met. It is also the task of leadership to make the best of communitarianism.*

There is nothing inherently good—or bad—about communitarianism. No ideology has a monopoly on sin or virtue. Stalin and Hitler were communitarians as are Lee Kuan Yew, and the leaders of Japan and Israel; even, it seems to me, Bill Clinton. And individualism, for all its glory—and there was much of that—justified slavery in the United States, at least in the eyes of Southerners, since slaves were deemed to be property, and property rights were sacred according to the dominant ideology. Furthermore, slavery was held to be consistent with community need as that need was defined by the southern states, a view justified in turn by the idea of states' rights, inherent in the doctrine of the limited state.

We may hope, therefore, that the world will make use of the best elements of individualism as it moves into the Twenty-First Century. Individualism promises democracy. The communitarian may or may not value democracy, regarding it as only one way of defining community need. Individualism argues for a voluntary consensus; the communitarian believes that it may be necessary to secure consensus through coercion (e.g., prisons). Partnership between government and business serves communitarian goals, but it also may bring fascism, so care must be taken to define clearly the terms of the partnership: its purpose, whether it is covert or overt, and so on. Holism without discipline and expertise is a sham and a deceit.

So there is danger built into this world ideology. The best way to avoid that danger is to be clear-headed and realistic about what we are doing and alert to the ideological implications of every act. Then we can make the best of globalization.

Finally, there is the challenge of meshing—not merging—the various national brands of communitarianism to create a legitimate basis for the transnational governmental mechanisms required to manage globalization. A reliable global consensus can only arise from national communities that know their interests and are confident that they are making best use of their resources. Global consensus springs from national strength, not weakness. It arises from a realistic sense of mutuality: The world prospers as long as everyone prospers. And national strength requires harmony between the nation's practice and its ideology.

For the United States to lead effectively in the creation of global institutions, such as the World Economic Organization discussed earlier, it needs not only economic and political strength, but a clear recognition of the ideological justification for that strength. That justification lies, as we have said, within a communitarian framework. Clearly, within that framework, the notion of community need requires recognition that the relevant community for many needs is the world, that realistically, in the long run, the national community need is inseparable from that of the world community.

Notes

INTRODUCTION

1. Figures assembled by Professor James L. Cash, Harvard Business School, using World Development Forum Data.
2. Daniel Bell, *The Coming of Post-Industrial Society* (New York: Basic Books, 1973), 373.

CHAPTER 1

1. Lester R. Brown, Hal Kane, and Ed Ayres, *Vital Signs 1993* (New York: W.W. Norton & Company, 1993), 74.
2. Lester R. Brown, Hal Kane, and David Malin Roodman, *Vital Signs 1994* (New York: W.W. Norton & Company, 1993), 76.
3. D. Keith Denton and Charles Boyd, *Did You Know?* (Englewood Cliffs, New Jersey: Prentice Hall, 1994), 43.
4. D. Keith Denton and Charles Boyd, *Did You Know?* (Englewood Cliffs, New Jersey: Prentice Hall, 1994), 43.
5. "A Survey of Multinationals," *The Economist*, March 27, 1993, 6.
6. C. Fred Bergsten and Edward M. Graham, "Global Corporation and National Governments: Are Changes Needed in the International Economic and Political Order in Light of the Globalization of Business?" unpublished manuscript, July 20, 1993, 8.
7. Office of Technology Assessment, *Multinationals and the National Interest* (Washington DC: Government Printing Office, 1993), 6.
8. D. Keith Denton and Charles Boyd, *Did You Know?* (Englewood Cliffs, New Jersey: Prentice Hall, 1994), 45.
9. "Cross-Border Investment Is High," *Chemical Week*, September 15, 1993, 5.
10. William W. Lewis and Marvin Harris, "Why Globalization Must Prevail," *The McKinsey Quarterly* 1992, no. 2: 116.
11. C. Fred Bergsten and Edward M. Graham, "Global Corporation and National Governments: Are Changes Needed in the International Economic and Political Order in Light of the Globalization of Business?" unpublished manuscript, July 20, 1993, 1.
12. "A Survey of Multinationals," *The Economist*, March 27, 1993, 6.
13. DeAnne Julius, "Global Companies and Public Policy," RIIA/Pinter, quoted in *The Economist*, June 23, 1990, 67, and Peter F. Cowhey and Jonathan D. Aronson, "A New Trade Order," *Foreign Affairs*, March/April 1993, 183.
14. Dennis Encarnation, *Rivals Beyond Trade: America versus Japan in Global Competition* (Ithaca: Cornell University Press, 1992).
15. "Cross-Border Investment Is High," *Chemical Week*, September 15, 1993, 5.
16. Debora Spar, "Foreign Investment and Free Trade in Canada in the 1990's," no. 793-032, Harvard Business School.
17. Bruce Scott, U.S. *Competitiveness in the World Economy*, Bruce Scott and George Lodge, eds., Chapters 1 and 2 (Boston: Harvard Business School Press, 1984); and Scott, *Economic Strategies of Nations*, forthcoming.
18. Quoted in Theodore Levitt, "The Globalization of Markets," *Harvard Business Review*, May-June 1983, 93.
19. Alan Farnham, "Global—Or Just Globaloney?" *Fortune*, June 27, 1994.
20. Office of Technology Assessment, U.S. Congress, *Multinationals and the National Interest* (Washington DC: Government Printing Office, 1993), 2, 3, 4, and 6.
21. Michael Porter, "Capital Disadvantage: America's Failing Capital Investment System," *Harvard Business Review*, September-October 1992, 65-82.
22. Cowhey and Aronson, "A New Trade Order," 183.
23. Lewis and Harris, "Why Globalization Must Prevail," 118.
24. Levitt, "The Globalization of Markets," 93-96.
25. Richard J. Barnet and John Cavanagh, *Global Dreams: Imperial Corporations and the New World Order* (New York: Simon and Schuster, 1994), 25.
26. Asahi Shimbun, *Japan Almanac 1993* (Tokyo: Asahi Shimbun Publishing Company, 1994), 237.
27. Jeremy J. Warford, "Environmental Management and Economic Policy in Developing Countries," Chapter 2 in *Environmental Management and Economic Development*, Gunter Schramm and Jeremy J. Warford, eds. (Baltimore, MD: Johns Hopkins University Press, 1989), 9.
28. Author interview, December 12, 1991. Taken from George C. Lodge, *The World Bank: Mission Uncertain*, no. 792-100, Harvard Business School, 1992, 12.
29. D. Keith Denton and Charles Boyd, *Did You Know?* (Englewood Cliffs, New Jersey: Prentice Hall, 1994), 76.
30. Author interview, October 5, 1991.
31. Ibid.
32. The discussion of GATT derives from Forest L. Reinhardt and Edward Prewitt, Forest L. Reinhardt and Edward Prewitt, *Environment and International Trade*, No. 794-018, Harvard Business School, 1993.
33. Paul Rauber, "Trading Away the Environment," Sierra, Jan.-Feb. 1992, 24, quoted in Forest L. Reinhardt and Edward Prewitt, *Environment and International Trade*, no 794-018, Harvard Business School, 1993.
34. *The World Bank Atlas 1993* (Washington DC: The World Bank, 1994), 7.
35. *The Economist*, April 25, 1992, 48.
36. Ibid.
37. Sharon Stanton Russell and Michael S. Teitelbaum, *International Migration and International Trade*, World Bank Discussion Paper #160, 1992, vii, 3, 5, and 35.
38. Samuel P. Huntington, "The Clash of Civilizations," *Foreign Affairs*, Summer 1993, 22-49.

CHAPTER 2

1. Thomas S. Kuhn, *The Structure of Scientific Revolutions* (Chicago and London: University of Chicago Press, 1962), 37.
2. William Manchester, *A World Lit Only By Fire* (Boston: Little, Brown, and Company, 1993) 116-117.
3. Howard M. Wachtel, *The Money Mandarins: The Making of a New Supranational Economic Order* (New York: Pantheon Books, 1986), 51, 53.
4. Lawrence G. Franko, "Global

Corporate Competition II: Is the Large American Firm an Endangered Species?", *Business Horizons*, Nov.-Dec. 1991, 14.
5. *The Economist*, November 20, 1993, 47.
6. Ibid.
7. Lester R. Brown, et al, *The State of the World* (New York: W.W. Norton & Company, 1994), 157.
8. George C. Lodge, *The World Bank: Mission Uncertain*, no. 792-100, Harvard Business School, 1992.
9. The World Bank Annual Report, 1991, 11.
10. The World Bank Annual Report, 1991, 3, and *Governance and Development* (Washington DC: The World Bank, 1992), 51.
11. Adapted from Mahbub ul Haq, *The Poverty Curtain: Choices for the Third World* (Pakistan: Ferozsons Ltd., 1983).
12. *The East Asian Miracle: A World Bank Policy Research Report*, published for the Bank by the Oxford University Press, 1993.
13. Quoted in *The Wall Street Journal*, September 27, 1993, 1.
14. Herbert Stein, "No Need to be Scared of NAFTA," *The Wall Street Journal*, September 29, 1993: op. ed. page.
15. Quoted in Bruce R. Scott, "Japan as Number One?" no. 387-005. Boston: Harvard Business School, 1988, 10.
16. Peter Sutherland, "If GATT Fails, We all Lose," *The Wall Street Journal*, October 19, 1993, op. ed. page.
17. Quoted in *The Straits Times*, November 26, 1993, 4.
18. D. Keith Denton and Charles Boyd, *Did You Know?* (Englewood Cliffs, New Jersey: Prentice Hall, 1994), 112.
19. Richard M. Levich and Ingo Walther, "The Regulation of Global Financial Markets," in *New York's Financial Markets: The Challenges of Globalization*, Thierry Noyelle, ed. (Boulder and London: Westview Press, 1989), 59.
20. I am indebted to Dr. Glenn Tobin for his description of this agreement. See Chapter 6 in Raymond Vernon, Debora Spar, and Glenn Tobin, *Iron Triangles and Revolving Doors* (New York: Praeger, 1991), 129-154.
21. Richard Elliot Benedick, *Ozone Diplomacy* (Cambridge, MA: Harvard University Press, 1991), 8 and 104.
22. *New York Public Library Desk Reference*, 2d edition (New York:

Prentice Hall General Reference, 1993), 65.

CHAPTER 3

1. C. Fred Bergsten, "The World Economy After the Cold War," *California Management Review* (Winter 1992), 52.
2. "Building a Competitive America," Competitiveness Policy Council first annual report to the President and Congress, March 1, 1992, 1.
3. C. Fred Bergsten, "The Primacy of Economics," *Foreign Policy*, No. 87 (Summer 1992), 4.
4. Published in daily newspapers.
5. Bruce R. Scott, *Japan D-1: A Strategy for Economic Growth*, No. 9-378-106, Harvard Business School.
6. Clyde V. Prestowitz, Jr., "Beyond Laissez Faire," *Foreign Policy*, No. 87 (Summer 1992), 67.
7. See Michael Porter, *Capital Choices: Changing the Way America Invests in Industry* (Washington, DC: Council on Competitiveness, 1992).
8. Lester C. Thurow, review of *Who's Bashing Whom?: Trade Conflicts in High Technology Industries* by Laura Tyson, *Foreign Policy*, No. 92 (Fall 1993), 189 and 191.
9. James Fallows, "Looking at the Sun," *The Atlantic Monthly*, November 1993, 99.
10. Christopher Wood, *The Bubble Economy: Japan's Extraordinary Speculative Boom of the '80s and the Dramatic Bust of the '90s* (Boston: The Atlantic Monthly Press, 1992) quoted in *The Wall Street Journal*, October 7, 1992, 39.
11. Paul Kennedy, *Preparing for the Twenty-First Century* (New York: Random House, 1993), 47-64.
12. J. Hirschmier and T. Yui, *The Development of Japanese Business 1600-1980*, 2d ed (London: George Allen and Unwin, 1982), 11, 19, 41, and 123.
13. Yasheng Huang, "The Strategies of Southeast Asian and Taiwanese Multinational Firms Investing in China," unpublished manuscript, 4-6.

CHAPTER 4

1. Kennedy, *Preparing for the Twenty-First Century*, 339.
2. Samuel P. Huntington, "The Clash of Civilizations," *Foreign Affairs*, Summer 1993, 22-49.
3. Ibid.
4. Thomas K. McCraw, "The Trouble with Adam Smith," *The American Scholar*, 61 (1992): 371.
5. Schumpeter, *Capitalism, Socialism,*

and Democracy, 312.
6. Tom Bottomore in his introduction to Joseph A. Schumpeter, *Capitalism, Socialism and Democracy* (New York: Harper and Row, 1950), xi.
7. Ibid, 312.
8. Ibid, x.
9. Max Weber, *The Protestant Ethic and the Spirit of Capitalism* (London: Harper Collins Academic, 1991).
10. Quoted in Michael Novak, *The Catholic Ethic and the Spirit of Capitalism* (New York: The Free Press, 1993), 41-42.
11. Ibid, 50.
12. Ibid, 149.
13. Ibid, 126, 134.
14. Ibid, 133.
15. John Paul II/Encyclical, *Veritatis Splendor*, Origins, (Washington DC: Catholic News Service, Oct. 1993), vol. 23: no 18, section numbers 32-37.
16. S. Gordon Redding, *The Spirit of Chinese Capitalism* (Berlin and New York: Walter de Gruyter, 1990) 43.
17. Ibid, 44.
18. Ibid, 47.
19. Ibid, 47.
20. Ibid, 47.
21. Ibid, 49.
22. Ibid, 52.

CHAPTER 5

1. George C. Lodge and Ezra F. Vogel, eds., *Ideology and National Competitiveness: An Analysis of Nine Countries* (Boston, MA: Harvard Business School Press, 1987) 317. See also Charles Hampden-Turner and Alfons Trompenaars, *The Seven Cultures of Capitalism* (New York: Doubleday, 1993) for an insightful comparison of managerial value systems in the United States, Japan, Germany, France, Britain, Sweden and the Netherlands.
2. *Veritatis Splendor*, Section 30.
3. Nicholas Leman, "The Myth of Community Development," *New York Times Magazine*, January 9, 1994, 50 and 54.

Index

A

Asian economic systems, 43-46, 104-105
Asian paradigm, 48-49, 69, 70-74

B

Basle Convention, 58
Bell, Daniel, xii
Bergsten, Fred, 28, 52
Boorstin, Daniel, 11
Bretton Woods system, 36-38
Business, role of, 74-77

C

Canada, foreign investment in, 7-9
Capital adequacy agreements, 55-57
Capitalism, 89-95, 101
Catholic tradition, 100-103
Centesimus Annus, 101-102
China, 62
    belief system in, 105-108
    investment in, 81-82
Civilization consciousness, 27
Cold War, xii-xiii, 27, 29, 32, 59
"Collective leadership," 28, 29, 51, 62
Committee on Foreign Investment in the United States (CFIUS), 15
Communism, 96-99
Communitarianism, 87, 90, 91-94, 103-105, 111-124
Community needs, 75-77, 92, 118-119
Competitive economic strategy, 71-73, 83
Confucianism, 105-108
Consensualism, 115-116
Convention on International Trade in Endangered Species

of Wild Flora and Fauna (CITES), 58
Convergence, globalization and, 10-28
Copernicus, Nicholaus, 35
Corporate objectives, 80
Corporate responsibility, 81-82
Cultural conflict, 16, 26-28

D

Daly, Herman, 21
Developing countries, 41-46

E

Earth Island Institute, 22
Eco-colonialism, 23
Education, 11-12
Environmentalism, 18-23, 57-58
Equality, 114-115
Euro Disneyland, 18
Eurodollars, 55, 56
European Community (EC), 15, 52
European Currency Unit (ECU), 14, 15
Exchange Rate Mechanism (ERM), 3-4
Exchange rate system, 36-37

F

Foreign direct investment (FDI), 4-10, 15, 54
Foreign investment, global impact of, 7-10
Foreign Investment Review Agency, 7-8

G

G-7 nations, 20
General Agreement on Tariffs and Trade (GATT), xiii, 22-23, 46-48
General Motors, 79
Germany, 62-63

Global consensus, 31, 85-108
Globalization, xi-xv, 1-29
    conflict and, 13-14, 17-18
    convergence and, 10-28
    decision making about, 28
    environment and, 18-23
    ideology and, 51-52
    literature of, xiv
    managing, 31, 33
    poverty and, 24-25
Goodland, Robert, 20, 21
Government-business intersection, 13, 16, 69
Government regulation, 76
"Group of Ten," 56-57
Gulf War, 2

H

Hierarchy, notion of, 114-115
Holism, 120-123
Human resource management, 12, 67
Human rights, 63
Huntington, Samuel P., 26

I

Ideology, 111-112
    examining, 86-89
    religion and, 99
Income distribution, 23-24
Individualism, 32, 51, 64, 87, 91-94
Industry-government consortia, 13
Interdependency, 3
Interests, global versus local, 14-15
International agencies, 20-23
International Centre for Settlement of International Disputes (ICSID), 54
International Monetary Fund (IMF), xiii, 9, 36-37, 39-41

Investment trends, 2-10

J

Japan
economic dominance of, 37, 39
economic recovery of, 62
economic strategy in, 10, 65-69
foreign investment by, 4-5
postwar development of, 48-49
trade deficit with, 37
Japanese companies, purpose of, 14

K

Keiretsu, 47, 108
Kennedy, Paul, 74, 85
Kuhn, Thomas S., 34, 35

L

Labor relations, 12
Laissez-faire paradigm, 32, 39
Leadership, global, 61-82
Lee Kuan Yew, 50
Legitimacy Gap, 87, 89
Less developed countries (LDCs), 21
Levitt, Theodore, 17
Locke, John, 93, 95

M

Management authority, sources of, 77-80
Marine Mammal Protection Act (MMPA), 22
Marx, Karl, 96
Mehta, Ashok, 97
Meiji restoration, 14
Mexico, foreign investment in, 8-10
Migrants, Third World, 25-26
Ministry of International Trade and Industry (MITI), 48
Mitsui Corporation, 80
Montreal Protocol, 57-58
Multinational corporations (MNCs), xiii, 1, 6, 14, 74, 81-82

N

Nationalistic corporations, 75
National systems, convergence of, 109
New United Motor Manufacturing, Inc. (NUMMI), 12, 79
North American Free Trade Agreement (NAFTA), 8, 9

O

Old World Order, 31-33
Organization for Economic Cooperation and Development, 24

P

Paradigm concept, 33-36
Perestroika, 36, 90
Populorum Progressio, 101
Poverty, 24-25
Preparing for the Twenty-First Century (Kennedy), 74
Producer orientation, 67
Property rights, 91, 98, 100, 101, 123
Protectionism, 16
Protestant ethic, 99-100

R

Rerum Novarum, 100-101
Ricardo, David, 47-48

S

Schumpeter, Joseph, 96, 98
Sematech, 13
Smith, Adam, 94-95
Socialism, 90, 95-99, 103, 104
Social rights, 117
States, communitarian, 120
"Structural adjustment" loans, 42
Structure of Scientific Revolutions, The (Kuhn), 33-34

T

Taoism, 107
Technology, xi, 11
Third World poverty, 24, 25
Trade, 2-10

American, 64-65, 72
investment and, 7
management of, 47
World Economic Organization and, 54

U

United Nations Commission on International Trade Law, 54
United States
communitarian drift in, 93
economic strength of, 64-74
global role of, 49-50
leadership of, 61-63
paradigm shifts in, 69-70
trade in, 37, 49

V

Veritatis Splendor, 102
Vogel, Ezra, 111
Volcker, Paul, 55-56

W

Warford, Jeremy, 19, 20
Wealth gap, 23-25
World Bank, xiii, 20-21, 41-46
World Economic Organization (WEO), 52-55, 59, 82
World ideology, 111-124
World power centers, 51
World Trade Organization, xiii, 20, 21-23, 46, 49

Z

Zambia, reform in, 40-41

THE

PARKER TWINS

S E R I E S

Captured in Colombia

JEANETTE WINDLE

Kregel
Publications

Captured in Colombia

Previously published as *Adventures in South America*.

© 1994, 1999, 2002 by Jeanette Windle

Published by Kregel Publications, a division of Kregel, Inc., P.O.
Box 2607, Grand Rapids, MI 49501. For more information about
Kregel Publications, visit our Web site: www.kregel.com.

Cover illustration: Patrick Kelley
Cover design: John M. Lucas

ISBN 0-8254-4147-1

Printed in the United States of America

1 2 3 4 5 / 06 05 04 03 02

A DEADLY FLOOD

It was the stillness and grayness that caught Justin's attention. He stopped struggling against the tightly knotted ropes cutting into his wrists long enough to draw a hot breath into his burning lungs. The cliff top above them was empty. The hoarse voices and the jingle of mules' harnesses had long since died away. The hail of pebbles and grit that had stung his face was over now, too.

No birds twittered in the wind-stunted tamaracks. And not a single cricket scraped the incessant song Justin had heard since his captors dragged him into the guerrilla camp. His sister and uncle, working at their own bonds, were silent. They had said all there was to say. Even the tangled branches of the bent cypress and junipers that lined the narrow creek and grew up the steep sides of the canyon hung silent and still. The only sound was a faint rushing in the distance that carried the promise of a faraway waterfall.

An onlooker might have thought it was snow that cast a cloak of ghostly white across the ground, the camp, and the three people tied fast to a branch that overhung the creek . . . if it weren't for the strange breathlessness and the taste of sulfur in the air. Even the prints of men and animals, and the dead grass where tents had stood just a short time ago, were slowly being covered.

Justin blew uselessly at the cloud of grayish white that drifted down from the evergreen needles to blind his eyes and choke his nostrils. Sweat trickled into his eyes and traced dark streaks down his face. He no longer felt the early morning chill of this high Andes gully.

Most of Justin's attention was focused on a broken piece of glass on the ground that offered hope of escape. But a corner of his mind eventually became aware that the quiet of the imagined distant waterfall had been transformed until it now resembled the grinding of an enormous cement mixer, churning rock and concrete in its massive metal belly. He looked up in surprise—then froze in fear.

Far up the mountain canyon, the eruption had fulfilled its promise. Released by the volcanic heat of the simmering Andes peak, thousands of tons of melted snow had plummeted downward, gobbling up dirt, boulders, trees, and any animals unfortunate enough to step in its path. Squeezed to unbelievable heights by the narrow canyon walls, the churning gray-brown mud flow—or *lahar*—now swept down the gully with enough force to bury a town.

The distant wall of mud and ice that met Justin's stunned gaze seemed to crawl at a turtle's pace, but Justin saw it scrape tangle-limbed trees and bushes from the canyon walls with the ease of a toddler snapping a toothpick in two. He saw a leaping wave sweep a boulder the size of a small house from the cliff top. It bobbed a moment, then disappeared below the surface.

Justin now pulled frantically at the ropes that held his hands outstretched overhead. Warmth trickled down his arms as the harsh strands cut into his wrists. He glanced upstream once more. Already the solid, gray-brown mass had doubled in size as it moved closer. He could see uprooted trees tossing about on the crest of the wave.

He tugged again, desperately, at his bonds, but there was no more time. Towering above the three small figures on the canyon floor, the *lahar* was now swallowing, one by one, the long line of evergreens that shaded the creek only half a mile upstream.

Justin stopped struggling. No longer afraid, he stared helplessly as the wave of mud and ice swept down upon the camp.

Chapter One

A STEAMING PEAK

"Justin, are we riding clear to Colombia like this?"

Nose pressed to the small round window of the DC-3, Justin Parker watched the distant carpet of the jungle canopy sweep under the wing just below him. A heavy wind tossed the treetops into a choppy, dusty green sea.

"Justin!" his twin sister, Jenny, repeated above the roar of the propellers. Running his fingers impatiently through short, red-gold hair, the husky thirteen-year-old reluctantly looked away from a mass of darkening clouds that drifted across the horizon.

Justin grinned as he noticed his sister's pale face and the folded paper bag in her hands, but he quickly changed his freckled face to a look of concern as he exclaimed, "Jenny, you look awful!"

"Thanks a lot!" Jenny answered, gold-brown eyes flashing indignantly. She sat up straight. One slim, tanned hand used the paper bag as a fan while the other pushed back damp, dark curls. But as another wind gust shook the plane, Jenny slumped back in the hard seat and moaned, "I'm going to be sick!"

"It's the altitude," Justin explained patiently. "These old planes don't have pressurized cabins."

Justin and Jenny Parker were opposites in more than just

8

appearance. Tall for his age, Justin was usually calm and even-tempered, but those who knew him well understood a certain stubborn set of his jaw. Steady, blue-green eyes noticed everything that went on around him.

As tall as her brother, Jenny moved through life at a run. But a strong streak of common sense rounded out her outgoing personality.

A flight attendant, her dark hair tucked up inside a blue cap, smiled at the twins and held out a tray. Jenny shook her head violently, but Justin reached for a plastic cup half-filled with Coca-Cola.

He had barely lifted the cup to his mouth when his seat seemed to drop away beneath him. Justin grabbed for his armrest as his stomach leapt into his throat. When the plane leveled off, he looked at the almost empty cup in his hand, then at the ceiling as something wet dripped down his neck. Another drop of Coca-Cola landed on his freckled nose.

"*Disculpa!* I am so sorry!" said the flight attendant, wiping a handful of paper towels across the light panel above Justin. Glancing around, Justin saw that he wasn't the only one to lose his drink.

"The plane fell!" Jenny gasped. "Uncle Pete, what happened!"

Across the aisle, a tall man with the build of a youthful Santa Claus wiped a paper towel across a full beard as red as Justin's hair. "We hit a down draft. The plane just dropped a few yards—nothing to worry about."

"Nothing to worry about!" Jenny wailed, clutching her paper bag again.

Shaking his head at the remainder of his drink, Justin

handed the cup to the flight attendant. "I guess I didn't want it, anyway."

"Oh, no!" Jenny wailed. Justin swung around as she motioned toward the window. The bank of storm clouds he had seen earlier was now just ahead—a menacing, dark mountain looming over the small plane. Moments later the interior of the plane turned to night as the storm closed around them.

The twins clutched their armrests as the small plane shook violently. Rain streamed down the windows. Looking over Justin's shoulder, Jenny gasped, "Justin, look! The wings!"

Justin again pressed his nose to the window. Just outside the window, the propeller fought against the driving rain. Lightning lit up the misty interior of the cloud, and Justin swallowed hard as he watched the wings shiver under another blast of wind.

As another flash of lightning crashed just beyond the wing tip, a light went on across the aisle. Swaying gently with the movements of the plane, Uncle Pete calmly held a stack of papers up to the dim glow of the cabin light. The man seated next to him, his eyes squeezed shut, was muttering what Justin guessed to be Spanish prayers.

Jenny eyed her uncle indignantly. "Uncle Pete, how can you work in this? We could be killed!"

Uncle Pete raised reddish brown eyebrows at the anxious expressions of his niece and nephew. "You aren't worried, are you, kids? These planes are used to this kind of weather. They don't have the power to get up above the clouds."

Laying the stack of papers carefully on his lap, he added thoughtfully, "Of course, this particular plane is a World War II leftover. I don't suppose it's been maintained too well. . . ."

As the sound of an infuriated kitten exploded from Jenny, he added hastily, "There's nothing to worry about, kids! Look! We're already breaking through the storm. We'll be in Santa Cruz in twenty minutes.

"And, no," he answered Jenny's original question as he turned back to his paperwork. "We won't be flying this crate clear to Colombia. We'll be flying to Bogotá tomorrow in a Boeing 727." Glancing at Jenny's still-pale face, he added, "With a pressurized, air-conditioned cabin, and well above any kind of weather!"

A top consultant for a major oil company, Triton Oil, Pete Parker spent much of his time jetting around the world, taking care of any problems that arose at the company's scattered work bases. His special hobby was befriending missionaries in the many countries he visited on business, and he liked to blame his size on their hospitality and the many new dishes he had to sample.

Justin and Jenny Parker had always looked forward to the interesting gifts and stories Uncle Pete brought on visits to their home in Seattle, Washington. When Uncle Pete decided to combine some vacation time with business in the small South American country of Bolivia, he had invited his nephew and niece to come along.

The last two weeks had been full of excitement as the twins tangled with a pair of Inca artifact smugglers in the highland city of La Paz, Bolivia, and stumbled over a counter-narcotics operation at one of Triton Oil's jungle bases.

Then, just this morning, as they boarded the DC-3 to leave the Bolivian jungle behind, Uncle Pete had received a request to check out the company's main Latin American office in Bogotá, the capital city of Colombia.

It was noon the next day when the loudspeaker at the front of the Boeing 727 first-class cabin announced that they were now over Colombian airspace and would be landing in Bogotá within the hour. Their appetites by now restored, Justin and Jenny bent over the lunch the airline had provided.

Justin lifted the tinfoil that covered his plate and sniffed gratefully at the perfect sirloin steak nestled beside a baked potato. Adjusting the flow of cool air above her, Jenny sighed with contentment as she peeled the gold foil from a wedge of French cheese.

The flight attendant had just cleared away the trays when the warning light above their seats blinked on. The twins quickly fastened their seatbelts for the landing. Jenny now sat beside the window, but Justin bent his neck to look over her shoulder. Still far below, a circle of snowcapped peaks enclosed a vast valley. As the plane curved downward, Justin could make out a patchwork of dark green evergreens and yellow-green mountain meadows.

"Uncle Pete, isn't Colombia on the equator?" he asked with surprise. "I thought it would be all jungle."

"Yes, it is on the equator," Uncle Pete answered without lifting his eyes from his spread-out briefcase contents. "And there is plenty of jungle. But the Andes Mountains here form a valley at about eight thousand five hundred feet in elevation. It's cool enough to have vegetation much like the mountains back home."

"It's beautiful!" Jenny said with awe, as pine forests and meadows bright with wildflowers rolled away below.

"Why are the capital cities all so high?" Justin asked, remembering the vast mountain crater in which the Bolivian capital of La Paz sat.

"Most of the main cities in the Andes were built in high mountain valleys," Uncle Pete answered, absently shuffling through a stack of computer printouts, "to get away from the heat and danger of the jungles. The Andes here in Colombia get a lot more rain, so they have more vegetation—"

His explanation was interrupted by an excited squeal from Jenny. "Hey, look at that! That mountain is smoking!"

Justin leaned over to study the mountain peak his sister was pointing at. The slightly lopsided peak was as snow-covered as its neighbors. But sure enough, from the snowfields rose clouds of steam—as though the mountain were indeed smoking.

"Is that a volcano?" he asked curiously.

"Most of the Andean mountains were once active volcanoes," Uncle Pete said, looking up again. "Hmm, that one does look like it's still alive! It must be the Nevada del Ruiz."

Laying down his papers, he added thoughtfully, "That peak made world news not too long ago."

Jenny could always sense a story. "Please tell us about it, Uncle Pete!"

Uncle Pete closed his briefcase and sat back. "Well, like most of its neighbors, the Nevada del Ruiz had been asleep—dormant—for many years. Then one day it woke up and blew its top. It wasn't much of a blow as volcanoes go—not much lava flow at all. But the heat of the volcano melted much of its snow and ice cap. Half the mountainside washed down, creating a mud flow more than forty feet deep that wiped out thousands

13

of farms. One entire town of twenty thousand people remains buried under the mud."

Justin eyed the steaming peak respectfully as the plane banked and left the mountain range behind. Still far below sprawled the city of Bogotá. Boxlike skyscrapers reached for a cloudless sky, and a maze of roads climbed over and under each other like some toy construction set.

"It's so big!" Jenny gasped.

"More than eight million people," Uncle Pete commented. "Bigger than New York City."

"Well, there should be some good shopping in a place that size!" Jenny concluded with satisfaction.

The plane touched down just minutes later. Slinging his handbag over his shoulder, Justin pulled his jacket tight against a brisk wind that whistled through the cracks of the inflated plastic tube that connected the Boeing 727 to the airport terminal.

As they trudged up the long corridor from the unloading gate, the twins eyed with interest the shops that lined both sides. They had stopped to admire some handblown glass swans when a voice questioned softly, "*Café*, señores?"

The two children whirled around. A square booth stood in the center of the wide hallway. On its side the words "Asociacion de Cafeteros Colombianos" were written under a picture of a man dressed in a poncho and sombrero. On the counter, a tall percolator steamed next to a collection of fine china cups. A smiling, dark-haired girl leaned over the counter. Catching their puzzled expressions, she repeated in careful English, "Would you like to try a cup of Colombian coffee?"

Jenny grimaced. "No, thanks! I don't like coffee."

Uncle Pete reached over their heads to accept a cup of coffee. "Try it, kids! You've never tasted coffee like this."

Justin breathed in the rich smell from the percolator. "I guess I'll try a cup!"

"I will make you my specialty," the girl offered. "*Café con leche*—coffee with milk."

Justin raised reddish brown eyebrows in surprise as he took a cautious sip of the milky brown liquid. It was sweet and strong but had none of the bitter taste he usually associated with coffee.

Jenny doubtfully sipped her own cup, then her eyes lit up. "Mmmm! It tastes almost like hot chocolate!"

The hostess smiled with pleasure. "It is pure, mountain-grown Colombian coffee—the best in the world!"

Jenny giggled. "Just like the commercials back home!"

Uncle Pete set down his cup. "Okay, kids, we need to check through customs and pick up our baggage."

In the center of the long corridor ahead stood what looked like a metal doorway just wide enough for one person. At table height beside it, a conveyor belt carried hand luggage through a similar—though much smaller—door. Soldiers in camouflage, assault rifles cradled across muscled bare arms, made sure that every passenger passed through the doorway.

The passenger in front of the Parkers had just set his handbag on the conveyor belt when someone with an American accent called, "Mr. Parker?"

A young man of medium height with clipped, dark hair pushed unhindered past the armed guards and stepped around the metal door. His gray business suit didn't hide the tough, wide-shouldered build of an athlete. *Or a soldier,* Justin thought.

His dark brown eyes were unsmiling as he handed a card to Uncle Pete. "Pete Parker, Triton Oil, right? I'm Steve Cardoza, American embassy. I'm here to pick you up."

"Well, I appreciate this," Uncle Pete answered, studying the card with a puzzled expression. "But it isn't necessary. I'm expecting one of my own men to pick me up."

"I'm afraid that won't be possible," Steve Cardoza answered shortly. He glanced around at the still-waiting passengers. "I'll explain later. This place is too public. Right now, let's get your things cleared through customs."

An impatient official was now waiting for the Parkers to move ahead. As Uncle Pete stepped through the metal doorway, Mr. Cardoza swung Jenny's handbag to the conveyor belt. Jenny hung back. "Why do we have to go through that? What is it?"

"It's an X-ray machine," Mr. Cardoza explained shortly. "It makes sure you're not bringing in anything you aren't supposed to."

"Drugs, you mean," Justin commented, remembering the customs search in Bolivia.

The embassy aide looked grim. "Not drugs. Bombs."

The surprised children meekly stepped single file through the doorway. As Justin walked through, an alarm sounded and a red light above the doorway began blinking. An unsmiling soldier moved to cut him off, then stepped back as Justin sheepishly pulled out the pocket flashlight that had triggered the alarm.

Justin noticed many other heavily armed soldiers as they pulled their suitcases from the baggage conveyor and went through another customs check. When they had repacked their suitcases, Steve Cardoza flagged a porter who wheeled the luggage to the parking zone. Here, too, alert and unsmiling soldiers patrolled back and forth, assault rifles held ready across their chests.

"Wow! Is there a war going on?" Justin whispered to Jenny as Mr. Cardoza unlocked the back of a dark blue minivan and tossed in the suitcases.

Giving the minivan a disappointed look, Jenny whispered back, "That's an embassy car? I figured it would be red, white, and blue with an American flag flying from the top!"

The embassy aide obviously had sharp ears. As he motioned them into the minivan, he remarked grimly, "In Colombia we'd rather not stand out. And yes, you could say there's a war going on."

Mr. Cardoza expertly maneuvered the minivan through a long line of buses and taxis. Justin was surprised to pass several more terminal buildings, the signs in front announcing the services of dozens of airlines. AVIANCA, the national Colombian airline, predominated. One of the terminals was air force, Justin guessed, eyeing the fighters and combat helicopters outside.

Mr. Cardoza turned onto a broad boulevard. Squat, gray factories stretched out alongside towering office buildings.

"Just like Seattle," Justin commented, feeling suddenly homesick for the busy streets of his home city. Then, as the embassy aide suddenly slammed on the brakes and cut across a lane of traffic, he added dryly, "Well, maybe not quite!"

Justin counted five lanes clearly marked on the road flowing toward the city, but he was startled to notice that seven or eight vehicles rushed abreast ahead of the van. With total disregard for traffic rules, the smaller cars zipped back and forth across the paths of buses and trucks while the larger vehicles seemed ready to ram anything that got in their way.

Jenny squealed as Mr. Cardoza changed lanes again, almost under the wheels of a massive refrigerated truck. Glancing back, the embassy aide's bronzed face broke into a grin. "It's not much like driving back home, but it's really a lot of fun when you get used to it. Kind of like the Indy 500."

Justin suddenly sat up straight. Just ahead, a mass of blackened rubble and the shattered remnants of a tall building broke the solid line of factories. "Wow! What happened there?" he asked. "It looks like the place exploded!"

Over the back of the seat, Justin could see their driver's strong hands tighten on the steering wheel. "Yesterday's bomb," he answered grimly. "The reason for all the stepped-up security at the airport."

"You mentioned a war, Mr. Cardoza," Uncle Pete spoke up quietly. "I haven't had much access to the news in the last couple of weeks, but I understood that the guerrillas here in Colombia were in the middle of peace talks with the government. I wouldn't have brought the kids otherwise."

"Gorillas!" Jenny exclaimed, looking puzzled. "How can monkeys talk to a government?"

Uncle Pete's sudden cough sounded suspiciously like a laugh, but he explained patiently, "Not the kind of gorillas you find in a zoo. *Guerrillas* are bands of terrorists who want to overthrow the government so they can take over the country for themselves. Is that essentially right, Mr. Cardoza?"

"Just call me Steve," the embassy aide said absently. Then

he added, "You're exactly right, Mr. Parker. And yes, the guerrillas have consented to peace talks with the government. But as you can see, there are plenty of stray bands still tossing bombs."

"Well, I appreciate your concern for the safety of American citizens," Uncle Pete commented. "But I still don't understand. There must be dozens of Americans flying in and out of Bogotá every day. Surely the embassy doesn't go to the trouble of picking them all up every time there has been a bombing!"

He added quietly, "There's obviously something else going on here. Maybe it's time you told me where you are taking us . . . and why my own men didn't come to pick me up."

"You'll see where we're going in just a minute," Steve answered politely. "My boss will be there to meet you. I'd rather let him explain."

They were now driving through a tranquil residential neighborhood. Just then they turned into a narrow side street lined with four-story brick buildings. High-pitched, excited voices broke the quiet. Steve slammed on the brakes as a group of dark-haired children kicked a tattered soccer ball right under the wheels of the minivan.

A shrill bark caught Justin's attention. Pressing his nose to the window, he realized that what looked like a dirty white dust mop on the sidewalk was actually a small dog. The dog rolled over and whined with contentment as a girl—long, dark hair covering her face—leaned down to scratch its belly.

The children scattered as Steve leaned on the horn. Muttering under his breath, he pulled up in front of one of the townhouses. Only a pair of soldiers with tiny American flags on the shoulders of their uniforms gave any indication that the building was anything other than an ordinary house.

"This is the American embassy guest house," Steve informed them as they piled out of the minivan. Nodding at the soldiers' salute, he took out a bunch of keys. The twins watched in awe as he unlocked first one, then another of a series of five locks. "We had a hand grenade tossed in here a couple of months ago. So we're careful about who enters embassy property."

Picking up his suitcase as Steve swung open the heavy metal door, Justin glanced down the long street. The children were still playing, the small, dusty white dog frisking around their feet. Suddenly, Justin heard a shrill whistle, and the dog broke free from the group of children. Just as Justin stepped into a wide, tiled hall, the dog dashed between his legs and into the hall.

"Get that dog!" Steve slammed the door shut and leapt for the dog. As he skidded across the polished tiles, the dog dashed back toward the door. Dropping his suitcase, Justin lunged for the dog.

Rolling over, Justin sat up, clutching the bundle of fur tight. Noticing a grimy handkerchief tied around a front foreleg, he stroked the trembling animal gently. "Did you hurt yourself?"

He untied the dirty cloth, and a rolled-up piece of paper fell to the ground. Unrolling the paper, Justin stared with astonishment as he recognized the insignia that had been cut from some brochure and pasted to one end of the sheet of cheap notebook paper. It was the insignia of Triton Oil.

"Well, what is it?" Jenny asked impatiently, peering over his shoulder. Then Uncle Pete reached down and lifted the piece of paper from Justin's hands. The hall fell silent as he read aloud, "Release our men at once or suffer grave consequences."

Chapter Two

TROUBLE FOR TRITON OIL

"Give me the dog!" Justin blinked in astonishment as Steve snatched the dog away. Carrying him across the hall, he ran his hands over the animal, even checking its mouth. "No explosives," he pronounced at last with relief.

Seeing the twins' look of surprise, he explained, "I've seen bombs delivered in some pretty strange ways."

As Steve put down the dog, Justin suddenly thought of something. Swinging open the heavy door, he peered down the street. It was now empty.

"Hey! Shut that door!" Something furry brushed against Justin's legs. Before he could move, the dog had dashed around the corner of the building. Steve clapped Justin on the shoulder as he started to apologize. "Don't worry about it, kid. The dog probably wouldn't have helped us anyway."

He, too, studied the empty street. "That was good thinking, though. I'd say someone paid those kids to deliver this message."

As they stepped back inside, a tall, thin man with honey-colored skin and tight black curls came down a wide staircase at the end of the hall. "What's all the commotion, Steve?"

He held out his hand to Uncle Pete as Steve introduced him. "This is Martin Bascom, Secretary to the American ambassador here in Bogotá—and my boss! Mr. Bascom, Pete Parker, consultant for Triton Oil."

Mr. Bascom led the group into a large living room off the hall while Steve explained what had happened. As they all sat down, Uncle Pete handed the diplomat the slip of paper they had found on the dog. "This seems to be directed at my company. What, exactly, is going on here?"

Instead of answering Uncle Pete's question. Mr. Bascom asked, "Mr. Parker, how much do you know about the situation here in Colombia?"

Uncle Pete rubbed his beard thoughtfully. "Well, I know that Colombia has one of the best records of democratic government in South America. They are not a wealthy country, but they've made a lot of social and economic advances over the last thirty years—including the development of their oil industry."

He added, "I also know that in the last few years guerrillas have brought the country to the brink of civil war and threatened to destroy every advance the government has made."

Mr. Bascom looked satisfied. "That's right. Guerrilla bands are the plague of Colombia. Each group is determined to overthrow the elected government and put themselves into power. The biggest is FARC—which is the Spanish abbreviation for the Armed Revolutionary Forces of Colombia. Then there is the ELN—or the National Liberation Army. And of course, there are dozens of smaller groups. Many are being funded by the drug trade."

As the twins sat up with sudden interest, he added, "Drug

traffickers use guerrillas as their private armies—paying them in weapons. Many of these guerrilla bands are better armed than the Colombian army. And they will do just about anything to achieve their goals—from tossing a bomb that kills dozens of innocent bystanders to blowing up the pipelines that carry oil across the country."

Uncle Pete's hazel eyes sharpened with interest. "Is that where Triton Oil comes in?"

Mr. Bascom nodded. "Two days ago, one of your American engineers was checking out your base in the eastern plains when he discovered two men setting an explosive to the pipeline near the oil camp. With the help of some local oil workers, he managed to capture them and turn them over to the Colombian police.

"It turns out that the two men were both members of some small guerrilla band. The Triton Oil office here has already received a phone call this morning, threatening to take action against the company if their men are not released."

An expression of worry clouded the man's face, but Mr. Bascom said firmly, "We really don't think there is much danger, but as a precaution, we have temporarily shut down your office and placed security guards at the homes of the two Americans who work there. Your head of operations here in Bogotá asked if we would have you picked up at the airport."

"I certainly appreciate your cooperation," Uncle Pete said, glancing at his watch, "but I would like to meet with the head of operations as soon as possible. Can that be arranged?"

"Of course!" Mr. Bascom stood up. "I'll give him a call and take you over myself."

The twins jumped up eagerly, and Uncle Pete frowned.

"A business meeting is no place for you two. You'd better stay here, where you can relax—and be safe."

Catching their look of disappointment, Mr. Bascom raised a hand. "There's no need for that. Lieutenant Steve Cardoza is on loan from the U.S. Marine Corps to help with our security. He will be responsible for your safety while you are here. The children will be perfectly safe doing some sightseeing with him."

Justin eyed with satisfaction the muscles that pressed against the seams of Steve's civilian clothes. "I *knew* you were a soldier!"

With a grin, the broad-shouldered Marine saluted smartly, then motioned toward the door. "Let's go!"

The quiet streets surrounding the embassy guest house could have been any middle-class neighborhood in North America. As Steve drove back onto a major thoroughfare, he asked, "Well, what would you two like to see first?"

"A pamphlet we got on the plane said something about the Gold Museum," Justin said.

"*I* want to go shopping," argued Jenny. "We saw the open-air market in Bolivia. It was pretty exciting, with all the Indian ladies sitting on the ground, selling their fruits and vegetables."

Steve looked from one to the other. "Tell you what. I'll show you how we do our shopping here in Bogotá. Then we'll hit that museum you mentioned."

Moments later, the minivan turned into a large parking lot. Across the front of a two-story glass and brick building several blocks long, a massive sign announced, *unicentro*.

"Hey, this is just a mall!" Jenny exclaimed with disappointment as Steve herded them toward the main entrance.

Inside, Justin read the signs that lined the vast, tiled corridor. "Wendy's, Burger King, Sears—just like back home!"

Steve grinned. "I'm afraid shopping in Bogotá isn't much different than in the U.S."

Jenny was inspecting a dress displayed in the window of an exclusive boutique. "Except for the prices! Look at this . . . $2,249! And that's American dollars! Who can afford to shop here?"

Leaving the mall with their savings intact, they drove toward the center of the city. Modern skyscrapers elbowed white colonial buildings with fancy iron balconies and red-tiled roofs. Studying a space-age office building whose tilted roof jutted toward the sky like a fighter jet taking off, Justin commented, "I sure didn't expect everything to be so modern and beautiful."

"Yeah, I don't understand why anyone would want to overthrow the government when they have such a nice country," Jenny agreed. "Those guerrillas must be awful people!"

"You kids have only seen the best part of the city," Steve commented, turning the minivan onto a narrow avenue lined with old, gray factory buildings. Soon the factories gave way to grime-stained apartment buildings. Doors swung on broken hinges, and scraps of lumber and cardboard darkened smashed windows. Startled, the teens sat up straight as even these buildings were left behind.

The houses just ahead—if you could call them houses—clung to the edges of a vast garbage dump. Scavenged boards, tin, and even old tires were nailed together to form crude shelters. Lines of threadbare laundry dangled between low roofs pieced together from scraps of metal.

"Hey, look at that!" exclaimed Jenny.

Under the flat bed of an abandoned trailer was a cardboard box that had once protected a freezer. An entrance had been cut in the front, and a sheet of torn plastic stretched over the top to keep out the rain. But what caught the twins' attention was the small boy whose tangle-haired, dark head was pillowed on a gunny sack in the makeshift doorway. A ragged sweater was his only protection against the chilling mountain winds.

"Does he *live* there?" Jenny asked in horror. "Where are his parents?"

The grim look was back on Steve's face. "He probably has no parents. There are hundreds of thousands of kids like him on the streets of Colombia. They are called the *gamines*—street urchins. They stay alive by running errands, stealing, even eating garbage.

"You asked about the guerrillas," he added as they left the dump behind. "Many of the guerrillas come from poor families such as these. They've seen their families suffer while most of the country's wealth is concentrated in the hands of just a few."

"No wonder they get mad," Justin said soberly, looking back at the flimsy cardboard home. "But if the government doesn't want the guerrillas to fight, why don't they do something to help?"

"The government *is* trying to do something," Steve answered seriously as he turned back onto a major boulevard. "But Colombia isn't a rich country, and improvement is slow. The guerrillas aren't willing to wait. They don't consider themselves criminals. They think of themselves as freedom fighters—fighting to free the poor from what they consider the 'oppression of the rich ruling class.'

"Unfortunately, while some guerrillas are real idealists who want to make the country better for the ordinary people, many just want to grab power and money for themselves. Instead of trying to change their country peacefully, they throw bombs and murder a lot of innocent people."

Glancing at their gloomy faces, he suddenly smiled. "Hey, kids, cheer up! On the whole, Colombia is a beautiful country, and we want you to enjoy your stay here."

Moments later Steve pulled up beside a wide plaza where thick-trunked trees spread leafy branches over stone benches, and marble fountains splashed rainbows in the late afternoon sun. "Come on, you two! You're about to see the most fabulous gold collection in the world."

Steve led the twins through the center of the plaza to a new-looking brick and glass skyscraper. Justin stopped counting stories after the first two dozen and studied the sign above wide glass doors. "Hey, this is a bank! I thought we were going to the Gold Museum!"

Steve grinned. "Yes, it is—and we *are!* The Gold Museum is housed in the bank because it contains most of Colombia's national gold reserve."

"You mean it's just a bunch of gold bars?" Jenny asked in disappointment. "Like the American national gold reserve at Fort Knox?"

"You'll have to wait and see," Steve answered. He motioned them into the bank lobby and bought their tickets. When a small group of other tourists had gathered, a guide led them toward a broad staircase. An armed Colombian soldier stepped in front of the group, while another brought up the rear.

The guide paused outside a heavy metal door like that of a bank vault. An armed guard stood in front of the door. As the door swung open, the guide motioned for the group to step forward, one at a time.

"What is he doing?" Jenny asked Steve.

"That door works like the X-ray machine you stepped through at the airport," Steve explained. "They're checking for burglary tools, as well as weapons."

The twins were surprised when Steve reached inside his jacket and pulled out a small pistol. With a rapid stream of Spanish, he handed the pistol and some identification papers to the guard.

"Hey, you sure speak good Spanish!" Justin complimented as the guard handed back Steve's identification but pocketed the pistol.

Steve grinned. "You pick up plenty of Spanish growing up in Southern California. That's what got me transferred to Colombia."

Justin and Jenny followed him into a large, empty room with no windows. Justin noticed a tiny video camera watching them from one corner. Across the room was another vault door. When the entire group was inside, the first door closed behind them.

"They sure aren't taking any chances with their gold, are they?" Jenny giggled a bit nervously as the light dimmed around them.

But her giggles ended in amazed silence as the second door slid open and the crowd of people moved into the lighted vault beyond. A soft yellow glittered on all sides, but not from stacks of heavy gold bars. Behind thick glass display windows, gold bracelets, rings, and necklaces were piled in careless abandon. Odd geometric designs etched cups and plates of solid gold, hammered out centuries before for an Indian noble's table.

"All that remains of Colombia's pre-Spanish riches," Steve said, looking amused at their open-mouthed awe. "It's the largest collection of gold artifacts in the world."

Jenny paused to examine a headdress that gleamed green against the delicate gold-work. Steve looked over her shoulder. "Those stones are emeralds," he told her. "The best coffee in the world isn't all Colombia produces. They also export most of the world's emeralds."

He leaned against a pillar. "You kids go on and look around. I've seen this often enough."

The twins moved slowly along the rows of display windows. They stopped suddenly as a dark-skinned warrior glared fiercely at them from behind a mask of solid gold. His out-thrust spear guarded a staircase that led to a lower level.

"He isn't real!" Justin said a little shakily as he realized the warrior was carved of some dark wood. From a lifeless chin jutted a pointed, golden beard. The gold helmet on the wooden head was topped with an ornate headdress of red, black, and gold feathers, and emeralds crossed a hammered breastplate. Golden earrings, curled like wood shavings, dangled from deaf ears.

"I *knew* he wasn't real!" Jenny answered scornfully as she started down the staircase. Justin looked unconvinced, but followed her to the lower level. Here tourists crowded around more showcases, exclaiming expressions of awe and greed in many languages.

Glancing up from an elegantly jeweled crown, Justin suddenly noticed that one face nearby didn't reflect awe or delight at the beauty that filled the vault. Her slim shoulders tight with concentration, a girl about the age of Justin and Jenny pressed against a glass window. The arrow-straight hair that cascaded below her waist was so black that it gleamed blue in the soft light of the display.

The girl moved slightly, and Justin caught a glimpse of delicate, pale features tight with anger. A thin hand hanging at her side clenched and unclenched as she stared at the heaped-up gold. *She must have come in at the last minute or I would have noticed her,* Justin thought. *She isn't like anyone I've ever seen!*

As if reading his mind, Jenny whispered, "She looks like a princess!"

Eyeing the neat but threadbare clothes, she added, "A princess in disguise, that is."

"I wonder who she is?" Justin whispered back

As though she had heard, the girl turned. Ice-blue eyes, fringed with impossibly long, black eyelashes, gave them a disdainful look. Then she turned her back to them.

"Come on, Jenny!" Justin said, flushing with embarrassment as he motioned Jenny toward a large, square glass case that stood alone in the center of the room.

"Wow! Look at that!" They forgot the strange girl as they bent over the lone object displayed in the glass case. Somehow afloat on a tiny artificial lake was a raft of gold logs only six inches long. At one end knelt a paddler, steering the raft with a long golden pole. In the center, his jeweled eyes blindly watching the horizon, stood an Indian prince, his tiny gold adornments hinting his relationship to the warrior upstairs. The haughty lift of the royal chin brought back to Justin's mind the proud face of the girl they had just seen.

"That piece alone could keep every homeless child in Bogotá off the streets for a month!" a voice said coldly in the precise, accentless English of a well-educated foreigner. The twins whirled around. Her silky fine hair falling in a shimmering curtain across her face, the girl they had noticed earlier leaned over the glass case.

"This gold should belong to the people of this country—all of it!" Her eyes were now hot blue sparks as she threw out a slim arm to include the rest of the room. "It should be sold—used to help the poor of this country. Instead, it's kept locked up for a bunch of fat, wealthy tourists to stare at!"

Startled at the bitterness in the girl's voice, Justin answered reasonably, "I thought it *did* belong to the people of Colombia. I mean, they said it was the *national* gold reserve. Doesn't that mean these things belong to everyone?"

"And they are so beautiful!" Jenny broke in, brushing her fingertips over the glass case as though to touch what lay within. She added, "And here, everyone can enjoy them—including the people of Colombia."

"Beauty can't fill a starving stomach!" the other girl answered coldly.

The murmur of tourists filing by filled an awkward silence. Then Jenny turned away. "Come on, Justin. I'm ready to go."

"Wait! Please! Don't go!" Her voice half-angry, half-pleading, the girl took a step toward them. "I'm . . ." The apology seemed to catch in her throat, then she said, "My name is Estrella."

She pronounced the name Es-tray-yu. As Justin mentally sounded out the strange syllables, she added, "It means 'Star' in your language."

Seeing Jenny's unfriendly expression, Justin held out his hand. "Why don't we start over. My name is Justin Parker, and this is my sister, Jenny. We're visiting your country with my Uncle Pete. He's an oil consultant. You may have seen the signs for Triton Oil. That's his company."

The girl's long lashes dropped to conceal a sudden gleam of satisfaction as Justin hurried on, "You sure speak good English! Where did you learn it?"

For a moment Justin thought the girl would refuse to answer, then she admitted, "My father was American."

Jenny's expression thawed noticeably. "Really! Then you're American like us! That's great!"

The blue eyes suddenly iced over again. "Do not call me American! *This* is my country!"

Justin and Jenny were both bewildered by Estrella's sudden changes of mood. Jenny answered rather coolly, "I just thought . . . I mean, your father . . . does he live here in Bogotá?"

Estrella was silent a moment, then she said reluctantly, "I have no father anymore."

"Oh, I'm sorry!" Jenny answered sympathetically. "Does your mother live here, then? Is *she* American?"

Justin saw the cold curtain drop again over Estrella's face. Elbowing Jenny, he whispered, "Don't ask so many questions! You're going to make her mad again!"

Jenny's eyes sparked hot gold, and she elbowed him back. "Look who's talking! You're the one who wanted to know who she is!"

Catching Estrella's wide-eyed expression, they both smiled sheepishly, and Jenny asked, "Don't you ever argue with your brothers?"

Estrella looked wistful. "I don't have any brothers—or sisters. And my mother died three years ago."

"Oh, that's awful! You aren't . . ." Jenny faltered. "You aren't one of those poor kids living on the street, are you?"

"You don't need to feel sorry for me!" Estrella answered proudly, "I have a new family now—a family of others like myself who have no home of their own."

Again she waved a slender arm around the room. "One day they will take all this gold and give it to those who really need it."

Justin raised unbelieving eyebrows. "Estrella, it would take an army to break in here and take out this gold—if anyone would be dumb enough to try!" He smiled encouragingly. "You're joking, aren't you?"

Her slim back straight as an arrow, Estrella answered firmly, "I am *not* joking! My family are special people. They are freedom fighters, and one day they will free our people from those who take all the wealth and keep it for themselves."

"Freedom fighters!" Justin repeated in a whisper. He and Jenny stared at each other in horrified understanding. Then Justin demanded doubtfully, "You mean your 'family' are guerrillas? Like the terrorists who threw that bomb and killed all those people yesterday? You can't mean that you're really a member of a guerrilla band!"

Chapter Three

HAUNTED!

The three children stared at each other for a long moment, then Jenny broke the silence. "You really live with terrorists?" she asked doubtfully. "How can *they* be your family?"

"Don't you dare call my family 'terrorists'!" Estrella's eyes were now the frozen blue of a winter sea.

"Yes, they are guerrillas. They work for the freedom of my people. But they are not like those mad men who throw bombs. They would not hurt anyone!"

Jenny looked scornful. "If they are so kind and peaceful, how do they plan on getting all the gold out of here and giving it to the people?"

"I . . . I don't know!" Estrella looked suddenly troubled, but she answered defiantly, "I just know they are good people. They found me on the street with no place to go, and they gave me a home . . . and food to eat. They even paid for lessons so that I would not forget the language of my father. I am very special for them because no other children are allowed."

She lowered her voice almost to a whisper. "Sometimes, though, I think it would be nice to have a friend my age, or . . . or perhaps a brother!"

Justin saw wistfulness behind the defiance in Estrella's eyes. He put out his hand. "Well, we'll be going back to the United States soon, but we'd sure like to be your friends while we're here!"

Estrella froze, scorn erasing the momentary softness in the blue eyes. She quickly put her hands behind her back. "The United States!" she repeated, her voice dripping with disdain. "What do Americans know about friendship? You are all alike. You pretend to care for people. Then you go away and leave them! Your friendship means nothing!"

Justin was too hurt and puzzled at her reaction to answer, but Jenny demanded angrily, "What do you mean by that? What do you know about Americans?"

"I knew my father!" Catching an astonished stare from a passing tourist, Estrella lowered her voice. "Daddy was an American—like you! He said he loved me, that he would always love me. Then one day he just left. I was only seven years old."

Her voice shook with anger and bitterness. "He never even bothered to write or send money. When my mother died, I would have starved if my family had not found me."

She drew herself up proudly. "No, I don't need any American friends. My family are all the friends I need!"

Jenny bristled with anger. "If you hate Americans so much, why did you stop to talk to us?"

Without waiting for an answer, she turned away. "Come on, Justin! Let's go!"

Justin started to follow, then stopped and said awkwardly, "Well, it was good to meet . . ." He was interrupted by a shrill whistle, and Steve called from the foot of the stairs, "Hey, Justin, are you planning on spending the night?"

Justin suddenly realized the lights had dimmed and that they were the only ones left in the vault. Even Estrella had disappeared. He hurried up the stairs. Ahead of him, Steve's clear baritone voice echoed down the stairwell as he answered Jenny, "So you really liked it, huh? Wait until you see Zipaquirá tomorrow. That's even better!"

At the top of the stairs, Justin glanced back. Estrella had stepped out from behind the display case where she had ducked. Perhaps it was only a trick of the light that made the young guerrilla girl look suddenly uncertain and lost as she stared up at them. Catching his glance, she ducked back into the darkness.

"Who's your little friend?" Steve asked as the guard returned his gun and he slid it into a shoulder holster. The rest of their group and even the guide had already left.

Jenny sniffed. "She isn't our friend! She made that pretty clear!"

The short dusk of the tropics had already fallen by the time they left the museum. Like so many fireflies, thousands of office windows twinkled against the black velvet backdrop of a starless night. In the plaza, underwater floodlights turned the fountains into rainbow-colored cascades of light.

Justin checked his watch. "Only six o'clock and dark already!"

"We're on the equator here," Steve explained. "Days and nights in Colombia are just about exactly twelve hours long. It's light from six A.M. to six P.M. year round."

As they followed Steve across the plaza, the twins told Steve all about the strange girl they had met. As they climbed into the minivan, Jenny concluded, "She sure wasn't very nice, was she, Justin?"

Justin nodded agreement, but that last glimpse of the young guerrilla girl's troubled face popped into his mind. "Maybe not, but I still feel sorry for her. She . . . I don't think she's very happy."

Jenny sniffed. "Well, we'll never see her again, so I guess it doesn't matter."

Turning the minivan back onto a major thoroughfare, Steve suddenly asked, "You say she was the one who came over . . . wanted to talk? Are you sure you didn't speak to her first?"

When Justin and Jenny emphatically shook their heads, the young Marine fell silent and seemed lost in thought as they drove back through the rush-hour traffic. As Steve swung the minivan off a traffic-congested overpass, Justin remembered his manners. "Thanks a lot for taking us, Mr. Cardoza."

"Yeah, that was great!" Jenny exclaimed.

"That's my job!" Steve answered. He looked at Justin. "I was telling your sister that I thought we'd head out to the salt mines at Zipaquirá tomorrow. There is less chance of anyone following us if we keep on the move."

There was a twinkle in his dark brown eyes as he added, "That's a good excuse for sightseeing."

The narrow street was dark and quiet when they arrived back at the embassy guest house, but two American soldiers still stood at attention in the doorway. The four-story building echoed with emptiness as Steve swung open the heavy metal door and ushered the twins into the wide hall. There was no sign of Uncle Pete or Mr. Bascom.

Leading Justin and Jenny into a gleaming white kitchen at the rear of the building, Steve lifted the lid of a large pot that simmered on the back of the huge stove. Handing Justin a sack of crusty rolls and a pat of butter, he carried the pot across to a dining room that could seat dozens of people.

"Doesn't anyone else live here?" Justin asked curiously as he looked around the long room with its empty tables.

"Yeah, if this is the American embassy, where are all the people?" Jenny added.

Steve grinned as he dished up three bowls of what he informed them was *sancocho*—a Colombian stew thick with unfamiliar ingredients. "The American embassy is in the center of town—with hundreds of people going in and out all day. This is just a guest house where we house VIPs—very important people, that is."

"And *we* are very important people?" Jenny asked impishly.

"Let's just say we want to keep you out of trouble," he answered. "At the moment, you Parkers are the only ones here. There are two security guards who double as cooks—if you can call what they do cooking! They are probably upstairs watching TV. And, of course, there are the soldiers on duty outside—though they don't sleep here."

Uncle Pete still had not returned by the time Steve showed the twins up two flights of stairs to where their luggage awaited them in adjoining bedrooms. But late that night, Justin awoke to hear Uncle Pete's familiar whistle from the bedroom next door.

The next morning, Justin and Jenny joined Uncle Pete and Steve for breakfast in one corner of the long dining room. One of the security guards was working in the kitchen, and, contrary to Steve's opinion, the cheese omelets were delicious. The twins had already discovered that the "TV" that so absorbed the security guards was actually a series of television screens that kept a distant eye on every inch of the property.

"How did your meetings go yesterday, Uncle Pete?" Justin asked, wiping his mouth on a napkin.

Uncle Pete set down his coffee cup with a sigh. "Allen Johnson, a young engineer on his first assignment here, was responsible for catching the two men who tried to blow a hole in the pipeline. He deserves a medal for it, but now the guerrilla band these two men belong to are threatening revenge on all our American personnel if we don't release them."

"Are you going to let them go, then?" Jenny asked, her eyes open wide.

"No, we're not. For one thing, the Colombian police have them in custody—not us. Besides, if we gave in to a threat like that, our workers would never be safe again. The terrorists would come back with another threat every time they wanted something."

"What are you going to do, then?" asked Justin.

Uncle Pete leaned back in his chair. "We'll let the Colombian police force take care of the two guerrillas. What happens to them is no business of ours. But as for Triton Oil, the engineers can't keep their minds on their work if they're worrying about their families. We've decided to pull all our married American executives out of Colombia and replace them with single workers. We'll have to step up security around our bases and office as well."

Uncle Pete turned a stern eye on his nephew and niece. "As

for you two . . . I want to get you home as soon as possible. I should be done here in a couple of days."

He stood up. "I'll be meeting with the chief of police and our office staff this morning. Steve tells me he has plans for you, so enjoy yourselves and stay out of trouble."

Steve stood up too. "Yeah, I told the kids I'd take them out to Zipaquirá. It's one of the biggest deposits of rock salt in the world—and a lot more!"

"A lot more what?" Justin and Jenny asked at the same time, but Steve just grinned and refused to explain.

A heavy mist blanketed the street outside, and the twins pulled their jackets tight. An hour later, they had left the last skyscraper behind. Cultivated fields and green pastures wet with fog made a patchwork against low, rolling hills. Fat Holstein and jersey cows munched contentedly behind neat barbwire fences. Brick-red farmhouses and barns reminded Justin of last year's vacation in New England.

Bordering the wide, paved highway were mile after mile of long sheds with peaked roofs of translucent green glass. Jenny cried out in delight as she caught sight of a flower stand in front of one shed. The stand was heaped high with carnations, roses, and strange tropical blooms.

"Those are greenhouses, aren't they!" she said with astonishment. "But why so many? You could grow enough flowers for the whole world in those!"

"Not quite," Steve answered. "But a good portion of the flowers you buy back home in the U.S. are grown in those greenhouses."

Justin had just noticed something more to his liking. A stand at the gate of a prosperous dairy farm announced in large letters, *Fresas con Crema.*

"Strawberries and cream," Steve translated as he stopped the minivan. "You can't leave Bogotá without trying the local strawberries and cream. They're delicious." A few minutes later, Justin and Jenny were nodding agreement over a bowl of oversized strawberries and cream too thick to pour.

The sun had burnt away the mist by the time they were back on the road, and they could now see the mountain range that ringed the high Andes valley. The cone-shaped snowcaps reminded Justin of the steaming peak they had seen from the plane. He told Steve what Uncle Pete had said about the strange peak.

"Yeah, that was quite a disaster! I wasn't in Colombia yet, but there was plenty about it in the news." Steve looked suddenly interested. "You saw steam, eh? Nevada del Ruiz must be simmering again. I hope she keeps a tighter lid on things this time!"

Jenny looked nervously at the ring of snowy mountains. "It . . . it isn't going to erupt again, is it?"

Steve laughed. "There's nothing for you to worry about, Jenny. The Nevada del Ruiz is eighty miles away from Bogotá. Besides, the seismologists—those are the scientists who study volcanoes and earthquakes—have been keeping a close eye on that mountain ever since the last eruption. The next time it goes off, everyone will have plenty of warning to get out of the way."

The highway was now winding down out of the vast mountain valley, and they soon left the snowy peaks behind. Palm trees and tropical flowers now mingled with the pine and cypress. Wiping a suddenly damp face, Justin pulled off his jacket. Jenny followed his example.

Noticing their movements without taking his eyes off the road, Steve commented, "Here on the equator, temperatures are pretty much the same all year around. But every time you drop a few hundred feet in elevation, you move into a new climate zone. If we dropped clear to the bottom of these mountains, you'd be in steaming-hot jungle."

Steve himself looked cool and tough in a T-shirt and jeans. Jenny made a face at him. "Do all Marines know as much as you do, Mr. Cardoza?"

"Steve!" he corrected automatically, then grinned. "Well, I do try to read up on all the countries I get stationed in."

A short time later, the winding highway dropped into a small town several centuries removed from the skyscrapers of Bogotá. A stone cathedral lifted its weathered spires and arches above low whitewashed homes with the black, wrought-iron balconies and red-tiled roofs the twins had noticed in the colonial sections of Bogotá. Modern green traffic signs reading "Zipaquirá— Catedral de Sal" pointed their way through narrow cobblestone streets.

"What does *Catedral de Sal* mean?" Justin asked, stumbling over the unfamiliar words. But Steve just shook his head. "You'll see!"

The road ended in a parking lot at the foot of a narrow concrete path that wound its way up a steep hill through cypress groves. As Steve locked the minivan, a long bus with "Zipaquirá" emblazoned across both sides pulled up beside them.

Steve and Jenny started up the steep path, but Justin paused to watch an assortment of foreigners—nearly all clad in the international tourist costume of shorts, T-shirt, and camera—pile out of the bus. The few local passengers were easily marked by their dark hair and solemn clothes.

Falling in behind the group of tourists, Justin stopped not far up the path to adjust his own camera. He had just focused the camera on the parking lot, when a 1968 Volkswagen Bug, newly painted bright red, roared into the camera frame. Snapping a picture, Justin lowered the camera for a better view as the classic car slammed to a stop at the far end of the parking lot.

Justin was more interested in the VW Bug than the slim, wiry man who jumped out. He was too far away for Justin to see his face, but his smooth movements and tight jeans gave the impression of youth. Justin hardly noticed the car's passenger until the young man hurried to the other side of the car. Justin caught a glimpse only of a straight back and a long, dark ponytail, as the young man took his passenger by the arm and hurried her off in the opposite direction.

"More locals," Justin thought, losing interest. He hurried to catch up to Steve and Jenny, now far up the path. He caught up with them near a cluster of long, low cement-block sheds, and what looked like some sort of mine diggings. Justin guessed that these were the salt mines, but before he could ask, Steve motioned him to move up the path.

The twins had to jog to keep up with Steve's long strides and were both out of breath by the time he stopped. They were standing on a wide terrace paved with stone blocks a yard across. To their left was a long, low building. From the brightly covered tables scattered outside, Justin guessed that it was a restaurant. A low wall on their right gave a clear view of the whole valley.

Just ahead, a high wire-mesh gate opened onto a wide, dark opening in the hillside. A loud chatter of different languages echoed like so many tropical parrots as the busload of tourists they had followed up the hill pressed around the ticket stand outside the gate.

Jenny collapsed against the stone wall and wiped her forehead. "Boy, am I out of shape!"

Justin eyed Steve's hard-muscled bare arms respectfully as the Marine lieutenant hurried over to join the line at the ticket stand. "I'll bet they lift weights in the Marines!"

He propped his elbows on the wide stone wall, then suddenly straightened up. Rubbing the heels of his hands against his eyes, he took another look. "Jenny!" he exclaimed in a low voice. "I think I'm being haunted by girls with long, black hair!"

Chapter Four

FOOTSTEPS IN
THE DEPTHS

The low, wide wall on which Justin was leaning ran along the top of the hill they had just climbed. From here he could see the entire valley—the burnt-red roofs and whitewashed walls of the small colonial town, nestled within a surrounding patchwork of green and gold fields. The salt diggings were spread out across the hillside directly below him. Scattered among the mounds of disturbed earth were long, flat ore-cars heaped with what Justin guessed was rock salt.

Leaning further over the wall, Justin rubbed his eyes again. Yes, he was right. In the shade of one of the ore-cars stood a small figure. The heaped-up salt ore cast a shadow across the face, but the long, black ponytail was unmistakable. The girl turned, one arm over her eyes, to study the mountainside above.

"What did you say?" Jenny asked, jumping up to sit on the wall.

"I said I'm being haunted by girls with long, black hair!" Justin repeated.

Jenny sniffed scornfully. "I'd just as soon not be, if they're all as unfriendly as the last one!"

"There she is again. See?"

Dangling her feet over the wall, she followed his pointed finger. "What do you mean? I don't see anyone but tourists!"

Justin looked again. The girl had disappeared. "There *was* a girl standing right there!" he insisted. "She must have ducked behind that cart."

His mind quickly flipped through its memory banks: He saw a young girl petting the white dog that had invaded the guest house; Estrella in the Gold Museum; the girl with a long ponytail who had jumped out of the red VW Bug. "That's the fourth one!"

"Justin!" Shaking her head with disgust, Jenny said reasonably, "*Most* Colombians have black hair! And at least half of them are girls! And probably a good part of those girls wear their hair long!"

Her explanation was interrupted by a now-familiar whistle, and she jumped off the wall. The rest of the tourists had disappeared. Standing alone outside the wire gate, Steve waved three small pieces of paper in the twins' direction. Jenny hurried across the stone terrace to join him. Still smarting from her sarcasm, Justin followed more slowly, stopping to read the signs warning tourists against rowdy behavior, loudness, and possible cave-ins—printed in English, Spanish, French, and German.

"This is where we go in," Steve informed them as he handed them their tickets. He motioned toward the dark opening in the mountainside. Justin and Jenny followed him out of the bright sunlight to where an impatient guard waited to collect the last tickets. Handing him the slips of paper, both twins looked around in surprise.

Ahead of them, a tunnel wide enough for a dozen people

abreast slanted endlessly downward, until it was lost in the inky-black of the mountain depths. Dim lights high above hardly disturbed the darkness, but the rough walls and even the tunnel floor shimmered with a faint light of their own.

The walls were protected by a heavy wire mesh. Justin touched a finger to the grayish-white, quartz-like rock that protruded through the mesh, then cautiously licked the tip of his finger. "Why, it's salt!" he exclaimed.

"That's right," Steve answered. "This whole mountain is made of pure rock salt. Come on! There's plenty more to see."

They hurried after the fast-disappearing group of tourists, their eyes gradually adjusting to the dimness as the sunlight of the entrance faded behind them. No one else was in sight now, but once, when their own hollow footsteps paused in front of a statue of a very young angel set into a wire-covered crevice, Justin thought he heard the echo of another pair of feet behind them. But the faint pitter-patter instantly died away, and no one joined them in the bright circle cast by the alcove floodlight.

This place is just plain spooky! Justin told himself as their own footsteps again drowned out any other sound. He stopped again as they came to the first of a series of tunnels that opened up on either side of the main tunnel. Pieces of lumber had been nailed across this opening, but Justin could see it would be easy to crawl over the makeshift barrier.

"Oh, no you don't!" Steve put a hand on Justin's shoulder as he stepped up onto one termite-eaten board to peer into the vast blackness beyond. "Those tunnels are blocked off because they aren't safe anymore. *And* to keep tourists like you from getting lost—maybe forever!"

"I wasn't going in," Justin answered hastily. "I was . . . I was just looking."

Justin didn't know how long he had been walking when the tunnel abruptly ended. All three stood still for a long moment, then Justin found his voice. "It's a church! A church built out of salt!"

Steve looked thoroughly pleased with their surprise. "Quite a sight, isn't it! This is the world-famous *Catedral de Sal de Zipaquirá*—Cathedral of Salt to you. The only one of its kind in the world!"

Opening before them into the sparkling heart of the mountain was a cavern so vast that the scattered busload of tourists seemed lost in its depths. The lights refracted diamond colors off every nodule of salt in the far-flung walls, dazzling their eyes after the dimness of the tunnel. Massive pillars of solid rock salt, gleaming faintly red in the floodlights at their bases, supported a vaulted ceiling so high that it was lost in what looked like star-strewn darkness. Rows of carved wooden benches ran between the pillars.

Above an ornate archway to their right, a trumpeting angel called them to step into his alcove. Grinning at the twins' shouts of wonder, Steve leaned against a salt pillar while Justin and Jenny inspected the shrine inside. Climbing to the top step, Justin suddenly noticed a green glow across the cavern.

"Wait for me!" Jenny ran after him as Justin hurried across the cavern. Reaching the grotto hollowed into the far end of the cavern, Justin was disappointed to discover that it was only a colored floodlight that caused the faint green sparkle of the walls. But he forgot his disappointment in the gentle beauty of the grotto.

A low wooden barrier protected the wide, gleaming steps leading up into the grotto from the dusty shoe marks of countless tourists. Leaning over as far as he dared, Justin saw that the altar that shimmered the translucent white of pure quartz was actually carved from one solid block of rock salt. As Jenny took his place at the rail, Justin read the multi-language sign that told how many tons the salt altar weighed.

Sitting down on one of the wooden benches, Justin slowly relaxed in the peaceful quiet of the vast salt cathedral. As he idly watched a flickering light shimmer over the cross that stretched out gold arms above the altar, his mind slipped back to that day at church camp last summer when he first realized how much it had cost Jesus to die on a cross for the sins of the world. That was the day when he and Jenny both had asked Jesus to be their Savior.

Justin didn't know how long he sat there before he realized that the short hairs on the back of his neck were standing straight up. He instantly recognized the prickly sensation. It had always come in handy when Jenny tried to sneak up on him. He turned his head cautiously, and seeing no one but Steve standing close by, he tipped his head back to study a tiny alcove above him.

Beside him, lost in her own thoughts, Jenny sat watching the green gleam of the floodlights. Justin stood up quietly and ambled casually over to the altar. Then he whirled around, quickly scanning the width of the cavern. He saw only a few scattered tourists, but the shadow behind one pillar a few yards to the right didn't seem quite natural.

Dodging quickly behind another pillar, he ran in that direction. But he caught only a slight movement, and the sound of running feet disappearing into the shadows.

Jenny was watching him curiously as he returned. "What's wrong?"

"I think we're being followed!" Justin informed her. Then, as she opened her mouth, he added, "And don't tell me it's just my imagination!"

"I wasn't going to!" Jenny answered indignantly. "But really, Justin . . ."

"Justin! Jenny! Come on! There's lots more to see." From a dozen yards away, Steve waved an arm toward the still unexplored areas of the salt cathedral.

The twins followed Steve toward a far-off, yellow-white beacon. A wooden barrier across the front of a small, well-lit cave brought them to a halt. Here they saw the Christmas story, the crystal-white salt figures radiating light in the beam of powerful floodlights. At one side, Joseph guarded watchfully as Mary bent over the sleeping figure of baby Jesus. Angels proclaimed glad tidings from above, and shepherds knelt in worship at the feet of the baby Savior.

The slight scrape of a shoe against stone echoed loudly in the absolute stillness. Justin whirled around—this time fast enough to catch sight of a thin, pale face just outside the circle of light. Jenny's exclamation told him she had seen the girl's face as well.

"Hey! Why are you following us?" he called. There was a startled gasp and the echo of running feet.

"You go that way!" he whispered urgently to Jenny. "I'll go this way!"

"Hey, kids!" Hardly noticing Steve's call, Justin circled at a run through the salt pillars. Ahead, he caught a glimpse of a slim running figure. Jenny caught up to him just as the running girl darted into a dark opening at the far side of the cathedral.

The twins followed to discover that the darkness led into a

poorly lit cave. The only exit was the opening they had just entered. Against the far wall, the pale beam of the cave's only spotlight full on her face, was the girl they had chased.

"It's Estrella!" Jenny said in astonishment. "Why did you run away from us?" The other girl tensed for flight as the twins walked up to her. Her delicate, pale features seemed thinner than ever with her long hair pulled back into a ponytail.

"That's not the right question!" Justin declared as he casually moved to block any escape. "Ask her why she's been following us!"

He looked at the young guerrilla girl. "You *have* been following us, haven't you?"

Estrella shook her head in a quick no, then—catching Jenny's unbelieving stare—she nodded reluctantly.

"I knew it!" Justin said. He added and subtracted a few memories. "I'll bet that was you in that VW Bug then, *and* up there on the hillside."

He looked triumphantly at Jenny, then knit reddish brown eyebrows together. "But why would you want to follow us? And how did you know we were here?"

Justin wondered if he had imagined the sly look in the blue eyes before Estrella lowered long lashes. "I . . . I heard that man you were with at the museum say you would be coming to Zipaquirá today. I . . . I don't often get to speak English . . . I thought it would be good practice."

When Justin and Jenny only stared at her with suspicion, she went on quickly, "No, that isn't true! I didn't come here to practice English. After you left yesterday, I was sorry I had been so unfriendly. I wanted to tell you how sorry I am, so you would not think badly of me. That is why I came."

Still suspicious, Jenny answered coldly, "Why do you want to be friends all of a sudden? We're still Americans, you know!"

Estrella bit her lip and looked away "Yes, well . . . I was wrong. It is not your fault that you are Americans. And I . . . I think I would like to learn more about my father's country."

Justin broke in. "Then why didn't you just come over and talk to us? Why did you run away?"

Estrella looked wary again. "I was frightened. . . . I didn't know how to speak to you. I was afraid you would be angry."

Her voice dropped so low that they had to strain to hear. "I . . . I think I need friends! Will you please forgive me and be my friends?"

Her lower lip quivered, and Justin softened immediately. Holding out his hand, he said gruffly, "That's okay. We all make mistakes."

Jenny didn't look impressed by the genuine pleading in her voice. "What about your 'family'?" she demanded. "You said they were all the friends you needed!"

Estrella hesitated, then admitted, "They are busy with other things. . . . Often they are gone. . . . There is no one young."

Straightening her back, she tilted her chin with a touch of her former defiance. "But if you do not wish to forgive, I will go! I will not beg for your friendship! Nor will I tell you the news I have come to give you."

"Jenny!" Seeing Jenny's crossed arms and tightened lips, Justin poked her in the ribs—*hard*. "Remember that verse we learned in youth group the week before we left?"

When Jenny looked blank, he added impatiently, "You know! Ephesians 4:32: 'Be kind and compassionate to one another, forgiving each other, just as in Christ God forgave you.'"

He emphasized each word, and Jenny joined in reluctantly halfway through the verse. As they finished, Estrella said oddly, "You believe in God?"

Jenny looked sheepish. "We sure do. But I guess you'd never know it—the way I've been acting!"

She put out her hand. "I'm sorry! I *would* like to be your friend."

"What's the big idea running off like that!" Turning, the three children saw Steve's silhouette against the brightness of the cave mouth. His swift strides brought him across the cave to their side. "I've been looking all over for you two!"

Catching sight of Estrella, his eyes narrowed, and he said in the coldest tones Justin had ever heard him use, "You're the girl who was talking to Justin and Jenny yesterday in the museum, aren't you! What are you doing here? Why are you following us?"

"She just wanted to see us again," Justin broke in hastily, surprised by the Marine lieutenant's anger. "She wants to be our friend, and we'd like to be hers!"

"Are you crazy?" Steve exploded. "Have you forgotten who she is?"

He caught Estrella by the shoulder as she started to move away. "So she just happened to show up again today, and she wants to be your friend! I'll bet she knows a lot more about who you are and what you're doing here than you think! Don't you?"

He addressed the last stern question to Estrella. Twisting away from his grip, she answered defiantly, "Okay, I do know who they are! I have heard on the streets about the two men who were taken by the police, and the man Parker who has come to decide their fate. When they told me of their uncle yesterday, I guessed who they were!"

The young guerrilla girl lifted her chin, wearing what Jenny had called her "princess look" the day before. "I followed them today to say that I was sorry and to be their friend. It was not hard to know where you would be! You speak very loudly in a crowded place."

As red tinged Steve's bronzed cheekbones, she added, "But I also came because I have heard news that is of great importance to them and to their uncle. If they have told you who I am, then you know that I have ways of finding out things."

"Why would someone like you want to help them?"

Estrella straightened her slim back proudly. "Because they are my friends! They have been kind to me, and I will be kind to them!"

Justin broke in feebly as the Marine lieutenant and the guerrilla girl stared at each other with dislike. "Just a minute, Estrella. What do you mean about Uncle Pete deciding those guys' 'fate'? He doesn't have anything to do with what happens to them! He couldn't free them if he wanted to!"

Ignoring him, Steve demanded coldly. "Okay, what exactly is this helpful news you've got?"

Cutting him off impatiently, Estrella turned to Justin and Jenny. "It does not matter if your uncle can free those men. It is thought that he can, and that is all that matters."

There was not even the sound of breathing in the small cavern as Estrella added with a dramatic movement of her hand, "I must speak to your uncle! He is in the greatest of danger!"

Chapter Five

KIDNAPPED!

Sudden loud footsteps startled the entire group. They whirled around to see who was there. Justin was sure he recognized the young man standing just outside the cave mouth as being the driver of the red VW Bug he'd seen earlier. Estrella's eyes widened when she saw him, and she whispered urgently, "I can't talk more! I must go!"

Justin protested, "But you can't just go like that! When will we see you again?"

"I will be at the house of Simón Bolívar tomorrow at three o'clock."

Before either Justin or Jenny could say a word, Steve said firmly, "Fine! I'll be there to receive any information you have."

Estrella shook her head. "No! I will speak only to my friends. Bring your uncle and come alone! I will tell *him* what I know!"

Ducking under Steve's outstretched arm, she darted across the cave floor. By the time Steve and the twins reached the entrance, both Estrella and the young man had disappeared.

There were still parts of the salt caverns that they hadn't explored, but Steve had obviously had enough sightseeing. He hurried the twins out of the salt cathedral and up the steep tunnel so quickly that they had to run to keep up.

Jenny finally broke into Steve's silence. "Steve, what kind of danger could Uncle Pete possibly be in? He didn't have anything to do with those guys! We just got here!"

"Yeah!" added Justin. "Uncle Pete couldn't do anything about those guys anyway! He isn't government or anything!"

"What he can or can't do doesn't matter," Steve answered grimly without slowing his stride. "Like your friend said, it's what the guerrillas *think* he can do that counts."

"Well, what *do* they think he can do?" Justin asked, puzzled.

Steve came to a stop. "By threatening Triton Oil property and personnel," he explained patiently, "the guerrillas are trying to force your uncle and the American government to pressure the Colombian police into letting those men go. I'm sure you realize that your uncle has a lot of influence in government circles."

Justin hadn't known this, and he listened closely as Steve continued. "What they don't realize is that both the American and Colombian governments have a rigid policy that they won't give in to threats. If they did, every American citizen abroad would be in danger. Terrorists would take them hostage to force the American government to give in to their demands. So even if your uncle would agree to use his influence to free those men, it wouldn't do any good."

He started walking again. "But the guerrillas don't seem to understand that yet. That's one reason we've got you and your uncle where you are—to keep you safe!"

The teens followed him in silence, but as they neared the entrance, Justin said quietly, "I guess I was pretty stupid, then . . . telling her our names like that yesterday!"

Steve stopped so suddenly that Justin slid into him. "Now

just a minute, Justin! Don't blame yourself. If there was fault, it was mine. I should have warned you not to speak to strangers."

A curious smile lit his bronzed face. "It just never occurred to me you'd find anyone to talk to in a foreign city. Anyway, what's done is done!"

He strode on ahead, nodding to the guard at the entrance, and pushed through the wire gate. The twins fell behind as the brightness of the early afternoon sun dazzled eyes now accustomed to the darkness below. Blinking, Justin commented, "Well, at least Estrella has decided to be our friend. With her help, maybe Uncle Pete can get this all cleared up right away."

Jenny frowned. "I don't know. It still seems pretty strange to me! Why should she go to all this trouble when we've only met her once? She sure changed her mind about being friends in a hurry!"

Justin paused, one hand on the gate. "She explained why she changed her mind. *And* she came all the way out here to warn us about Uncle Pete being in danger. I'd call that pretty nice. Anyway, you promised you'd be her friend!"

Glancing sideways at her brother, Jenny teased, "She's awfully pretty, isn't she?"

Red crept up the back of Justin's neck. "You know that's not it! It's just . . . oh, I don't know!" He shook his head. "There's just something about her. . . . I think she really does need friends."

He added, "I mean, look at us! We've got a great family *and* lots of friends! I wonder how it would feel to lose it all."

Jenny suddenly looked ashamed. "Yeah, I guess you're right. We did promise to be friends. Anyway, if Uncle Pete really is in danger . . ." She darted across the terrace to where Steve was leaning over the stone wall, waiting for them to catch up. "Steve, we *are* going to meet Estrella tomorrow, aren't we?"

Following Jenny, Justin caught Steve's sudden frown. "I don't know, kids. It could be risky. If this girl knows all about *you,* who knows how many others do too? Maybe you'd all better sit tight until we can get you out of the country."

Jenny looked like she wanted to argue, but Steve stood up. "We can't decide anything until we've talked to your uncle and Mr. Bascom, so let's get going!"

As they hurried down the winding path, Justin scanned the parking lot below. There was no sign of the little red car or its occupants. He suddenly realized he hadn't told Steve and Jenny about the car or the driver he'd recognized later in the caverns.

"Good work," Steve said approvingly when Justin finished describing the car, the young man, and Estrella's reaction to him. "That could be a useful piece of information."

Both Uncle Pete and Mr. Bascom, the embassy secretary, were at the guest house when they arrived. Over supper, Steve briefly outlined the events of the last two days. To the twins' surprise, Mr. Bascom seemed very interested in the young guerrilla girl, asking questions until Justin and Jenny had repeated all they could remember of their conversations with Estrella.

When they had finished, Uncle Pete raised his eyebrows at Mr. Bascom. "This whole situation still makes no sense! I can understand this guerrilla band threatening Triton Oil. But how could they possibly know anything about me—or even that I'm in the country?"

Mr. Bascom shrugged. "These groups have ways of getting information. They could have bribed a secretary—or even a janitor—to snoop around the Triton Oil office. Who knows? What matters is that they obviously *do* know about you."

"Yeah, and somehow that information got around to whatever group this girl calls her 'family,'" added Steve. "News travels fast on the street."

He frowned. "Of course, that's assuming this Estrella's telling the truth. I don't trust that girl! Maybe it would be safest just to pretend we never met her."

Mr. Bascom disagreed. "This girl could be a valuable contact for our intelligence gathering bureau. I would certainly like to know what information she has to pass on." He shook his head. "But I don't know that I want to involve the kids."

Steve said thoughtfully, "I could go alone, but I'm sure she wouldn't show unless she saw the kids. Now, if there was some way we could stake out the place. . . . That way, if it's a trap . . ."

Uncle Pete slapped a hand against the table. "Now, just a minute! I'm not putting Justin and Jenny in any position where they will run a risk of being hurt!"

The twins had been listening while the adults talked, but Justin couldn't keep quiet any longer. "Uncle Pete, Estrella wouldn't do anything to hurt us! She's our friend! If we don't show up tomorrow, she's going to think we lied when we said we'd be her friend."

Jenny spoke up in support. "I agree with Justin. We did promise to be her friend. Besides, if she does know something, then maybe the police can catch those guys, and your company can get back to work." She grinned impishly. "Then Steve won't have to baby-sit us anymore!"

"Yeah, if you're in danger, Uncle Pete," Justin added, "we really should find out about it. We don't want anything to happen to you! We just want to talk to her. What could possibly happen?"

Uncle Pete's green eyes twinkled as he looked from one pleading face to the other. "It seems I've heard that from you two before. All right, we'll go—but only if Steve takes the proper security measures."

As Justin and Jenny started to protest, he raised a stern hand. "No, I don't care what this girl said. I'm not taking you anywhere alone!"

"Don't worry!" Steve put in. "I'll hide a couple of guys in the bushes. She won't even know we're there."

The next afternoon, Mr. Bascom brought the minivan around to the front door of the guest house. Steve had left an hour earlier with two other Marines whose duty it was to protect the American embassy. As they pulled away from the curb, Justin noticed a group of children playing soccer at the end of the block. *Looks like the same bunch as before,* he thought idly. But he saw no sign of the little white dog.

"I'll drop you off at the entrance," Mr. Bascom told the Parkers as he turned onto a six-lane avenue lined with business offices. "Anyone watching will think you've come alone. You will then leave here with Steve. He should have his men staked out around the grounds by now."

"Do we really *need* to go through all this spy stuff just to talk to a girl?" Justin muttered to Jenny.

"Don't ask me!" Jenny whispered back. "It seems pretty silly!"

From the driver's seat, Mr. Bascom said sternly, "We've learned the hard way here in Bogotá not to take any chances."

"Exactly what *is* this house of Simón Bolívar?" Uncle Pete put in quickly, as the twins flushed with embarrassment.

With a smile, Mr. Bascom looked back at Justin and Jenny. "Can either of you tell us who Simón Bolívar was?"

Justin answered hesitantly, "Wasn't he the guy who helped South America get its independence from Spain? Like George Washington back home?"

"That's right!" Mr. Bascom nodded approvingly. "He was also the first president of Colombia. We are going to his family mansion here in Bogotá. It's now open to the public."

Leaving the office buildings behind, he drove through a wide intersection, then pulled to a stop halfway through the next block. Jumping out onto a broad cement sidewalk, Justin looked both ways as the embassy minivan drove off. There was little traffic at this hour of the afternoon, and no one else shared the sidewalk as far as he could see.

Above Justin's head, untrimmed cypress trees leaned over a weathered stone wall to run feathery green fingers through his hair. Justin followed Jenny and Uncle Pete to the heavy metal gate that swung between tall stone pillars. As Uncle Pete dug the small entrance fee from his pocket, the guard handed tickets through a barred stone window and swung open the gate.

The gentle, green oasis on the other side of the gate was unexpected, and as the click of the heavy latch shut out the bustle of the city, Justin felt that he had stepped back into another, quieter century. Even the roar of distant traffic was cut off by the gentle rush of wind through the evergreens.

The three Parkers walked through a maze of oddly cut yew hedges that bordered a series of spouting fountains, stone statues, and small ponds where goldfish glinted in the afternoon sun. Tucked into odd corners, and blazing from formal, carefully tended beds, were the flowers, their colors splashed across the garden like a child's spilled paint box.

Justin paused to look across the maze of green. It was a warm weekday afternoon. The only visitor in sight was a middle-aged tourist taking pictures of the flowers. If Steve and the other security agents were somewhere in the mass of shrubbery, they were too well hidden to be seen from where Justin stood. The idea of terrorists and danger suddenly seemed ridiculous.

Uncle Pete stopped in front of the square, two-story mansion at the far end of the garden. The usual burnt-red tiles of the roof contrasted with the blinding white of the old adobe walls. Flower pots nodded colorful heads from the black iron balconies overhead. Glancing at his watch, he announced, "Three o'clock on the dot. Do you see any sign of your friend?"

Justin shook his head reluctantly, and Jenny suggested, "Maybe she's inside. Why don't we take a look?"

"Good idea," Uncle Pete agreed. "If she doesn't show, you'll get a history lesson out of the afternoon, at least."

As they filed through the tiled entryway, Justin discovered that the entire house was wrapped around a large courtyard. In the center, a few stunted citrus trees in pots sheltered another fountain. High pillars held up a veranda that circled the courtyard. In its shade, rows of hand-carved doors opened into high-ceilinged, whitewashed rooms. Heavy ropes across the open doors kept visitors from entering.

There was no sign of a guide or Estrella. *Maybe she's just late,* Justin thought as he followed Jenny and Uncle Pete along the veranda. Although a small part of his mind stayed alert for the telltale prickle at his neck that would inform him of spying eyes, he decided to enjoy the tour.

He peered over Jenny's shoulder into a room that was once a study. The room looked as though the nineteenth-century liberator had just stepped out for an afternoon stroll.

One corner of the veranda opened into a long room where finely embroidered chairs, imported from France a century before, sat around highly polished tables. Paintings by famous European artists looked down from the walls, and a crystal chandelier hung unlit from the mural-covered ceiling.

In every room, treasures of china and silver peered out of locked glass cases. Justin and Jenny followed Uncle Pete up one of the broad, tiled staircases that curved up to the second floor from each corner of the courtyard. Here, too, a row of carved-wood doors opened out onto a wide balcony that circled the courtyard.

Justin whistled as he pointed out a four-poster bed with a faded silk canopy in the master bedroom. "Look how small that bed is! People must have been awfully short back then."

Reading a sign, Justin mentally translated the centimeters to inches. "Wow! That guy was only four feet ten inches tall!"

Jenny giggled at a set of the liberator's clothes preserved in a glass case. "*I* couldn't even get into those."

As the two children followed Uncle Pete down the far staircase, Justin paused again to scan the courtyard. "I wonder what's keeping Estrella!"

"Maybe she never meant to come," Jenny suggested idly, leaning over the rail to watch a pair of bright yellow birds. "Maybe she was just pulling our leg."

Justin bristled. "Don't be ridiculous! There could be a hundred reasons why she's late."

"Let's get a move on, kids!" Uncle Pete was waving at them from the top of a stairway that led below ground. Forgetting their argument, the twins hurried to catch up and followed Uncle Pete down toward the servants' quarters and kitchen.

They entered a vast underground chamber dimly lit by a few barred windows high on the wall. Copper utensils and ladles hung from its low rafters. Brick ovens built into the earthen walls were still blackened with a century or two of soot, and a rusty, three-legged pot was perched in a fireplace large enough to roast an entire ox. A heavy iron spit showed that it had probably been used for that very purpose.

As they emerged back into the afternoon light, Uncle Pete glanced at his watch. "Well, kids, it doesn't look like your friend is going to show. This has been an interesting outing, but I have work waiting."

"Yeah, let's go home!" Jenny agreed. "She's obviously not coming."

"Can't we wait just a little longer?" Justin begged, scanning the courtyard one last time. "We might not get another chance to find out what she knows."

Uncle Pete shook his head firmly. "It's already four o'clock. If she planned to show, she would be here by now. Come on. We'll try to locate Steve and get a ride home."

In the tiled entryway, the twins used the last of the savings they had brought along for the trip to buy a covered silver sugar bowl—supposedly a copy of Simón Bolívar's and incredibly low in price. Silver was plentiful and still quite cheap in Colombia, Uncle Pete explained.

Trailing a few feet behind as they threaded back through the maze of walkways that led to the gate, Justin saw with disappointment that the garden was empty. Even the solitary tourist was gone, and if Steve and the other agents were there, they were well hidden.

"Justin! Jenny!" Justin instantly recognized the cool, precise girl's voice. Pointing, he announced triumphantly, "Look! I told you she'd come."

Dark-shaded blue eyes were peering through the grillwork of the iron gate, then a slim arm waved through the opening. Justin and Jenny hurried to the gate, Uncle Pete close behind. "Estrella, where were you?" Justin demanded. "We were just about to leave!"

What they could see of Estrella's expression looked uneasy. "I . . . I could not buy the ticket to get in. I have been waiting here for you to come out."

Uncle Pete bent down to look through the grillwork. "Kids, would you introduce me to your friend?"

"Oh, yes." Jenny turned hurriedly to Uncle Pete. "Uncle Pete, this is Estrella. Estrella, this is my uncle who you wanted to talk to."

Uncle Pete studied the slim, pale features closely. "If you want to talk to me, come on in. We'll take care of your ticket."

They could see Estrella shake her head, then she stepped out of sight. "No, I can't let you do that," her voice floated stubbornly from the other side of the gate. "If you wish to hear what I have to say, you must come out here and speak with me."

Uncle Pete glanced around the garden, and Justin guessed that he was looking for some sign of Steve. "All right," he said at last, looking exasperated.

Pushing open the gate, the three Parkers stepped out onto the sidewalk. Justin looked up and down the street. It was empty of pedestrians, and the only traffic was a long, black Mercedes-Benz limousine moving in their direction a couple of blocks away.

"Hi, Estrella! We thought you weren't coming!" Estrella looked surprised at Jenny's quick hug, but she hugged her back and shook Justin's outstretched hand.

"Estrella, I'm glad to meet you, but we can't stay here long." Uncle Pete looked down kindly at the young guerrilla girl. "Why don't you go ahead and tell me what you have to say—and how you learned about us."

Moving away from the twins, Estrella stared up at Uncle Pete. Her speech sounded rehearsed as she answered calmly, "I hear many things in the street. When Justin and Jenny told me their names, I knew who you were. They were kind to me and promised to be my friends, so I decided to help them."

Her voice died away as she glanced up the street. Justin followed her gaze, but saw nothing but the black limousine now only a block away. Uncle Pete's big foot tapped impatiently, but he repeated gently, "Well, what is it that you heard?"

Estrella opened her mouth, but her voice was suddenly drowned out by the loud gunning of an engine. Startled, Justin looked up to see the Mercedes-Benz now hurtling down the street toward them. The mirrorlike one-way glass of the windows hid any sign of a driver. As it neared the four on the sidewalk, the limousine suddenly braked and a rear window slid down.

Justin glimpsed a black hood and a gloved hand clutching an egg-shaped object. Then, as a black, leather-clad arm reached through the window and made a smooth overhand toss, Estrella shouted, "Run!"

Justin instinctively jerked away as she grabbed at his jacket and caught Jenny by the hand, and she hissed, "Don't be stupid!"

With more strength than they would have guessed possible, the young guerrilla girl shoved Justin and Jenny away from the car. Stumbling back against the stone wall, Justin watched as the egg-shaped object tumbled end over end through the afternoon sun. From the corner of his eye, he saw Estrella cover her head with her arms. Then, with a blast of thunder, his world exploded!

Chapter Six

THE SEARCH FOR UNCLE PETE

Justin lay unmoving, one cheek against the cement pavement where the explosion had thrown him. His lungs felt deflated. He vaguely sensed that someone lay beneath him, but he couldn't move. Lifting his head cautiously, he choked as a sharp odor and dust rushed into his lungs.

Several yards beyond the gate, dust and black smoke drifted up from a gaping hole in the stone wall. Chunks of concrete and shattered stone littered the sidewalk. *How could they possibly have missed us?* he wondered numbly. Then, as he blinked the dirt and debris from his eyes, he again felt his breath snatched away.

The rear door of the black limousine stood open, and a tall, hooded figure all in black was shoving Uncle Pete into the back seat. Another slim, black-hooded figure—Justin couldn't tell whether it was a man or a woman—scanned the sidewalk, while balancing a machine gun with an obviously experienced hand.

Justin tried to shout, but his voice came out in a squeak. Before he could even move, the first hooded figure had climbed in beside Uncle Pete. The one with the machine gun slammed the door shut and jerked open the front door. The door was still open when the engine roared and the Mercedes-Benz moved smoothly away from the curb.

"Justin, you're squashing me!" a muffled voice gasped from beneath him. "Get off!"

Justin rolled over and struggled to his feet just as the heavy gate in the stone wall clanged open and Steve ran out, followed by the other two Marines. *Nice of you to show up!* Justin thought savagely, before he realized that no more than a minute had gone by since they first stepped out of the gate.

Holding an army-caliber pistol high with both hands, the Marine lieutenant took in the scene with one glance. Dropping into a crouch, he brought the pistol down expertly to bear on the black limousine. But whatever he planned to do, it was too late. Still picking up speed, the Mercedes-Benz was already far down the block.

It had all happened so quickly that Justin stood unmoving, staring down the street in frozen dismay. Part of his mind registered Jenny and Estrella struggling to their feet behind him. Grabbing his arm, Jenny cried out, "What happened? Where's Uncle Pete?"

Justin motioned hopelessly after the speeding car, which at that instant turned a corner and disappeared. The other two security agents had lowered their guns. One was shouting into a walkie-talkie while the other scanned the debris. Steve walked back toward them, frustration all over his bronze features.

"Okay, kids!" he snapped. "What happened? Where is Mr. Parker?"

Jenny was looking around in a daze, one hand rubbing sudden

tears from her dust-covered cheeks. She choked, "I . . . I don't know! They took him away!"

Putting an arm around his sister, Justin got out an answer. "Some men in that big, black car—I saw them throw the bomb. Then they shoved Uncle Pete in the back and took off."

Justin's arm dropped as Jenny moved away to stand in front of Steve. Looking angrily up at the broad-shouldered Marine, she demanded, "Why did you let them get Uncle Pete? You said you were watching us! You said we'd be safe!"

"You *were* safe!" Steve snapped an answer. "Inside that gate! Why did you leave the property? Don't you have any sense?"

"Estrella called us out," Justin explained wearily. "She wouldn't come in. We didn't think a few minutes would hurt anything."

Steve seemed to notice the young guerrilla girl for the first time. He looked down at the dirt-streaked, thin face with cold anger. "I might have known you'd be in on this!"

Estrella looked just as angry as the Marine lieutenant. Turning to Justin, she stormed, "Why is he here? I told you to come alone!"

"I was the one who insisted on coming. I was sure you weren't to be trusted. And I was right, wasn't I?" Steve caught Estrella by the shoulders. "You planned this, didn't you! You're in more trouble than you've ever been in your life."

Justin caught a look of fear in the blue eyes as Estrella protested, "I know nothing of this, I swear! I stayed outside because I had no money for the ticket."

She turned to the twins. "You tell him."

"We'll see!" Steve muttered as Justin and Jenny nodded agreement. Estrella looked faintly triumphant when Steve checked her pockets and found them empty. "You see? It was of this danger that I came to warn you. Those were the men who wanted to harm your uncle."

Steve was still angry. "Didn't you look around, girl? Those men probably followed you all the way here!"

Estrella pulled herself up proudly. "Don't blame me! How do you know they didn't follow you? It wouldn't be hard to find out where you are staying!"

Justin had a sudden mental picture of the band of children outside the embassy guest house. He raised his hands to his still-ringing ears, suddenly exhausted and desperately wishing he could shut out the angry voices. "Who cares whose fault it was! They've got Uncle Pete! We've got to get him back!"

He dropped his hands back to his side and turned to Steve. "Estrella couldn't have anything to do with this. She saved our lives when that guy threw the bomb. If it's anyone's fault, it's ours for going outside the gate."

Steve looked suddenly tired, the anger draining from his face. "I'm sorry, kids. I've no right to yell or to blame anyone. It's just that this was supposed to be such a simple operation."

A siren interrupted him, and moments later the street was crowded with army vehicles and Colombian soldiers. With the ease of much practice, a pair of military police threw up a heavy rope along the sidewalk. One of the Marines hurried over, holding out a few glinting fragments. "Looks like an Army-issue grenade they threw."

Steve nodded agreement as he glanced over the fragments, then led the three children away from the roped-off area. Justin saw the dark blue embassy minivan screech to a halt behind a police jeep. Mr. Bascom climbed out, and Steve hurried over to talk to him.

As Justin slumped against the stone wall to wait, he noticed for the first time the painful sting of his face and hands. Wiping the grit from his skinned palms against his jeans, he touched one cheek cautiously. His fingers came away red-stained, and he realized that he must have scraped it against the concrete pavement when the blast sent him flying.

As the two girls came over to stand beside him, he noticed that Estrella was limping and that the knees of her worn jeans were torn and red-stained. Jenny had a long scrape down one arm. Their hair and clothes were as coated with chalky dust as his own.

"Kids!" Justin stood up as Steve waved the children over to the minivan. "Dave and Mac will take care of the local police." He indicated the other two security agents who were talking with a Colombian army officer inside the roped-off area. "Mr. Bascom and I are taking you back to the guest house."

As the twins climbed into the back of the van, Steve looked down at Estrella, who stood alone on the pavement, looking very dirty and a little lost. He added without his former anger, "You, too. We'll have a few questions to ask you."

The rest of the day had the unreal quality of a bad dream. Mr. Bascom kindly refrained from asking any questions until the three children had all bathed and changed—Jenny lending Estrella a spare pair of jeans and T-shirt—and Steve had administered basic first aid to their cuts and scrapes.

Only when they were eating the last of another pot of Colombian *sancocho*, the Colombian stew they had eaten their first evening there, did Mr. Bascom take Steve and the three children, step by step, over every detail of what had happened since he had dropped the Parkers off earlier in the afternoon.

When they finished, Mr. Bascom said heavily, "Well, kids, I can't tell you how sorry I am about this. Be sure that we will be doing all we can to get your uncle back."

Running long fingers through his receding tight curls, he eyed Estrella sharply. "So you knew something like this might happen?"

"I heard that there were men who wanted to capture Justin and Jenny's uncle—to keep him until you let your prisoners go. It was for this reason that I came today," Estrella shrugged. "I am sorry that I was too late."

Justin's mind seemed to clear for the first time since the kidnapping. He said thoughtfully, "Those guys who took Uncle Pete must have been from that guerrilla band who tried to bomb the oil line—the ones who have been threatening Triton Oil. Well, you've got two of their guys in prison. Maybe they'd know where those guerrillas might have taken Uncle Pete!"

Mr. Bascom looked approvingly at Justin. "That's good thinking. You can be sure the Colombian police are going to be questioning those two men pretty thoroughly."

He looked down at the young guerrilla girl. "What about you, Estrella? Can you think of any place they might have taken Mr. Parker—or anyone who might be able to find out?"

Estrella nodded. "I will do all I can to help find my friends' uncle. I have many ways of finding things out."

She added hesitantly, "But there is one thing. I . . . my family left the city today. I . . . I stayed behind to warn my friends. I don't know where I will stay."

Justin spoke up immediately. "Well, I'm sure you can stay with us. Can't she, Mr. Bascom? . . . Steve? . . . I mean, she stayed behind just to warn us."

His back to the children, Steve leaned over and spoke quietly to Mr. Bascom. Justin barely caught Mr. Bascom's soft answer. "It might be the best way to keep an eye on her."

Steve nodded to the waiting children. "You're certainly welcome to stay, Estrella. We'll appreciate any help you can give us."

Still pink around the eyelids, Jenny had been staring down at her empty bowl. But at this, she looked up and smiled at the young guerrilla girl. "She can sleep with me. I've got plenty of extra clothes—even an extra toothbrush."

Estrella nodded satisfaction. "That is good. Then I will go out now and see what news I can find. I will be back tonight to sleep."

"Oh, no you don't!" Steve suddenly stood up. "No one is going in or out of this building except myself and Mr. Bascom. We aren't taking any more risks. If Estrella is really anxious to help, she can just tell me what she knows, and I'll check it out myself."

His expression was so discouraging that Estrella didn't argue. She said glumly, "If that is what you wish! But I can't promise that my friends will speak with you."

Mr. Bascom rose to his feet as the security guard Justin had seen in the kitchen that morning came in to collect their empty dishes. "Well, kids, I don't think there is anything more we can do right now. Steve, why don't you write down any contacts or information Estrella can give you and begin working on that. Justin and Jenny . . ."

As he paused, Justin suddenly realized that what he wanted most in the world right now was to talk to his parents. As usual, Jenny echoed his thoughts. "Mr. Bascom, could we please call Mom and Dad?"

"Just what I was going to suggest." Mr. Bascom again ran his fingers through his tight, black curls and sighed. "I imagine they'll want you on the first plane home."

Leaving Estrella and Steve bent over a notebook, he led the twins to the next room and showed them how to dial the international area code.

"You go first!" Jenny told Justin. "You're better at explaining."

Justin waited impatiently as the dial tone buzzed in his ear, then sighed with relief as he heard his mother's warm voice say, "This is the Parker residence."

But his relief turned to dismay as the voice went on, "We are unavailable at the moment. Please leave your name and number after the beep."

His father's voice suddenly broke into the taped message, "Pete, Justin, Jenny—if you should call, we'll be back in a few days. I managed to finish that project sooner than expected, and Helen and I decided to get away. . . ."

As his father's voice continued, Justin looked blankly at Mr. Bascom. "They went camping! It . . . it's just the answering machine. They won't be home for three more days."

Mr. Bascom took the phone from Justin and spoke crisply into the receiver, "Mr. and Mrs. Parker, this is Mr. Marvin Bascom from the American embassy in Bogotá. Your children are fine, but we would appreciate you getting in contact with us at your earliest convenience. Our phone number is . . ."

He rattled off a line of numbers, then hung up. Turning to the twins, he explained, "We need to get in touch with them as soon as possible, but I didn't want them thinking something has happened to you."

Justin slumped into a chair. He hadn't realized how much he had counted on hearing his parents' reassuring voices. "What do we do now?" he asked.

"We'll keep you here under guard until we hear from your parents," Mr. Bascom answered firmly. "Then you'll be on the first plane home—with or without your uncle!"

Dropping into another chair, Jenny said hesitantly, "But . . . but you'll have found him by then, won't you?"

Mr. Bascom faced the two children squarely. "Look, I'm going to be honest with you. We could find your uncle in a couple of days. But Colombia is a big country. We don't even know if your uncle is still in Bogotá. Sometimes it takes months to recover a hostage taken by guerrillas. Sometimes . . ."

He broke off, and Justin finished for him, "Sometimes you never get them back."

Justin jumped to his feet. "Sometimes they kill them, don't they? They could be hurting Uncle Pete right now!"

Mr. Bascom patted him on the shoulder. "Don't worry, Justin. I'm sure your uncle is just fine. They won't hurt him as long as they hope to trade him for their two men in prison. And by the time they realize the government won't trade . . ."

He hesitated, then went on, "Well, we'll just have to make sure we've found him by that time."

Estrella came into the room just then, followed by Steve, who seemed very satisfied with the scribbled notes he was reading over. A short time later, the three children climbed the stairs to their rooms. Justin joined the girls in Jenny's room as Jenny showed Estrella the extra twin bed and dug out a spare sweat suit.

It wasn't yet their usual bedtime, but as Justin stretched out on Jenny's bed, he realized how tired and sore he was.

Echoing his thoughts, Jenny gave a mouth-splitting yawn.

Estrella smiled slightly. "It would be well if we went to sleep. There is nothing more we can do tonight."

At her words, Justin suddenly straightened up. "Oh, yes there is!"

He looked at his sister and knew she'd had the same thought. Estrella paused with one hand on the bathroom door. She stood there unmoving as Justin and Jenny bowed their heads and, first one, then the other, prayed that God would protect Uncle Pete, wherever he was, and bring him safely back.

When they had finished, Estrella asked curiously, "Do you really think God is going to hear your prayers?"

The twins looked at each other again and smiled for the first time that evening. Justin answered, "We *know* He does!"

"Carlos says that God is an invention of the rich and powerful to keep the poor under their thumb," Estrella remarked, still with her hand on the doorknob. "If the poor pray to God for help, they will not think to fight those who are oppressing them."

But she spoke thoughtfully rather than with scorn, and as she left the room, she added, "I once knew someone who spoke about God as you do."

Much later, Justin was still awake, staring into the darkness above his bed. Tiredness pressed on his eyelids, but his mind would not stop going over and over the events of the afternoon. He was envying the two girls sleeping peacefully next door when a light tap at the door startled him into sitting up.

"Justin, are you awake?" he heard his sister whisper. He felt a weight settling on the far end of the bed.

"Yeah, I'm awake," he whispered back. "You couldn't get to sleep either?"

He felt her shake her head. "No. I've been thinking!"

Giving up any attempt to sleep, Justin asked, "Yeah? What about?"

"I've been wondering," Jenny said, still in a whisper, "Do you think it could really have been Estrella who brought those guerrillas to kidnap Uncle Pete?"

"What?" Justin sat up, his exclamation almost a shout.

"Shh!" Jenny hissed, then added, "Well, what if Steve was right! I mean, don't you think it's strange that those guerrillas showed up right after Estrella called us out of the gate?"

"No, I don't," Justin answered flatly, reaching over to switch on a lamp that stood on a wooden table beside the bed. Jenny blinked at the sudden light as he demanded, "Have you forgotten she saved our lives when that grenade went off?"

A knock at the door startled them into silence. The door opened, and Estrella looked in. "I woke to find Jenny gone. Is there something wrong?"

As Justin and Jenny quickly shook their heads, Estrella joined them on the twin bed. Drawing her knees up to her chin, she wrapped her arms around them and said hesitantly, "I am sorry that you cannot sleep. I, too, am very sad about your uncle. I wish I had never asked you to meet me."

Throwing a glance at Jenny, Justin interrupted gruffly. "It wasn't your fault, Estrella. Anyway, we sure appreciate the way you're helping us get him back."

"*If* we ever get him back!" Jenny said, wiping at suddenly overflowing tears. "Oh, Justin, what if we never . . ."

"Justin! Jenny! Please do not be so sad!" Even Jenny could not mistake the genuine sympathy in Estrella's voice. She jumped off the bed. "Please do not cry, Jenny. You must not worry! Your uncle *will* come back to you soon. I promise you! I, Estrella, will find him myself!"

Chapter Seven

I FOUND HIM!

Justin and Jenny stared at Estrella in surprise. Jenny demanded, "How are you going to do that? You're not even allowed to leave the building!"

Estrella looked scornful. "Do you really think they can keep me here if I want to leave?"

Justin thought of the locked, heavy metal doors, and the surveillance cameras he had seen in the halls.

He said slowly, "I don't see how you can possibly get out. You know they'll just stop you if they see you."

"There are ways," Estrella answered vaguely. She added sharply, "I *must* get out. No matter what Steve says, the people I have told him of will not speak to him as they will to me."

"Well, why don't you tell Steve that," Jenny said reasonably. "Maybe he could take you along with him or something."

"No!" Estrella shook her head sharply. "If they saw that I did not come alone, they would not speak to me, either."

"I still think you should talk to Steve," Jenny argued. "It could be dangerous for you out there."

"No, I will not talk to that man again! You know he doesn't like me. He would just try to stop me. Besides, there is no one trying to kidnap *me!* Why should I be caged up here like a prisoner?"

Estrella looked from one to the other. "If you want your uncle back, you must promise to keep quiet . . . or I will not be able to help you."

Jenny opened her mouth to argue further, but Justin, wearily rubbing his eyes, interrupted, "Let her try, Jenny! We've got to do anything we can to help Uncle Pete. Anyway, it's time we all get back to bed."

"Good! Tomorrow I will see what I can find out!" Estrella started toward the door, and Jenny reluctantly followed her. Turning out the light, Justin soon fell into a troubled sleep.

There was no further news about Uncle Pete the following morning, and the next three days settled into a pattern of waiting. Steve was often gone, and when he was there, he was usually on the phone or sifting through the pile of reports that a Colombian police officer dropped off twice a day.

It was noon on the first day when Mr. Bascom informed the three children that the embassy had received a ransom note. "We were right. It's the same group that threatened your uncle's company. They want to exchange him for their two members in prison."

"What are you going to do?" Justin asked.

"There's nothing we *can* do," Mr. Bascom answered grimly. "You know the government's policy about giving in to kidnappers."

As he left the room, Jenny turned to Estrella and said desperately, "Estrella, you've got to find him soon!"

Estrella squeezed her hand sympathetically. "Don't worry! I will find him in time."

Estrella often slipped away, but she was never gone long and managed to be there every time Steve or Mr. Bascom reported any updates on the search for Uncle Pete. As they had promised, the twins said nothing about her occasional disappearances. But Justin couldn't restrain his curiosity.

The afternoon after the kidnapping, Justin decided to try to leave the building for himself. He made his way through darkened hallways down to the basement, but was still yards from the backdoor when a security guard tapped him on the shoulder.

"You don't want to go out there," the guard said, kindly but firmly.

"I didn't really want to go out. I just wanted to see if I could do it without being caught," Justin answered with a grin. He gave up trying to figure out how Estrella managed to leave the guest house undetected.

The twins discovered that the security guards' row of surveillance screens weren't the only TV sets in the guest house. They located a large recreation room on the third floor. Here, the security guards relaxed when they were off duty. Occasionally joined by Steve, Mr. Bascom, or one of the guards, the three teens spent most of their time there—reading magazines, playing board games, deciphering the Spanish news broadcasts on the big-screen TV, or just talking.

It was after Justin's attempt to defeat the security system, as the three children huddled on the floor over an antique Monopoly game, that Justin suddenly remembered something. Glancing up from a pile of paper money, he asked, "Estrella, who's Carlos?"

When Estrella looked up in surprise, he added, "You know . . . you mentioned him the other night."

"Yes, I had forgotten I said his name." Estrella hesitated, then went on. "Carlos is the leader of my family. It was he who found me on the streets; he made me a part of his band."

Looking up from the board, Jenny asked curiously, "How old were you when you joined his band?"

Estrella dropped her paper money. To Justin's surprise, she answered readily. "I was nine years old the day Carlos found me on the street. I remember very well. . . . I was looking at a magazine I found in a barrel. I was cold and hungry—I had been hungry for so long! To forget my stomach, I was reading out loud the words I knew on the page. Then Carlos spoke to me. He took me to a *panaderia*—a bakery."

Estrella suddenly smiled, her completely charming smile that the twins had seen so seldom. "I remember that I ate so much I was sick! But he was not angry. He spoke to me other days, and one day he took me to meet his band."

She spread her hands out. "And that is all! I have been part of his family ever since. Perhaps some day you will meet them and see how kind they are."

Jenny had lost interest in the Monopoly game. In a rapid-fire series of questions, she demanded, "Where did you go after Carlos took you to meet his band? Do all your family live together? How many are there? Do you go to school?"

When Estrella seemed reluctant to answer, she pleaded, "Come on, Estrella! We've told you all about us. Now we'd like to hear about you!"

When Justin added his persuasion, Estrella continued. "Well, I told you that my family—Carlos—paid that I might better learn my father's language. Carlos took me to a school. I studied English and all the other things children study in school—writing, arithmetic, science. I lived there for a long time with many other girls who did not have families close by."

"It sounds lonely," Jenny commented.

"I had food to eat and a place to sleep!" Estrella answered. "That is what matters. And Carlos came often to take me to visit the rest of my family."

Seeing that the twins still looked interested, she went on. "They have a big house. I do not know how many there are—perhaps a dozen, perhaps twenty. They come, they go. They have important things to do. When I grew bigger, Carlos let me do things for them—carry messages sometimes, translate English words, speak to . . ."

She broke off suddenly, and Justin added curiously. "Well, I guess that *was* pretty nice of them to do all that for you. But aren't you awfully young to be a guerrilla? You're no older than *we* are. Didn't you say there weren't any other children in your family?"

"Yes, I am the only one," Estrella answered proudly. "Children are not allowed in the freedom fighters. But I am *special* . . . their—how do you say it in English?—their mascot."

Jenny looked puzzled. "I still don't understand! Steve says there's thousands of kids who live in the streets. What made them pick *you* for their band?"

"Because she speaks English." Justin commented idly as he put away the Monopoly board. He looked up as Estrella's hand froze in midair. "I mean, it must be pretty useful!"

Forgetting the scattered pair of dice she was reaching for, Estrella said in a whisper, "It . . . it *was* an English magazine! I remember now. Carlos asked me how I knew the words."

She jumped up. "No, it was not because of that! They are kind. They *care* about me. I am glad to use my English to help them!"

At that moment the door swung open and Mr. Bascom walked in, ending their conversation. The twins scrambled to their feet, eagerly asking if he had any news for them.

Mr. Bascom looked serious as he shook his head. "And I'm afraid the Colombian police haven't been able to get any information out of those two prisoners. If they do know where this bunch is hiding out, they sure aren't telling!"

Mr. Bascom asked if Justin and Jenny had heard from their parents yet, and when they glumly admitted they hadn't, he left again abruptly. None of the teenagers felt like playing games or talking after that, so they decided on an early bedtime.

On the second morning, Justin looked up from a battered checkerboard as he caught a familiar name. A shot of a steaming, snowcapped peak filled the TV screen. Estrella wasn't there to translate, so he called over to Steve, who was leafing through that day's newspaper. "Hey, Steve, isn't that the mountain we saw spouting steam? The one that erupted and buried that town?"

"The Nevada del Ruiz," Steve confirmed, lowering the paper. "It sounds like it's going to do more than spout steam! They're warning of another eruption any day."

Studying Jenny's red checkers with care, Justin said idly, "I meant to ask you before—how could that mountain do so much damage? I mean, I can see a volcano burning up a town. But you'd think you could just climb out of the way of melting snow!"

"Justin, I don't think you've got the picture. I remember watching that disaster on the news." Steve folded up the paper before continuing. "Just imagine literally hundreds of tons of snow melting from the heat of that eruption. You've got as much water as the Niagara Falls rushing down the mountain canyons, scraping away dirt and boulders and trees . . . carrying it all down into the valleys. It's called *lahar*—that mixture of ice, mud, rock, you name it.

"By the time the *lahar* reached Armero, it was a river of sticky mud and rock forty feet high. . . . That's taller than most of the buildings. Most people were sound asleep when that mud slide swept over the town. I saw the pictures—you couldn't even see the church steeple!"

"Oh, that's awful!" Jenny shuddered as she absently moved a checker piece. "What's going to happen this time? Are they going to move all the people?"

"They won't need to evacuate this time," Steve reassured her, listening closely to the rest of the news clip. "They say this will be a fairly small eruption, and the seismologists can tell exactly how the snowcap will melt. The only things up that way are uninhabited mountain gullies. Hikers are being warned to stay out of the area. The mud will probably catch a few wild animals and lost cattle, but that's all."

Just then Justin took advantage of Jenny's lack of concentration to jump her last four checkers. Jenny's cries of indignation quickly drove the news story from their thoughts.

Estrella came in a short time later. After a short talk with her about his scribbled notes and as soon as the lunch dishes were cleared away, Steve left the guesthouse. Estrella showed no signs of going out again, but one of the security guards decided to spend the afternoon with them in the lounge, so the twins were unable to ask her if she had made any progress.

After supper, Jenny and Estrella were alone again in the lounge. Estrella was translating the international news for Jenny when Justin walked in and tossed a newspaper onto the coffee table. "Hey, look what the guard gave me!"

Jenny and Estrella quickly joined him around the spread-out newspaper. At the top of the front page was the title, *The Miami Herald,* and Jenny instantly forgot the newscast when she recognized a photo halfway down the page. It was one of Uncle Pete, probably dug out of some old company file.

Justin read aloud, "The United States government is presenting strong protests to the Colombian guerrillas over the kidnapping of a prominent American citizen. The FARC and ELN, Colombia's largest guerrilla groups, have denied all involvement in the kidnapping."

Looking over his shoulder, Estrella interrupted sarcastically, "Your government is always using its power to lean on those less fortunate. What right do they have to make demands here?"

"Don't you think they have a right to protest when someone kidnaps one of their citizens?" Justin answered in surprise.

"And don't say '*your*' government," Jenny added hotly. "If you have an American father, then *you* are an American citizen, too!"

Estrella clenched her fists. "Don't you call me that. I want nothing of my father's! I will never be American!"

Brown and blue sparks clashed as the two girls stared at each other. Justin said mildly, "Lay off, Jenny! She's just repeating what someone told her."

As the two girls lowered their angry eyes, he dropped into an armchair and said, "Estrella, you never did tell us about your father. Do you still remember him? Who was he? Why did he go away?"

Sitting down on the sofa, Estrella answered slowly, "Yes, I remember him. He . . . he was a big man with eyes as blue as mine. I . . . I used to run to meet him when he came home each night. He would throw me up to the ceiling and laugh. My mother would laugh, too. That is what I remember best—the laughing, the happiness! His name was . . . yes, I do remember . . . it was Gary Adams."

She pronounced the name with an odd foreign accent. "But I did not call him that. He taught me the American word . . . 'Daddy.' He always spoke to me in English and was proud that I learned his language better than my mother. He went away often, but my mother always told me he had gone to his country on business and that he would be back. And he always did come back. Until one day . . ."

Estrella stared blindly at the blank wall opposite her, her eyes focused on long-ago memories. "I remember . . . I was going to be eight years old. He hugged me when he left. He told me he loved me . . . that he would be back soon . . . that he would bring me a present for my birthday!"

Estrella sat stiffly on the edge of the sofa, tears trickling down her face. Jenny moved over and put a sympathetic arm around her as she continued, almost in a whisper. "He never came back! He never even sent a letter! We waited and waited!

"My mother spent the money he had left. Then she got sick. If only I could have brought a doctor, but there was no money even for medicine. It was his fault she died! And then they said I had to leave. I could pay no rent."

She shrugged Jenny's arm away angrily. "I was on the street for months! Do you know what it is like to live on the streets? To have no one who cares if you live or die?"

Justin tried to imagine life without Mom, who would always drop what she was doing when he dashed in from school to ask in her gentle voice about his day. Or without Dad, squealing into the driveway every night in the Trooper with some crazy new idea for a family outing. He had a sudden mental picture of a forlorn little boy huddled in a drafty cardboard box. He said slowly, "Yeah, we've seen it. It's awful!"

"I'll never forgive him!" Estrella said fiercely, wiping at her cheeks with the back of her hand. "I'll never forgive my father for what he did to my mother . . . and to me!"

There was an uncomfortable silence. As Estrella stared down at her clenched fists, Justin suddenly remembered something his youth group leader had said the Sunday before they left Seattle. "I'm really sorry about your father, Estrella. It's been terrible for you."

He added hesitantly, "But you can't keep hating your father for the rest of your life! God says to forgive other people just like He forgave all the bad things *we've* done."

"God!" Estrella replied scornfully as she jumped off the couch.

"You two sound just like Doña Rosa! Always talking about God and telling me to forgive my father!"

"Doña Rosa?" the twins chorused together, trying to pronounce the name as Estrella had: *Do-nee-u Ro-su.* "Who's she?" asked Justin.

Then Jenny demanded, "I thought you said you didn't have any friends . . . just your 'family'! Who's this Doña Rosa?"

"Doña Rosa is . . ." Estrella sat down again, looking shamefaced. "Well, you know how I told you about Carlos finding me on the street?"

They nodded, and she went on. "That was true, but not all the truth. One day soon after Carlos found me, I was at the garbage heap. I was looking for something to eat. This lady . . . she had brought her garbage . . . I knew her and she knew me. She had once lived in our neighborhood—she sewed clothes for my mother and me.

"She was so sorry to see me there. She took me to her home. Her husband was kind to me, too. I was there many weeks. They talked like you . . . like those words you said in Zipaquirá. . . . I can't remember them all."

Looking at her brother, Jenny repeated, "Be kind and compassionate to one another, forgiving each other, just as in Christ God forgave you."

"Yes, Doña Rosa was like that . . . kind and compassionate. She kept telling me I must forgive my father and forget what he had done . . . that I would never be happy until I forgave him."

Her expression softened suddenly. "I wonder sometimes what happened to Doña Rosa. She cried when Carlos took me away.

She and her husband had no children of their own. They wanted me to stay forever!"

"Why did you leave, then?" Jenny asked, confused. "It sounds like they were nice people!"

"I didn't like her words," Estrella admitted. "I was very angry. Then Carlos found me. The people on the street told him where I had gone. He told me that God was a lie . . . that Doña Rosa and her husband were foolish.

"One day Doña Rosa had to move . . . her husband had a new job. They wanted me to go with them, but Carlos came and told me that he had a place for me . . . that with him I could fight against people who would leave children to starve in the street."

Estrella waved an expressive hand. "So I went with him . . . and that is all."

Jenny sniffed. "Well, it seems to me it would have been smarter to stay with this Doña Rosa."

"Yeah, Doña Rosa was right . . . about forgiving your father, I mean," Justin added.

Estrella jumped up again. "It is easy for you to say this!" she stormed angrily. "If you were me, you would not forgive either!"

She turned and ran from the lounge, leaving the twins looking blankly at each other. After a long moment, Justin shrugged and said, "Well, I guess she really has had it pretty rough!"

"Yeah, I don't know *what* I'd do if Dad just disappeared," Jenny frowned. "No wonder she doesn't trust Americans."

Estrella didn't reappear that evening, but Steve showed up briefly before they went to bed. As he read through his usual stack of reports, Justin asked him, "Steve, how would you find someone who's missing?"

When Steve looked up in surprise, Justin explained, "It's Estrella's dad. Do you think you could find out what happened to him?"

"Well, if you know his name and when he was last in Bogotá, I suppose we could do some checking," Steve answered thoughtfully. He looked suddenly interested. "What did you say his name was?"

Steve promised to look through the embassy passport records for any information about a Gary Adams. Estrella was in bed when the twins went upstairs and was nowhere to be found when they got up the next morning. She didn't appear for breakfast, but neither Steve nor Mr. Bascom were there, and the security guard who dished up scrambled eggs and bacon only made a comment about kids sleeping in while soldiers—meaning him!—had to slave for their country.

When Estrella still hadn't appeared by eleven o'clock, Justin began to feel uneasy. She had never been gone this long, and Justin knew Steve or Mr. Bascom would be certain to ask where she was if she didn't show up soon. As though his thoughts had summoned them, Steve and Mr. Bascom chose that moment to walk into the lounge together.

Steve looked frustrated as he continued whatever conversation he had been having with Mr. Bascom. "It just seems like every lead that girl gives us comes to a dead end!"

He stopped short as he caught sight of the twins. "Don't worry, kids! We're sure to find your uncle any time. We're doing all we can!"

But he didn't sound at all convincing, and the twins exchanged a worried look. Jenny made a slight motion with her head, and

Justin followed her out of the lounge and back upstairs. Shutting the door to her room behind them, Jenny said with determination, "Justin, don't you think it's strange that every tip Estrella has given Steve has come up a dead end?"

Justin sat down on the bed. "No, I don't! You know Estrella told us people wouldn't talk to Steve."

"Well, Estrella hasn't come up with anything either, has she!" Jenny answered. "I'm beginning to wonder if she's really trying."

Justin walked over to the barred window and stared down at the dusty alley. "Cut it out, Jenny! I'm worried about Uncle Pete, too. But you can't blame Estrella!"

"I'm not blaming her!" Jenny slid off the bed and joined him at the window. "I'm just asking questions that need answers. Like why, if Estrella has hated Americans for so many years, did she suddenly decide to talk to us at that museum?"

Reading Justin's thoughts before he could answer, she added, "Yes, I know she was sorry for being so rude and wanted to be our friend. But why did she come over to talk to us in the first place? She must have known we were Americans the minute we opened our mouths!

"And there at Simón Bolívar's house! It just seems too much of a coincidence that those guerrillas showed up right after Estrella called us out."

"Jenny, she saved our lives!" Justin answered impatiently. "Why would she do that if she wasn't doing her best to help us?"

"Oh, come on, Justin! That bomb didn't come anywhere near us, and you know it!" Jenny answered scornfully. She looked suddenly exasperated. "What's got into you, Justin? Usually, *you* would be the one asking questions—and wondering what Estrella's up to!"

Justin shook his head stubbornly. "This is different. I *know* Estrella was telling the truth when she said she wanted to be our friend. I can tell she really cares about us!"

Before Jenny could argue further, the door slammed open. Both Justin and Jenny were startled into silence as Estrella burst into the room, her pale features ablaze with excitement. Justin cast a glance of triumph at his sister as Estrella announced, "I've found him! At last, I have found your uncle!"

Chapter Eight

BETRAYED!

"Estrella, that's great! Where is he? Is he okay? How did you find out?" Justin and Jenny's questions tumbled over each other. Jenny—her suspicions swept away—was as excited as Justin.

Justin started for the door. "Well, come on you two! We've got to find Steve right away! Once Estrella tells him where Uncle Pete is, Steve can take his men in there to get him out in no time!"

"Just one moment!" Estrella blocked the doorway. "You do not understand. I cannot tell Steve where your uncle is. I do not even know!"

Bewildered, Justin demanded, "But, Estrella, you said you found him!"

"I have learned where he is, but I don't know exactly how to get there," Estrella explained. She added quickly, "But that does not matter. I have a friend who does know. He will help us find your uncle."

Sitting on the edge of Jenny's bed, she told them how an acquaintance had admitted that he had heard rumors of an American hostage. "I told him that your uncle was a friend of mine and begged him to tell me what he knew. He was frightened and would tell me nothing at first, but at last he told me that he knew the man who takes supplies to the group that holds your uncle. From this man he learned where your uncle is being held."

"Then your *friend* will help Steve and the soldiers rescue Uncle Pete!" Justin said with satisfaction.

"No!" Surprised at her violent response, the twins stared at Estrella. The young guerrilla girl jumped to her feet. "No! Have you forgotten who I am? Never will I deliver freedom fighters into the hands of the soldiers—not even for you! Nor would my friend ever lead soldiers to the camp."

The excitement drained from Justin and Jenny's faces. Jenny demanded angrily, "Why did you bother finding him if you aren't going to tell us where he is? You promised to help us rescue him!"

"But of course I will help you!" Estrella said with a shrug of her slim shoulders. "It is very simple. I will take *you* to your uncle—and no one else!"

The twins stared at Estrella skeptically. Justin found his voice first. "Are you crazy, Estrella? You don't really think three kids can walk into a guerrilla hideout and just grab Uncle Pete, do you?"

Estrella looked very pleased with herself. "I told you this man I know will help. He has everything planned, and he will be armed. There are no more than two guards where your uncle is. It will not be difficult."

"Well, that's great, Estrella," Justin said, a little doubtfully. "You've certainly been a great friend."

Estrella stared at Justin, a strange expression flickering in the black-fringed, blue eyes. She looked away. Turning toward the door, she said in a hard voice, "Well, are you coming with me or not?"

This time it was Jenny who blocked the doorway. "Just a minute! Justin was right. This is crazy! You haven't even told us where we're going! Is Uncle Pete still in Bogotá? How long will we be gone? What do we need to take with us?"

Planting her feet firmly, she crossed her arms. "I'm not moving from here until I get a few answers!"

Seeing Jenny's determined expression, Justin added his support. "Come on, Estrella! We're your friends! You can at least tell us where we're going!"

Estrella looked sulky, but at last shrugged her shoulders. "I guess it does not really matter. You will find out soon enough."

She pointed at Jenny's jacket lying in a heap at the foot of her bed. "We are going into the mountains, so you will need that. It is not far—an hour or two past Armero. We will have your uncle back here before dark."

Justin nodded agreement, but Jenny shook her head with a frown. "I don't know. I think we should at least leave a message for Steve—let him know where we're going. What if something goes wrong? He won't have any idea where we are!"

Estrella's pale cheeks were stained red with anger. "No! If you tell Steve anything, I will leave and so will my friend. You will never see your uncle again!"

Justin looked at his sister, his jaw set with determination. "Jenny, we have to go! If we hadn't talked Uncle Pete into going with us that afternoon, he wouldn't be in this fix. You know Steve said they might never find him. If there's even a chance we can get him back, we've got to try!"

There was a long moment of silence, then Jenny nodded. "Yeah, I guess you're right. We don't really have much choice."

"Then let us go!" Estrella said urgently. "We have already wasted much time!"

"Just a minute. I'll get my jacket." Justin dashed next door and picked up his jacket from the chair where he had tossed it. He was pulling it on when he paused. *Jenny's right,* he thought suddenly. *No matter what Estrella says, we can't just run off without telling anyone. Steve would think we'd been kidnapped, too.*

Grabbing the newspaper he had brought up the day before, he tore a strip from the broad margin that edged the paper. Pulling out a pencil, he scribbled rapidly, "Steve, Estrella's taking us to Uncle Pete. The mountains—an hour or two past Armero. Don't worry about us. We should have Uncle Pete back by tonight."

He was looking for a place to put the note when he had a sudden thought. Unfolding it, he hastily added a rough sketch of the VW Bug he had seen at Zipaquirá. Folding the note into a tiny rectangle as he hurried into the connecting bathroom, he stuffed it into the frame of the mirror over the sink.

He had just returned to the other room and was pulling on his jacket when Estrella pushed open the door. She looked around the room so suspiciously that Justin was glad he hadn't left the note on the table as he had at first planned. She asked impatiently, "What is taking so long?"

"Just had to use the bathroom! I'm ready to go now," Justin answered hastily, zipping up his jacket and following her into the hall.

The twins and Estrella walked casually down the wide stairs.

There was no one in sight. Estrella led them down a dark passageway toward the back of the house and into an unlocked room piled high with cardboard boxes and barrels.

Half-used buckets of paint stood in one corner, and remnants of rope and other odds and ends hung on the walls. Justin grinned to himself as Estrella paused behind a tall stack of boxes to pry out the screen that covered an air vent. So *this* was how Estrella had been getting out of the house!

The tunnel behind the vent screen was too small to permit the passage of an adult. Estrella and Jenny wormed their way through with ease, but Justin had to force his wider shoulders through the narrow space. He was breathing hard by the time he tumbled out behind the girls into a small, dark room. From the clink of cutlery and the odors filtering through the cracks in a wooden door, Justin guessed they were in one of the kitchen storerooms.

Crouching behind a pair of large, galvanized metal cans that— judging by the smell!—held a month's supply of the guest house kitchen's garbage, Estrella pointed toward a faint red light that indicated one of the surveillance cameras high on the ceiling in the opposite corner of the small room. Then she motioned toward a dark, square opening in the floor, sheltered from the view of the moving camera by the garbage cans.

Estrella disappeared feet first into the opening, and Jenny reluctantly followed her. Then Justin swung his feet into the opening and found himself sliding quickly down some sort of metal chute—obviously meant for the kitchen garbage. His shoulders jammed as the chute leveled out at the bottom, and he felt a momentary panic until the two girls tugged him free.

Justin carefully climbed off the pile of black plastic bags of garbage that lay at the foot of the chute. He was standing in a dusty alley that ran along the back of the guest house. The sun was shining, but a cold breeze whistled down the alley, and Justin pulled his jacket close.

"Wow!" he said with admiration as he peered back up the dark garbage chute. "Estrella, how did you learn about this?"

She shrugged. "Buildings are much alike. There are few from which one cannot escape."

She seemed nervous as she urged the twins quickly down the alley. Justin, too, looked back frequently as Estrella led them through several small side streets, but no one seemed to have discovered their escape. About three blocks from the guest house, Justin suddenly caught sight of a familiar red Volkswagen Bug. Lounging against the side of the car was the young driver he had seen at the salt cathedral.

"Hey, I've seen that guy before! He's your friend, isn't he?" Justin exclaimed. Estrella abruptly stopped and demanded, "How would you know about him?"

"I saw him with you at the salt cathedral," Justin explained. "I had a feeling he might be the man you were talking about!"

Estrella looked displeased, but she admitted as they reached the red car, "Yes, this is Alejandro. He will take us to your uncle."

She added something in Spanish, and the young man, who looked only half-a-dozen years older than Justin, straightened up. Pulling off a pair of sunglasses, he stared down at Justin and Jenny, his dark features cold and unfriendly. Then he growled something to Estrella and opened the car door.

Pushing the twins toward the open door, Estrella said impatiently, "Come on! He says we must hurry!"

Justin instinctively disliked the young man. Reluctantly, he followed Jenny into the back seat. Estrella climbed into the front seat beside the driver. Ignoring the twins completely, the young man she had called Alejandro slammed on the accelerator, barely missing an oncoming truck as he zoomed onto a main avenue.

Though fast, the young man was not a good driver. He pushed in and out of the heavy traffic with complete disregard of traffic laws. In the front seat, Estrella and the driver were speaking quietly together in Spanish. Justin leaned over to whisper to his sister, "I don't trust this guy. I hope Estrella knows what she's doing!"

Her knuckles white as the car swerved to miss by inches what seemed a certain collision with a bus, Jenny whispered back, "You were the one who wanted to come!"

Justin had no answer to that. He watched alertly as they left the city behind, and quickly recognized this as the highway Steve had taken to the salt cathedral. But they soon turned onto a two-lane paved road that headed directly toward the great mountain range that surrounded the valley of Bogotá.

No one spoke as Alejandro slowed through several small towns with whitewashed buildings. There was little traffic, but occasionally Justin heard the drone of an airplane. And once, he glimpsed a helicopter lazily tracing patterns overhead.

He leaned forward suddenly as he caught sight of a familiar-looking snowcapped peak ahead, its heavy, gray-white plume drifting up to lose itself in the bank of clouds that was closing in over the mountains.

"Hey, Jenny, there's that mountain again—the Nevada del Ruiz! Look at all that smoke! Maybe it's about to erupt!"

"It always looks like that," Estrella answered from the front seat in a bored voice.

Justin was about to tell her what they had seen on the news when, without even slowing down, Alejandro turned onto a dirt road that wound up into the foothills of the mountain range. All three children clung to their seats as the dirt road grew narrower and bumpier. The cloud cover seemed to drop to the ground, and fog soon blotted out all but the road directly ahead.

The VW Bug hit an extra large bump that crashed Justin and Jenny against the roof of the car, then Alejandro slammed to a stop. Climbing out, he hurried around to the back of the car. Opening the passenger door, Estrella stepped out, pulled the seat forward, and motioned impatiently to the twins. "Come on! We have to walk from here."

They climbed out. The fog pressed in around them, but Justin could see that the dirt road had ended on a ridge of the mountains. They were above the tree line here, but in the gullies sweeping downward on either side were stunted cypress, tamarack, and junipers.

A strong, icy wind blew through their jackets. Justin took in a deep breath that stung his lungs with cold, then sniffed at the air again. "What's that smell?" he demanded. "It smells like rotten eggs!"

Estrella looked impatient. "I don't smell anything. Come! We have no time to waste."

Alejandro had opened a door of the little car and yanked out a backpack. He lifted the pack to his back, then pulled out a machine gun.

Jenny gasped as the young man checked the gun for bullets

and slung an extra belt of bullets over one shoulder. "What does he need that for?"

"Yeah, we wouldn't want to shoot anyone!" Justin said with determination.

"And how did you think we would get your uncle out?" Estrella replied scornfully. "Do you think you can just say 'please' to the guards, and they will let your uncle go?"

She added smoothly, "Of course we will not hurt anyone. If the guards see that Alejandro is armed, they will let your uncle go without any shooting."

Alejandro slammed the car door shut, and his sharp words whirled the children around. Estrella translated his order. "We are leaving the car here. We must go that way."

The three children followed Alejandro up the bank where the road ended and along the top of the mountain ridge. There was no path, but they picked their way across the springy, mosslike grass that cloaked the mountain meadow with green. Justin's tennis shoes were soon soaked through, and he could see that Jenny was shivering. Though she wore only a thin windbreaker, Estrella seemed immune to the cold.

Alejandro came to a halt at the edge of a gully. With his machine gun, he pointed out a faint animal trail that led down into a tangle of evergreens. The same wind that bit through their clothing had carved these evergreens into short, twisted forms not much taller than a man.

No one else seemed to notice the odd smell that still caught at the back of Justin's nostrils, and he wondered if he could be imagining it. As the two girls scrambled down the trail ahead of him, he paused to wipe his fog-wet face with a jacket sleeve. He looked with keen interest at the gray-white streak left on his sleeve.

A sudden blow to his back pushed him down the trail. Justin looked up angrily. Alejandro, his dark eyes cold and watchful, pointed his machine gun impatiently down into the gully. Estrella, already at the bottom, called up to him, "Justin, come! We have not much time!"

Justin scrambled down hastily to join his sister and Estrella. As they threaded their way through the evergreen thickets, Justin glanced back at Alejandro, his machine gun cradled easily across his arms as he brought up the rear.

Pushing a soggy branch out of his face, Justin muttered loudly, "I thought he was supposed to be leading us, not taking us prisoner!"

Estrella, at the front of the single file line, looked back. "He is making sure no one follows us."

Justin was suddenly reminded of the note he had tucked into the bathroom mirror. He wondered if Steve had found it.

The fog had rolled away by the time Alejandro finally brought them to a stop. They had been climbing up and down one gully after another for more than an hour, scrambling over logs, wading across shallow streams, and occasionally breaking into the welcome short grass of a mountain meadow.

Now they were on flat ground—a small mountain plateau choked with underbrush. Here the evergreens grew tall, in the shelter of the mountain ridges that pressed close overhead. The trail they now followed bore the obvious marks of human feet, but they could see only a few feet ahead, and Justin had lost all sense of direction.

Alejandro pushed them into the partial shelter of a tangled thicket, and the twins squatted down to rest while Estrella and Alejandro held a whispered conference. The growling of his stomach reminded Justin that they had missed lunch.

Estrella walked over and squatted down beside them. "The camp is just ahead—down in a canyon. Alejandro and I will check out the camp—to make sure there have not been any changes since our last information. You two will stay here out of sight."

Justin protested. "Why should we stay here? Wouldn't it be safer if we all stuck together?"

"You do not know how to move silently as we do," Estrella answered flatly. "You would bring danger to us. If you stay here out of sight, you will be safe enough. We will be back in just a few minutes. If there are still just two guards, we will take you in to get your uncle."

Estrella jumped to her feet as Alejandro snapped out a Spanish order. At the sight of his scowling face and expertly held machine gun, Justin didn't argue. Alejandro and Estrella disappeared without a sound into the underbrush, and Justin admitted to himself that he could never move that quietly.

The twins huddled further into the thicket. The tangled branches of a pair of junipers trailed to the ground around them, but there was room enough to lean upright against their intertwined trunks. Here, the weak rays of a late afternoon sun couldn't reach their damp clothing, and without the exercise of walking to warm them, both children were soon shivering.

Justin glanced over at his sister. Her dark curls were plastered to her head, and her lips were blue with cold. She frowned. "I hope they come back soon! At this rate we'll never get back before dark!"

In fact, no more than five minutes had passed when they heard a twig crack on the path just outside the thicket. Justin whispered eagerly to his sister, "There they are! Let's go."

But it was neither Estrella nor Alejandro who poked a head into the thicket where they crouched. Justin's mouth fell open as Steve Cardoza squatted down on his haunches and, holding a branch out of his face, said softly, "Hello, kids!"

"Steve! How did you find us so fast?" Justin exclaimed. The enormous relief he felt made him realize how much he had counted on Steve finding his note. Now everything would be all right!

As Steve dropped the branch behind him and joined them in the thicket, Jenny demanded, "How did you find us at all? Estrella's going to be really mad when she sees you here!"

Justin sheepishly told his sister of the note he had left behind. "I was afraid you wouldn't see it!" he told Steve.

"You couldn't have been gone long when I came up to look for you," Steve explained quickly in a low voice. "I searched your rooms up and down once the security guards confirmed you weren't in the building."

He looked approvingly at Justin. "That sketch of the car— that was good thinking. I remembered what you'd told me about Estrella's acquaintance in the red car, and got on the phone right away to a friend over at the Colombian Air Force. I asked him to call out a couple of helicopters to check out every mountain road leading out past Armero for a red Volkswagen Bug."

Justin suddenly remembered the helicopter he had seen

tracing patterns overhead—what seemed like hours ago. Steve went on, "Of course, I knew there was a good chance you might have taken a different vehicle, but it was the only lead we had. And it paid off!"

He grinned. "I was already at Armero when the helicopter radioed that they'd seen your car heading up this way. I found the VW abandoned at the end of the road and followed your tracks. None of you took much care to cover them. I'm sure glad to find you here safe and sound."

His grin suddenly disappeared as he leaned forward. In a stern whisper, he demanded, "Now tell me what ever possessed you to go off like this! This is the most stupid stunt I've ever seen! Don't you know better than to let that little guerrilla friend of yours talk you into something like *this?* You could have been killed!"

Both children squirmed under his sharp words, but Justin defended Estrella. "Estrella didn't want anyone to get hurt. She said you'd bring in soldiers and maybe get some of the guerrillas killed—and Uncle Pete, too! She and her friend have it all planned. There are only two guards, and Alejandro can take care of them. They'll be back in just a few minutes, and we can get Uncle Pete out without any shooting!"

Steve shook his head grimly. "It was still stupid! Anyway, we'd better try to get your uncle and get out of here. This is a very dangerous place to be right now."

"What do you mean?" Justin asked curiously

"I mean that we're too close to the Nevada del Ruiz. Don't you remember they announced yesterday that they were expecting another blowup?"

"But you said it would just be a little one—that the mud and snow would just go down the mountain canyons!" Jenny protested. Her voice trailed off as she caught her breath.

"That smell! It was *sulfur!*" Justin exclaimed suddenly. He brushed at the faint powdering of gray-white dust that coated his jacket. "This dust must be ash falling!"

"That's right," Steve added grimly. "And that melt-off will be heading this way. These guerrillas obviously don't pay close enough attention to the news."

He turned to leave the thicket. "By the way, Justin, it's unlikely that you'd find only two guards in a guerrilla camp. Which way did you say Estrella and her friend went?"

Crawling out of the thicket behind him, Justin pointed out the direction. In spite of the tongue-lashing, he had to admit that the presence of the tough Marine lieutenant was enough to send his optimism soaring.

Steve said calmly, "I'll take a look. You two stay here and don't move!"

"Oh, please, can't we go along?" Justin protested. "We'll be quiet!"

Steve nodded curtly, his keen eyes expertly scanning for any movement. "Okay! But you step where I step and do what I do—and don't make a sound!"

Jenny, holding a branch back to look out of the thicket, made no move to follow them. When Justin looked back at her in surprise, she said, "I'll wait for Estrella. Someone has to tell her where you are."

They had only moved a few dozen yards through the thick undergrowth, Justin following Steve's footsteps as quietly as he could, when they heard faint voices. Dropping to his stomach, Steve hissed, "Get down!"

He wriggled forward through a tangle of brush, then stopped. Wriggling up beside him, Justin's heart skipped a beat as he saw what had frozen the Marine lieutenant to this spot.

About thirty feet below them was a wide gully—almost a narrow valley—pierced through the center by a rapidly moving stream. Two crude thatched huts perched on the bank of the creek and, directly below the brush thicket where Steve and Justin crouched, several small Army-style tents had been erected to form a circle with the huts and the canyon wall. At least half-a-dozen men huddled around a bonfire in the center of the circle.

That's a lot more than two guards! Justin thought angrily. *I never did trust that Alejandro! I hope he didn't lead Estrella into a trap!* But it wasn't Alejandro who walked that moment into the smoky light of the fire, laughing and clinging to the arm of a tall, slim man with a commanding stride who carried a machine gun slung over the other shoulder.

"It can't be Estrella!" Justin whispered blankly. "But . . . but it is!"

Chapter Nine

THE GUERRILLA CAMP

Justin stared in horror at the scene below, trying to persuade himself that Estrella was a prisoner. But just then, the tall commander bent his head to speak to Estrella and her tinkling laugh rang out in response. He shook his head numbly and whispered, "I don't understand! She's our friend! What's she doing down there?"

Steve reached over and grabbed Justin by the wrist. "Don't you get it? That's Estrella's guerrilla band down there—her 'family'! She led you into a trap!"

Turning his head to catch Steve's grim expression, Justin made a discovery. "You aren't surprised! Did you know?"

"I never did trust that girl!" Steve answered bluntly. "I've been checking around her old neighborhood. This morning one of the neighbors told me they'd heard a couple of men from her band were arrested. I was on my way to ask Estrella about it when I found you gone."

Steve began to slither backward. "Your uncle is probably in one of the tents—or one of those huts. Let's go get Jenny. We'll have to go for help and hope they don't move your uncle before we get some soldiers up here."

Justin watched the scene below a moment longer. He shook

his head in amazement as Estrella laughingly greeted the other men around the fire. She had seemed so sincere. He could have sworn she desperately wanted their friendship. There had to be an explanation!

"Justin!" At Steve's urgent command, Justin began to wriggle quietly backward. He was out of the brush and about to stand up when he heard a sudden thud and a grunt of pain.

"Steve?" he called quietly.

There was a rustle in the tangled brush beside him. Justin froze as he heard heavy footsteps, then slowly turned his head. He stared at the combat boots planted firmly inches from his nose. They were dusty and scuffed, and very, very real. His eyes rose slowly upward to focus on a gun held in rock-steady hands.

Justin slowly rolled over and sat up, raising his arms in the air. The gun didn't waver, and his gaze moved upward to meet a pair of young, black eyes that burned with hatred. He turned his head cautiously. Steve lay on the ground a few feet away, blood streaming down one side of his face from a cut on his head. Standing over him was an older guerrilla with a machine gun cradled in one arm.

Steve groaned, then slowly sat up. As soon as the two guerrillas saw that he had regained consciousness, they motioned for their two captives to stand up. Aware of the gun only inches from his stomach, Justin jumped to his feet, carefully keeping his hands in the air.

Shaking the blood from his eyes, Steve didn't move fast enough for their two captors, and the older guerrilla jabbed him in the stomach with the butt of his machine gun. Wiping a hand across his face, Steve swayed to his feet.

Just then Justin heard his sister's angry voice. "Let go, Alejandro! You're hurting my arm!"

A moment later, Alejandro—smiling for the first time since they'd met him—shoved Jenny into their midst. Catching sight of her brother, Jenny exclaimed breathlessly, "Justin, I don't know what's got into Alejandro! Have you seen Estrella?"

Her voice trailed off in a gasp as she caught sight of the two armed guerrillas. "You mean . . . Alejandro's one of them? One of the guerrillas?"

She looked around as the two guerrillas, their guns trained on their three captives, spoke in Spanish with Alejandro. "I suppose they got Estrella, too!" Jenny continued.

Justin shook his head wearily and motioned toward the gully. Estrella was now seated on the edge of a roughly built picnic table beside the fire. Jenny stiffened as Estrella's voice suddenly rang out in a laugh. "I knew it!" she said angrily. "I never did trust her!"

Alejandro suddenly barked out an order, and Justin's captor used his machine gun butt to push him toward the edge of the cliff. Stepping around the bushes, Justin caught sight of a very steep trail that cut diagonally across the cliff face, down into the gully.

As he started down the path, he saw that the gully widened into an open valley downstream. But about half a mile upstream, it narrowed into a bottleneck canyon that wound up into the hills. Half-slipping down the steep trail wide enough only for one slim person, he caught a faint glimpse of snowy peaks upstream, stained with the red of sunset.

Two women were clearing a pile of dirty metal plates from

the picnic table when their captors shoved Steve and the twins into the circle of tattered tents and huts. Everyone in the camp paused to watch their approach, and Estrella hopped down from the table, waving a slim arm.

"Justin! Jenny! You're all right, aren't you?"

She motioned toward the slim, dark man who leaned unmoving against the picnic table. "I told you that you would meet Carlos one day."

Her welcoming smile turned to a scowl as she noticed Steve. "What is *he* doing here?"

The man she had called Carlos didn't even look at the children as he barked out an order, and the two guerrillas who had captured Justin and Steve shoved the Marine lieutenant toward one of the huts. Carlos followed them, leaving Justin and Jenny standing alone with Estrella. Justin quickly scanned the camp, but any thoughts of dashing into the darkness evaporated at the sight of Alejandro lounging against a nearby tree, machine gun cradled and ready.

Confusion fought with anger as Justin turned to the young guerrilla girl and demanded roughly, "Estrella, what's going on? Where's Uncle Pete?"

A shrill bark rang out. A little dog with tangled, dusty white hair dashed out from behind a tent, and suddenly everything became horribly clear to Justin. "You were the girl with the dog— the one who sent that message to Uncle Pete! You've been in this all along!"

As Estrella leaned down to pick up the dog, Jenny added scornfully, "Yeah, it was no 'accident' when you met us at the Gold Museum, was it? I'll bet you'd been following us the whole time! You were the one who led the guerrillas to capture Uncle Pete. And you pretended to feel so sorry for us!"

Estrella flushed with embarrassment as Jenny looked her up and down with disgust, and Jenny added impatiently, "What I don't understand is, why this silly play-acting? Why didn't you just take us all at once?"

For the first time since her greeting, Estrella spoke up. "They did not want you—only your uncle. But he will not cooperate. Carlos told me to bring you here so that your uncle will do as he is told."

She lifted her chin defiantly. "You don't understand! Your uncle's people took our friends—Eduardo and Paco. Now they are in prison. It is only fair that we should take your uncle. With his help, we can get them out."

"There is a difference!" Justin answered shortly. "Those men were criminals. Mr. Bascom said two men were killed when they tried to bomb the pipeline. The police had every right to put them in jail."

Estrella's eyes flashed. "No! That is not true. They wouldn't kill anyone! Nor will anyone hurt you. All we want is to get Eduardo and Paco out of jail."

Her expression was half-pleading, half-defiant. "Don't you understand? They are my family. I *had* to help get them out!"

Justin said bitterly, "So you pretended to be our friend. And all the time it was just another of Carlos's orders. I suppose all that time you were out 'looking for Uncle Pete,' you were just going out to get orders from Carlos. How could I have been so stupid!"

Justin didn't often lose his temper, but when he did, all his friends knew to get out of his way. The hot anger and hurt that had been building up since he had first seen Estrella in the guerrilla camp tightened into a hard lump in his chest.

Clenching his fists, he exploded, "You are a liar and a cheat, Estrella! We were your friends! We cared about you, and you were pretending and lying to us all the time!"

"But I *am* your friend! I would not hurt you!" Estrella stepped forward just as Alejandro moved to separate the three angry children.

As the young guerrilla shoved the twins toward one of the tents, Justin glared back at Estrella. "I'll never forgive you for this, Estrella! Never!"

The tent Alejandro took them to lay back under a cluster of tamaracks. A guard stood at attention in front. As Alejandro raised the tent flap and shoved the two children inside, Justin and Jenny caught sight of a bound and gagged figure half-sitting, half-lying at the far side of the tent.

"Uncle Pete!" Jenny cried joyfully, almost knocking him over with her exuberant bear hug. "You really *are* here!"

"At least she told the truth about something," Justin muttered as he quickly knelt behind his uncle. "Come on, Jenny! Help me get him untied."

Jenny yanked off the dirty strip of cloth that had served as a gag, while Justin struggled with the tight knots that bound Uncle Pete's hands behind his back. Uncle Pete didn't look at all pleased to see his niece and nephew. The instant the gag was off, he said gloomily, "So they got you, too. I overheard their planning, but I hoped you wouldn't fall for it."

Justin finally loosened the last knot. As the rope fell to the ground, Uncle Pete rubbed his swollen wrists and looked sternly at his niece and nephew. "How could you fall for that girl's story? Didn't you have more sense than to try to rescue me single-handedly?"

Both twins looked shamefaced, and Uncle Pete sighed, "Well, it's done now. Okay, tell me what happened."

They had only a few minutes to recount the happenings of the last few days when the tent flap lifted again and a guerrilla motioned to the three to step outside. He, too, carried a machine gun—obviously the favorite weapon of the guerrillas—and waved it toward the three Parkers as he led them back to the fire.

It was pitch dark now, and the only light was that of the campfire. The whole group of guerrillas had gathered, and Justin counted eight men and three women. All were dressed in mismatched bits of civilian clothing and Colombian army uniforms.

Steve also was there, a rough bandage now covering the gash on the side of his head. His battered face was expressionless, but his eyes were alert. *He'll do something to get us out of here,* Justin thought hopefully. But Steve's hands were tied tightly behind him, and one guard kept a gun trained on his back.

A brisk wind whistled down the canyon, and Justin was suddenly aware of how cold he was in his still-damp clothing. A branch snapped in the fire, and the flames flared up, casting red shadows across the angry face of the tall leader of the guerrilla band.

"Señor Parker, you have been very uncooperative!" he snapped in strongly accented English. "Our comrades have not been released."

Still clutching her dog, Estrella sat on the edge of the picnic table, intently watching as the guerrilla leader waved a threatening arm. "Now we have your family and this American spy. Surely your government will consider the four of you an adequate exchange for release of our comrades."

Uncle Pete looked regretfully down at his niece and nephew, but he shook his head firmly. "Carlos, I have explained this to you before. There is nothing I can do to secure the release of your men. Neither your government nor ours will give in to your demands. Extra hostages won't make any difference at all!"

Estrella was suddenly at Justin's side. She whispered urgently, "You must convince him to let our friends go! Please!"

Carlos looked furious. "Do you think I am a fool? You are an important man, Señor Parker. Your embassy will do what you command. You and your family will not leave here until our demands are met."

Steve took a sudden step forward. "We can't stay here! Like I told you already, we've *all* got to get out of here—and soon!"

He motioned toward the surrounding mountain peaks, now masked by darkness. "The Nevada del Ruiz is due to erupt again soon, and this place will be right in the path. Have you forgotten Armero?"

The events of the last hour had driven the strange odor in the air out of Justin's mind, but he suddenly realized the smell of sulfur had grown stronger. Carlos's sharp features showed uncertainty, then his expression hardened. "I have already told you that this is nonsense. If this were so, we would have heard about it."

"Only a small eruption is expected. If you'd been listening to the news you would have heard about it. It won't reach any towns, and there aren't supposed to be any people in this area. But you're right in the canyon! You should at least move up to high ground."

Steve looked around impatiently at the rest of the small band. "Haven't you seen the smoke rising from the mountain?"

The rest of the guerrillas stared back blankly, unable to understand Steve's words, but Carlos answered curtly. "There is always smoke above the Nevada del Ruiz."

"But is there always ash falling? Look at my coat!" The thin film of gray-white ash was clearly seen against the dark brown leather of Steve's coat.

The guerrilla leader ran a finger down his own sleeve, then spit on the ground. "It is nothing but dust blown by the wind— the same dust we have seen since we camped here."

Before Steve could say anything else, he added sharply, "This is but a trick to escape from here, but it will not work! We will wait no longer. Your embassy will be informed tonight of your capture. They have until morning to announce the release of our comrades. If it doesn't happen, . . . then you will all be very sorry you ever came to this country!"

Carlos snapped an order, and Alejandro and another guerrilla herded the captives back toward the tent. While the other guerrilla stood guard, Alejandro roughly bound their hands and feet. As they left the tent, Justin slumped against the tent wall next to Jenny, his bound hands on his pulled-up knees.

Wearily resting his forehead against the rough ropes, he said in a voice too low to be heard by anyone but Jenny, "This is all my fault! I was so sure Estrella was our friend. If only I hadn't believed her!"

"She fooled the rest of us, too—even Steve!" Jenny whispered back.

That wasn't quite true, but Justin felt better. Jenny really was a great sister, he thought gratefully. She never rubbed it in when a guy was wrong.

His thoughts were interrupted as Steve whispered urgently into the darkness, "Mr. Parker, we've got to get out of here tonight!"

He added, still in a whisper, "Mr. Parker, I wasn't bluffing about the danger. I figure we don't have more than a day before that melt-off comes shooting down this canyon. We've got to get to high ground!"

Uncle Pete was silent, but Jenny whispered, "How can we escape? We're all tied up!"

"Yeah, and what about the guards?" Justin added quietly. Steve's low voice suddenly carried a note of amusement. "I picked up a few tricks in the Marines. I can be out of these ropes in ten minutes. As for the guards . . . well, it's pitch dark. This band is pretty amateur. It wouldn't be hard to evade them. How about it, Mr. Parker? Are you willing to try?"

There was a moment's silence, then Uncle Pete answered slowly, "Lieutenant Cardoza, I think you do have an excellent chance of getting out of here. But we aren't trained soldiers. We can't move as quietly or as quickly as you can. They'll be checking on us, and once they discovered our escape, they'd be after us in a second. We'd just slow you down."

Steve sighed. "I'm aware of that. But I'm willing to risk it if you are."

"No," Uncle Pete whispered decisively. "Our chances of escape are too small. And if we failed, we'd never get another chance. You'd better go for help. We'll cover for you here."

Steve sounded relieved. "That's probably the best plan. I'll go as soon as the camp is quiet. It'll take me a few hours to get to a main road, but I should have help here by morning."

He broke off abruptly at the sound of voices approaching the tent. The tent flap opened, the distant glimmer of the campfire making only a slight difference in the darkness. A small figure slipped in. Justin heard a thump, and the sound of a striking match—then the red-yellow flicker of a candle lit Estrella's unhappy face.

"Justin. Jenny." The candle dripped wax and sent long, wavering shadows across the tent floor as Estrella leaned down to pick up the bundle she had dropped. "I knew you would be cold so I brought you some blankets."

Seeing their bound hands and feet, Estrella set down the candle. Shaking out the pile of heavy wool blankets, she carefully draped a blanket around each of the prisoners.

"Thanks a lot, Estrella," Jenny said gratefully as Estrella tucked her blanket close.

Uncle Pete and Steve, on the side of the tent opposite the twins, nodded their thanks. But Justin, snuggling into his own blanket, just said grudgingly, "While you're in here, why don't you do something useful—like untie our hands!"

"No!" Justin wondered if he had imagined the sudden look of fright on Estrella's face. Then she frowned. "No, I cannot let you go!"

"Yeah, I forgot, you're one of them!" Justin answered sarcastically. "Why don't you just go away and leave us alone!"

Instead of leaving, Estrella squatted down in front of Justin and Jenny. "Please, I know you are angry with me. I . . . I don't want you to hate me. I want to explain."

Pushing back the long hair that fell over her slim shoulders, she pleaded, "Carlos did tell me to be your friend. And he told me to bring you here. You see, Carlos and my family have done everything for me. How could I say no when they needed my help?"

"Yeah, so you pretended you needed friends—that you really liked us!" Justin interrupted with a growl. "You sure fooled me!"

"But I was not pretending! Well, perhaps at first . . ." Estrella's low voice shook a little. "When I knew you—how you loved each other even when you quarreled, how you were kind to me when I am not even of your country—then it wasn't pretend anymore. I was glad to be your friend. And when I saw how sad you were about your uncle, I was very sorry."

"You call this being a friend?" Justin growled. He lowered his voice as Uncle Pete and Steve looked in their direction. "Carlos is planning to kill us tomorrow if you don't get your men back!"

Estrella looked surprised. "But I told you already that no one will be hurt. Carlos just talks that way to make the police let Eduardo and Paco go. They promised me they would not hurt you if I brought you here. No matter what happens, you and your uncle will be released unharmed."

She added soothingly, "So you see, there is nothing to worry about. Now you will stop being angry and be my friend, will you not?"

Jenny looked doubtful as Estrella stopped speaking, but Justin was furious. Looking hard at the young guerrilla girl, he whispered sarcastically, "Do you really think we're stupid enough to fall for your lies again? Did Carlos send you in here? Does he think we'll tell you our escape plans or something if you're nice to us?"

Estrella's chin went up proudly. Leaning forward, she hissed, "You talk about God and forgiveness—but do you forgive?"

Justin didn't answer, and she jumped to her feet so fast that she bumped her head on the ridge pole of the tent. They had been talking too softly for the adults to overhear, but now Estrella almost shouted, "I should have known better than to be friends with you! *You* are the liars—like all Americans!"

She grabbed the candlestick and turned to storm out of the tent when Steve called out quietly, "Speaking of Americans, I found out what happened to your father."

Estrella froze, then turned around slowly. Justin exclaimed with sudden interest, "So you did check it out! That's great!" He glanced at Estrella, and his excitement turned into a scowl.

"That's right. I checked the embassy records for a Gary Adams traveling from Bogotá to the U.S. that year, and then ran his name through the Interpol computer."

Looking up at Estrella, he said gently, "Your father never did leave you, Estrella. He was in a car accident in Miami and was killed instantly. He didn't have any close relatives in the U.S., and I guess the insurance company that settled everything didn't know he had a wife and daughter in Colombia."

"My father didn't leave me?" Estrella looked dazed. Shaking her head, she whispered, "I . . . I have hated him for so long! I went with Carlos because I hated him."

"Yes, I know," Steve said gently. "You joined the guerrillas because they were fighting those so-called rich men like your father who would leave a little girl out in the streets to starve."

"And all the time he was . . . " Estrella suddenly whirled around. The candle dropped unnoticed to the floor and went out as she plunged through the tent flap.

Justin was blinking his eyes in the sudden darkness when Jenny spoke up quietly. "Justin, don't you think you were a little hard on Estrella?"

"I don't want to talk about it," he muttered. Rolling over on his side, he nestled into his blanket. Faint rustlings told him that the others were also trying to get comfortable. Only the occasional twitter of a bird settling down for the night and the chirping of crickets disturbed the sleeping camp.

Justin stared into the darkness. At least his angry thoughts took his mind from the gnawing hunger pains and growing discomfort in his bound arms and legs.

She lied to us! he told himself fiercely.

That was what really hurt. He had trusted Estrella—given her his friendship—and now they were all in great danger because of her. He didn't believe for one minute that those hard-eyed men and women around the campfire had any intention of letting them go as easily as Estrella claimed.

He tried to get to sleep, but somehow Estrella's angry words echoed in his mind, *You talk about God and forgiveness! You are the liars . . . the liars . . . the liars!*

"Stop moving around!" Jenny said crossly. "I'm trying to sleep!"

Justin lay still and finally dozed off. It seemed only minutes later that he was disturbed by a movement at the end of the tent. A firm hand touched his shoulder.

"I'm leaving now." Justin could hardly hear Steve's whisper. "I've left my blanket humped up in case the guard looks in before morning. I'm sorry I have to leave you tied up, but it's better they think you don't know anything about my escape."

Soundlessly, he dropped to the floor of the tent. Justin sensed rather than heard Steve lift the canvas wall of the tent just enough to thrust his head and shoulders through. He lay flat on his stomach for a long moment. Justin knew that Steve was scanning the area, checking for guards. Then, without a whisper of a noise, Steve was gone.

Chapter Ten

DANGER IN
THE CANYON

Justin awoke coughing. Lying on his side, his head pillowed on something hard, he wondered for a moment where he was. He shifted position, and a twinge of pain shot up his numb arms and legs. Instantly, the events of the last few days flooded into his mind. He now realized that a sharp rock under the canvas beneath his head was digging into his ear.

He struggled to a sitting position, noticing that the wool blanket had slipped from his shoulders. Although the mountain dawn usually was bitterly cold, the air seemed strangely warm and thick. He breathed in deeply and almost choked as the biting smell of sulfur burned his lungs. Outside, a rooster—probably destined for the big cooking pot Justin had seen the day before—announced the dawn, and the first light began to replace the darkness inside the tent.

Justin had been awakened twice during the night as a guard briefly flashed a powerful flashlight around the tent. The guard had done no more than glance at the humped-up blanket that marked the spot where Steve had been. Cold fear suddenly struck Justin's empty stomach as he realized that Steve hadn't returned yet. The guard would check again any minute now. In full daylight, he would have to notice that one of his prisoners had escaped.

Beside him, Jenny stirred and sat up. She grimaced, cautiously moving her bound arms and legs, then bent over in a sudden coughing fit. At the sound, Uncle Pete, too, raised his head from where he leaned in a sitting position against the side of the tent. His keen eyes took in his wide-awake nephew and niece.

"Well, kids," he said softly, "it looks like Steve didn't make it back."

"Yeah, and smell the air!" Justin answered. "We've got to get out of here!"

"What are we going to do, Uncle Pete?" Jenny asked anxiously.

Before Uncle Pete could answer, the tent flap lifted. But instead of the guard they expected, Estrella slipped in, a sharp knife in her hand. Justin turned his head away as she knelt to saw at his bonds.

Estrella explained briefly, "You will not need these during the day. I will take you down to the river to wash. Then there will be something to eat."

As the ropes binding Justin's hands and ankles fell to the ground, she turned to Jenny, who smiled at her in her usual friendly fashion. Estrella didn't smile back. She looked as though she hadn't slept. She cut through the first strand of the rope that bound Jenny's ankles. "We must hurry. It looks like a bad storm is coming."

She glanced over Jenny's shoulder at the other end of the tent, and the black-fringed, blue eyes widened in sudden horror. The knife dropped from her hand as she demanded, "Where is Steve? Where did he go?"

Fear pinched her thin features as she grabbed frantically at the heaped-up blanket that had taken Steve's place. "No, he can't be gone!"

Forgetting her errand, she ran from the tent. Justin grabbed at the knife and finished sawing through the half-cut rope, then freed Uncle Pete. Rubbing at swollen hands, Uncle Pete said soberly, "There's going to be trouble, kids. I wish you were out of this, but it's too late now."

He looked steadily at the two of them. "I don't know how much more time we have, but there's one thing we can do right now. Let's pray."

Bowing his head, Justin nodded in agreement as Uncle Pete prayed for Steve's safety, and that he would bring help soon. But he opened his eyes in shock when Uncle Pete added, "Help us to be Your witness to our captors. They, too, need Your love."

They don't need love, Justin thought bitterly. *They need punishment—especially Estrella!*

Angry shouts arose outside the tent. Lifting his head, Uncle Pete said quickly in a low voice, "No matter what happens, kids, don't forget that God is in control of every situation—even this one!"

Just then, the tent flap was yanked back. The guerrilla who had stood guard all night thrust his head through the opening. His black eyes narrowed with anger as he caught sight of Steve's empty blanket. Shoving his machine gun through the flap, he angrily motioned for the three Parkers to step outside.

The dawn was slowly lightening the steel gray of the sky as they emerged from the tent, but there would be no sun that morning. The air was not so heavy out here, but a sharp smell of sulfur still burned Justin's nostrils if he breathed in too deeply.

Justin thought at first it was fog that shrouded the camp with ghostly white. But as he scuffed a sneaker against the ground, he realized that the ground, the tents, and even the trees were cloaked with a thick layer of gray-white dust.

Ash! he thought grimly. *It's coming down faster!*

The guerrilla leader was over by the picnic table talking to Estrella, the rapid motions of his hands expressing his anger. Estrella looked upset. Breaking off at the sight of the Parkers, Carlos marched over and struck Uncle Pete hard across the face.

"Where is the American spy? How has he escaped?" he demanded angrily.

Rubbing his bruised face, Uncle Pete answered evenly, "I don't know. I was asleep."

The ring of truth in his voice seemed to convince Carlos, and he turned his hot, angry gaze toward the twins. Justin was afraid that the leader would question him, but after a long, searching glance, Carlos turned to the guard who still stood there, his gun trained on the small group of hostages.

"Imbecile!" he shouted. The guard backed up, fear on his dark face, as Carlos switched to angry Spanish. The young guerrilla was trembling by the time Carlos stopped shouting, and Justin wondered what threat could have frightened him so.

Ignoring the guard, Carlos turned again to Uncle Pete. "You knew of this escape, did you not?"

Uncle Pete faced the guerrilla leader steadily. "Yes, I knew he would try to escape. He knew this place was dangerous, and he didn't want to be caught in this canyon when the eruption hit."

Uncle Pete reached out a hand and rubbed it against the tent. His fingers came away coated silvery white. "Can't you see he was telling the truth? You must at least move to high ground!"

Estrella moved to Carlos' side and whispered urgently. The guerrilla leader glanced at the strange gray cast of the sky, then reached out and fingered the ash. "There is often ash in these mountains, but we will move out."

Justin gave a sigh of relief, then froze as Carlos gave him a cold, dark stare. "Do not think this will help you escape! If the American spy should now make his way back, we will not be here."

Motioning toward his hostages, he snapped at Estrella, "Tell the others to begin packing up at once. Then take care of these."

Estrella was back within seconds. She led the Parkers to a crude outhouse, then down to the river to wash, the guard—a different one this time—stayed a few feet behind, machine gun ready. Justin scowled to see Jenny chatting quietly with Estrella as they completed a quick wash without soap or towels. Jenny might be softening toward Estrella, but he, Justin, wasn't about to let the young guerrilla girl fool him again!

The camp was already swarming with activity by the time they walked back from the river. The tents were now flat on the ground, and the guard motioned for Uncle Pete to sit nearby, with his back against a tree near the edge of the river. Perching on a large boulder, the guard cradled his gun across his knees. His black eyes didn't move for an instant from Uncle Pete's face, but when Estrella said something to him in Spanish, he nodded and allowed her to lead the twins over to the campfire.

A sizzling smell of something frying twisted Justin's stomach with hunger. Several of the guerrillas were still eating, huddled close to the warmth of the fire. Justin's mouth watered as Estrella handed him an enamel plate piled high with cakes made of finely-ground corn about the size of pancakes, but much thicker. Each was sliced and stuffed with a fried egg.

"Arepas," Estrella said, putting an enamel mug in his other hand. Justin growled a reluctant thanks as he took a sip of the strong, sweet *café con leche* (coffee with milk) he had already learned to enjoy. Estrella handed Jenny her food, then hurried away with a plate and mug for Uncle Pete.

Squatting down by the fire, Justin hurriedly chewed one of the thick corn cakes. Biting into her own *arepa*, Jenny looked across the clearing to watch Estrella carry a bundle of blankets over to a pack mule.

Swallowing, she demanded, "Justin, do you have to be so mean to Estrella? You're hurting her feelings!"

"So what?" Justin growled, stuffing the rest of the *arepa* into his mouth. "She's done a lot worse than that to us!"

Jenny looked exasperated. "Justin, you are so stubborn! You make up your mind about something, and nothing can change it! Like Estrella—at first, you decided she was our friend, so you wouldn't listen when I warned you about her."

Suddenly hurt, Justin snapped, "I already said I was sorry! I was wrong! She had me fooled. What more do you want?"

To Justin's surprise, Jenny answered thoughtfully, "I don't think you *were* wrong! I think she's telling the truth. She really did want to be our friend—at least after she got to know us. You *felt* that—that's why you were so sure she wouldn't hurt us."

She made a helpless motion with her coffee mug. "You know what I mean! I can't explain it very well. Anyway, the only mistake you made was thinking she couldn't be our friend and still lie to us about Uncle Pete and all this. She really believes these guys aren't going to hurt us—and maybe she's right!"

She leaned forward, waving an *arepa* right under his nose. "But that isn't the point! The point is, now you've decided that Estrella is a jerk and our worst enemy, so you've made up your mind to hate her for the rest of your life. And you're not going to let anyone change your mind about that, either! Mom always says you're so 'sensible' and 'determined.' Well, I think you're just plain pig-headed!"

Justin set his jaw stubbornly and refused to answer, but his sister's words had hit home. He knew that holding grudges was one of his worst faults. For the first time, he began to wonder what he would have done if he'd been in Estrella's shoes—and his anger slowly began to ebb away.

Justin felt much better with a stomach full of *arepas* and *café con leche*. He couldn't quite smile when Estrella collected their dishes, but he didn't scowl, either.

It was beginning to drizzle as the twins walked back to join Uncle Pete, and a strong wind stung Justin's face with what felt like blowing sand. In spite of the drizzle, the still-falling ash was beginning to give the camp the look of a silvery Christmas card. A tiny pebble struck Justin's back as he ducked under the shelter of the trees. Others followed, hitting the ground like a shower of tiny hailstones.

"It won't be long now!" Uncle Pete commented as Justin and Jenny squatted beside him. His expression was as calm as ever, but Justin knew he was worried as he looked up at the canyon and murmured, "Where could Steve be?"

Carlos shouted angrily, and the guerrillas began to work faster. The tents had been rolled into bundles, and two of the guerrillas were leading pack mules up the steep path to the top of the gully when a shout caught Justin's attention. It was Alejandro, and Justin suddenly realized that he hadn't seen the young guerrilla at all that morning.

Alejandro jumped out of the way of a pack mule and ran into camp. Carlos strode over, asking a sharp question in Spanish. Alejandro shook his head and poured out an answering flood of words. Justin caught his breath at the look on Carlos's face as he snapped a sharp response, then marched over to the three hostages.

Uncle Pete rose to his feet as Carlos announced coldly, "Your embassy has not done as we demanded. Our men have not been released. Now we are out of time. If the American spy finds his way back, this place will be filled soon with soldiers."

He looked at Uncle Pete thoughtfully. "Do you truly think that your people will not give in to our request? Even if you write and demand it?"

Uncle Pete's gaze was steady as he answered firmly, "My embassy will not give in to terrorist demands, no matter how long you wait. And I wouldn't want them to give in to threats for my sake."

The guerrilla leader turned somber eyes on the twins. "And what about your family? Would you risk their lives just to keep two of my men in jail?"

Uncle Pete sighed heavily as he, too, glanced down at his niece and nephew. "You know I would do anything to protect Justin and Jenny. But it doesn't make any difference. Even if I could persuade my embassy to deal with you, your own government would refuse to release the prisoners. Why don't you just let us go and be done with it all!"

Carlos didn't answer. Justin held his breath as the guerrilla leader stared at them for a long moment. Then, shrugging his shoulders as though he had made a decision, he walked away and shouted an order.

The last of the guerrillas, backpacks over their shoulders, began to move up the narrow trail to the top of the gully. Within moments, the campsite was abandoned, except for the Parkers and their guard. The shower of stones and ash was growing heavier, and Justin and Jenny followed Uncle Pete further into the shelter of the cluster of trees.

Carlos walked over, his own machine gun slung across his back and a pistol in a holster at his side. Alejandro came behind him, carrying a coil of nylon rope. He motioned to their guard, and he, too, headed toward the cliff.

Justin jumped to his feet, relieved that they were at last moving out. When Alejandro began roping his hands together in front of him, he wasn't surprised. The guerrillas were obviously making sure that they wouldn't escape along the way. Alejandro moved along to Jenny and Uncle Pete, quickly looping the same rope around their wrists and pulling it tightly.

Carlos stopped in front of Uncle Pete. "I thought you would wish to know that the American spy was right. We have just heard on the radio that the volcano is again melting the snow on the Nevada del Ruiz. They were careful to announce that no towns or haciendas are in danger."

He gave a sign to Alejandro. Then, to Justin's shock, Alejandro looped the remainder of the long rope around a low limb of the tree. He yanked it so hard that their hands were pulled overhead.

"What are you doing?" Uncle Pete demanded sternly. "If you've heard that the snow is melting, then you know there will be floods through these canyons. Tie us up and leave us at the top of the gully if you aren't taking us with you. But don't leave us here!"

Carlos just turned and walked away. Alejandro gave them a nasty grin and made a taunting remark in Spanish, then began knotting the rope tightly to the branch. Realizing with horror just what Carlos had in mind, Justin kicked Alejandro sharply in the shins. Alejandro kicked back, knocking Justin's feet out from under him. The ropes cut deeply into his wrists as he struggled to regain his footing. Alejandro tied a final knot, then walked away.

Justin glanced up at the cliff face. Estrella was halfway up, a heavy bundle on her back. He shouted bitterly, "So your friends won't hurt anyone, Estrella? So much for your promises!"

Justin's shout brought Estrella to a halt. Even at that distance, he could see the horror on her face as she took in the situation. A moment later, she had dropped her bundle and was flying down the path. Carlos had stooped to pick up a last small bundle of personal items. Estrella rushed at him, screaming, "What are you doing? You cannot leave them here!"

Carlos only paused to swing his pack to his shoulders as he answered loud enough for the Parkers to hear clearly, "Why should we leave witnesses?"

"But you promised not to hurt them!" Estrella pounded him on the chest with her small fists as she shouted, "You cannot leave them here! They will die!"

The guerrilla leader grabbed her wrists, raising his voice. "Do not be stupid! The government will not exchange our men even for three of them. They are no good to us now. They would just slow us down."

Estrella broke away. She flew at the knots, trying to untie them as she cried, "They did promise not to hurt you! They did! Please believe me! I did not know they would do this! Please forgive me!"

As Carlos pulled her away, Jenny answered softly, "We do believe you, Estrella. Don't worry. We'll be all right! Maybe the eruption won't even come here."

Uncle Pete said quietly, "You'd better go, Estrella. Your friends are waiting for you."

"No, I won't go! Not until Carlos lets you go!"

Carlos grabbed Estrella by the arm. "You will do as you are told! You, at least, are still of some use to us!"

He lapsed into Spanish as he forced her across the clearing. Estrella looked back pleadingly, and Justin suddenly knew that he had something to do before it was too late.

"Estrella!" he called. Estrella stopped in spite of Carlos' scowl and iron grip, and Justin added, "I'm sorry I was so mad at you, Estrella. I *do* forgive you!"

Estrella didn't answer. She stood for a moment with her head bowed, and Justin realized with shock that she was crying. With a Spanish curse, Carlos pulled her away. She didn't look back again as he pushed her up the trail. Moments later, the path and the cliff top above were empty, and the Parkers were alone.

"Okay, kids," Uncle Pete said. "Let's figure out a way to get out of this mess."

Fifteen minutes later, Justin admitted to himself that there might not be a way out. They had tried to loosen the rope, but Alejandro had tied the knots too well, and the branch over which he had hung the rope was well out of reach of even Uncle Pete's outstretched arms. Uncle Pete encouraged the two children, even making jokes as they stumbled over each other in an attempt to free their upstretched hands, but Justin saw that the cheerful smile that split the red-gold beard didn't reach his somber eyes.

Justin couldn't see his watch, but he guessed that it was about mid-morning. The shower of rocks had slowly dwindled away, and even the ash fall was lessening. The sky grew a shade less gray. Relaxing a moment against his burning wrists, Justin caught the faint roar of a distant waterfall. His spirits began to lift.

"Maybe the eruption is over," he declared with relief. "Nothing has happened after all. Maybe we can just wait for Steve to show up. He should be here any minute." He didn't let himself even wonder if something might have happened to Steve.

Uncle Pete shook his head. "It isn't the volcano we have to worry about—it's the runoff. Whether the eruption is over or not, that water and mud will still be heading down these canyons."

He looked down. "See if you can find something we can use to cut us loose."

As Justin scanned the ground at his feet, Jenny cried triumphantly, "Look! There's a broken pop bottle!"

The shard of glass lay against the side of the tree trunk. Jenny was closest. "Try to kick it over here!" Uncle Pete said urgently.

But Jenny couldn't quite reach it. "Just a minute! I'll take my shoes off." In seconds, she had kicked off one sneaker and wriggled out of a sock.

"You'll cut yourself," Justin protested as Jenny tried to grab the broken bottle between two toes.

"I don't think that really matters right now," she panted. Finally successful, Jenny began pulling the piece of broken bottle slowly toward her.

Justin's eyes were glued on the shard of glass slowly moving toward them, when he suddenly realized that the waterfall sound he had heard earlier had grown much louder and seemed to be closer. Justin raised his head. He stared upstream in disbelief, and a desperate fear wrapped around his lungs.

Still far up the gully, its gray-brown mass squeezed almost to the top of the sheer cliff tops by the narrow stone sides of the canyon, was a solid, moving wall of rock and mud. Justin watched in helpless horror as the *lahar* spawned by the Nevada del Ruiz swept relentlessly down toward the camp.

Chapter Eleven

UNEXPECTED HELP

The far-off mass of mud and ice was still hardly visible against the dirt-brown color of the canyon walls. It seemed to move so slowly that Justin wondered momentarily if he was mistaken. He glanced over at his sister, who had just managed to grab the piece of broken bottle between both feet. When he looked back up, he was shocked to see how much the wall of mud had grown in just that split-second of time.

A gasp beside him as Jenny dropped the piece of glass told Justin that she, too, had noticed the swelling wave of mud. Panicking, Justin yanked hopelessly at the ropes that stretched his arms upward, ignoring the sharp pain as the twisted strands cut into his wrists. He heard the frightened sobs of his sister, but there was no time for words.

The rush of a waterfall rose to the rumble of a mountain-sized cement mixer as the churning mass of boulders and mud grew with every breath. Justin caught sight of the massive roots of an uprooted evergreen giant tossed onto the crest of the wave like a broken twig.

He sagged against the ropes, not bothering to struggle further. He was past feeling any fear. He spared a brief thought for his parents—they would be so sad when they heard the news. Then he bowed his head and whispered quietly, "Dear God, I guess it'd take a miracle to get us out of this one!"

Then it happened—so suddenly he was sure he had imagined it. A soft voice spoke in his ear, "Come! We must leave here!"

He lifted his head to see Estrella standing on tiptoes in front of him. Her face was tense with fear, but she was already reaching up to saw at the ropes that twisted around his wrists.

"Estrella!" he cried, his shout jerking Uncle Pete and Jenny around. "You came back!"

Estrella didn't stop sawing for a second, but she gasped, "I could not leave you here. I ran away from the others."

The knife she held was an old—and dull—kitchen knife. She had sawed only part way through the knotted strands, and sweat already beaded on her forehead. Justin quickly glanced at the approaching wave of *lahar*. It was much closer now, and no longer looked solid. His sharp eyes could pick out the boulders, branches, even dead animals that dotted the heaving, slick surface of the mud.

"Estrella!" he cried urgently. "It's too late! Save yourself."

"No!" Estrella cried, sawing harder. "I will not leave you again!"

"Just cut this rope up here!" Uncle Pete shouted over the churning rumble of the advancing mud. He motioned with his head toward the single strand that stretched their arms up toward the branch just above his hands. "If you cut this, the rest of the ropes will fall off."

Estrella rushed to Uncle Pete's side, but the rope was well over her head and out of reach. In an instant, she managed to roll a small boulder up beside him. Perching on it, she began to saw frantically, still straining to reach the rope. The towering, gray-brown wall had now reached a thick belt of cypress and tamarack trees that lined the riverbed only half a mile upstream. Justin held his breath as they were broken off and smashed under the relentless movement of the *lahar*. Within seconds they were gone, and thousands of tons of mud, ice, and debris pushed through the bottleneck of the narrow canyon into the wider valley which spread on down the mountainside.

It was this that gave them hope. The mad rush of the oncoming river of mud slowed a little as it spread out to fill every nook and cranny of the now broader gully. And at that moment, Estrella's knife broke through the rope. The strands that had been so tight instantly loosened, and the Parkers quickly shook off the ropes.

"Come on!" Estrella cried, her voice tight with fear. She began sprinting toward the cliff, the others close behind. Jenny paused long enough to snatch up shoes and socks, but her long legs shot her past both Justin and Estrella.

Running faster than he ever had in his life, Justin glanced upstream. The wave of *lahar* had dropped in height as it spread out sideways into the valley and spilled over the lower far bank of the gully. But it was now so close that it loomed high over the small, running figures, blotting out the skyline. Justin reached the bottom of the cliff right behind his uncle and Jenny. Estrella, still out of breath from her run to save them, had fallen slightly behind.

The path that they had been herded down the day before was nothing more than a narrow trail carved out of the cliff face by generations of wild animals. Steep enough that climbers occasionally had to use hands to pull themselves up, it was hardly wide enough for one person. Uncle Pete was already climbing rapidly, his powerful hand yanking Jenny up behind him.

The river of mud was still dropping in height. It was now a race to see if they could climb far enough up the path to escape the reach of the thundering wave as it swept past.

Justin scrambled faster. He kicked his foot loose from a tangled root system that, washed free by mountain rains, was spread out across the path. He grabbed at a clump of grass as he lost his balance. He sure didn't remember this trail having so many obstacles on the way down! Uncle Pete and Jenny were now yards above him.

A sudden scream rose above the deafening roar of the oncoming torrent. Justin glanced backward. Right behind him, Estrella lay flat on her stomach, her foot caught in the root system that had just tripped him. He saw her tug frantically at the root that trapped her, sobbing with fear, but she couldn't pull free. He hesitated only a split second.

"No!" Estrella cried as she saw him turn back. "Don't stop!"

The *lahar* had almost reached them, and the heaving, churning gray-brown mass still reared yards above their heads. Already Justin felt the moisture that splashed ahead of the wave. There was no time to think.

Reaching down, Justin tugged at the root with all the force he could manage, allowing Estrella to pull her foot free. Then, with a single motion, he pulled the still-sobbing girl to her feet and pushed her ahead of him up the trail.

There was only time to take three steps. They had almost

made it. It was the very crest of the wave that Justin saw sweeping over them. He gave Estrella a powerful shove up the path, then grabbed for an overhanging branch. He managed to gulp a lungfull of air, then the *lahar* passed over his head.

It was much colder than Justin had imagined. He had forgotten that the river of mud fed from the melted snow and ice of the Andean glaciers. He was so cold that he hardly felt the branches, rocks, and other debris that battered his body.

Holding his breath and keeping his eyes squeezed shut, he clung to the branch with all his strength, fighting the relentless pressure that tried to pull him downstream.

Long seconds passed before the level of the *lahar* dropped enough that he could pull his head out of the mud. Shaking his head hard to clear the mud from his eyes, he glimpsed Estrella just beyond him, clinging to an overhanging tree as the mud flow washed her up to the waist.

He had just raised his head to search for his sister and uncle when he felt a movement under his hands. A heavy branch had slammed into the stunted juniper he clung to, tearing it away from the cliff side. Before he could grab for another hold, Justin was swept out into the icy, sticky, racing river of *lahar*.

Justin's eyes were still filmed over with mud, but he caught a brief, misty glimpse of three figures on the part of the path that was still visible. At least the other three had made it! The screams of the two girls rose above the roaring in his ears as he was carried helplessly down the valley.

Justin kicked to stay afloat, struggling wildly to keep his head out of the mud. Something nudged at his legs, then he caught sight of a branching set of antlers as a dead deer swept by him.

He no longer felt so cold. In fact, he didn't really feel *anything* anymore—not even his arms and legs. The mud oozed up over his mouth. His head felt as heavy as lead, and it seemed it would be so easy just to let himself slip down into the mud. He was so tired!

He hardly felt the bump. Lifting his head with an effort, he saw a log as long as his body floating beside him. Moving along at the same speed as he was, it seemed to be lying still. The broken branches that still extended from the log kept it from rolling. Bunching up numb, exhausted muscles, Justin grabbed for the log just as a sudden wave crashed over his head.

The wave receded, leaving Justin choking. Blinking the mud once more from his eyes, Justin gratefully draped his arms across a couple of branches and rested his weary head against the log. As long as he could hold on, he still had a chance of getting out of this.

A jolt brought his head up. The log had bumped into something large and bulky. Under the coat of sticky gray-brown, Justin made out faint black-and-white markings, then a long head. It was a Holstein cow that probably had wandered away from some highland farm and was taking a drink at the river's edge when the *lahar* struck.

Justin thought it too was dead until a low moo protested helplessly. He caught a glimpse of pleading, large brown eyes, then a sudden undertow pulled the cow below the surface of the mud. Justin held tightly to the log, fighting the pull of the undertow. The next time he looked up, the cow was gone.

As the mud flow spread down into the widening gully, the cliff top dropped until now it was no more than a high bank running along one edge of the valley. The other side of the valley now stretched out flat into a heavily forested plateau. As the *lahar* spread out across the plateau, the river slowed even further.

There seemed to be currents in the mud flow, because the log Justin clung to had begun to drift toward the high bank. Justin heard a shout and eased his head to one side. Three distant figures were racing along the edge of the gully.

He heard a deep call. "Justin! Are you all right?"

Justin raised a leaden arm in answer to the call and heard a glad shout in response. He could now make out his uncle running along the edge. With new strength, he tried to kick himself closer to the shore. There were branches and trees growing there, and he might still be able to pull himself out.

But just at that moment a new force grabbed at him with an iron grip. He felt himself being carried away from the bank as some undercurrent swung him around in a vast circle. He clung desperately to the log as it whirled around, faster and faster.

A whirlpool! he thought faintly. *I'll never get out of this!*

He had just enough time to take a deep breath before the whirlpool sucked him under the heaving, rolling surface. Clutching frantically at the broken branches of the log, he felt himself pulled down, down. He couldn't even kick against the immense weight of the icy mud that pressed him from all sides.

He couldn't feel whether his numb fingers still clung to the log. He was desperately fighting the urge to breathe when a blinding pain struck across the side of his head. A burst of fireworks exploded somewhere behind his eyelids, then everything went black.

Chapter Twelve

RESCUED OR . . . ?

From far away down a long, dark tunnel, Justin heard the murmur of voices. He knew something had happened, but he couldn't remember what. He knew he should get up . . . find the voices . . . but he was too tired to move.

The voices came nearer. This time he caught the words.

"Will he be all right, Uncle Pete?" It was the tearful voice of his sister. "He's so cold!"

"He's breathing, anyway," answered Uncle Pete heavily. Justin could hear the worry underlying the steady voice. "He needs blankets and a warm bed."

He tried to open his eyes, to tell them he was fine, but his tongue felt heavy and his eyes were glued shut. He felt something wet against his face. The weight lifted from his eyes, and he opened them slowly.

A somewhat blurry Estrella bent over him, holding a handkerchief that still dripped muddy water. As his vision slowly focused, she leaned closer. Seeing his open eyes, she cried out joyfully, "He is awake!"

Uncle Pete's face swam into view. His hazel eyes were full of concern, but the red-brown beard smiled as he asked calmly, "Justin, are you all right?"

Justin attempted a nod, but a sharp pain shot through his head as he moved, and he shut his eyes again. He tried to speak, but he couldn't seem to pry his mouth open. He felt Estrella's handkerchief again and realized it was mud that choked him.

"Don't try to get up!" Uncle Pete ordered firmly. Justin felt his uncle's big hands moving expertly over his arms and legs. He winced as Uncle Pete touched a sore spot on the side of his head.

"Doesn't look like anything is broken," Uncle Pete said at last in a relieved voice. "He'll have a good collection of scrapes and bruises, and he's got a nasty bump on the side of his head. He must have banged it against something."

Justin opened his eyes again. This time, everything stayed in focus. He turned his head slowly. He was lying on a grassy bank. The numbness was leaving his body, and he began to shiver violently.

Uncle Pete moved to tuck a jacket closer around him. Looking up, he saw that neither Uncle Pete nor the girls wore their jackets. Uncle Pete was without a shirt as well. Cautiously turning his head again, he saw his own mud-soaked jeans, shirt, and jacket stretched over a branch. Uncle Pete's mud-streaked, once-white shirt was tossed over a bush. He had obviously used it to towel Justin dry.

Estrella knelt beside Justin, her face tear-streaked. "You should not have come back for me! You could have been killed!"

The drying mud crackled on Justin's cheeks as he grinned weakly. "Look who's talking!"

A thin, smoky haze still hid the sun, but it was no longer cold. Gradually, Justin stopped shivering and began to feel warm under the blanket of jackets. He tried to sit up, and this time Uncle Pete didn't stop him. Uncle Pete helped him prop himself against a tree trunk, and he sat quietly until the world stopped turning circles around him.

He looked out over the bank. A gray-brown lake now filled the entire valley as far as he could see. He suddenly remembered the whirlpool pulling him down into darkness. "What happened?" he asked faintly, one hand on his still-aching head. "How . . . how did I get here?"

Uncle Pete picked up the jacket that had tumbled from his shoulders, and tucked it back around him. "Well, as soon as you were swept away, we got up to the top of the cliff and started running downstream. We finally saw you holding onto that log. When you waved, we knew you were alive. Then, when your log started swinging toward the bank, I climbed down, hoping to cut you off."

His expression was suddenly bleak. "I almost had you, but you swung away again and then . . . you just disappeared! We thought you were gone."

"It was a whirlpool," Justin murmured, suddenly shivering again. "But how did I get out?"

"You were under for quite some time," Uncle Pete continued. "At least it seemed like it. Then, all of a sudden you popped up again—still holding on to that log. The whirlpool must have tossed you to the surface. We couldn't tell if you were alive or not. You swung around in a wide circle. On the second time around, you came close enough for me to grab you."

Justin suddenly noticed that Uncle Pete, too, was covered with the gray, slimy mud from the waist down. "You were unconscious, but I managed to grab you before you were dragged away again. The current was so strong, I was afraid both of us would be swept downstream. But Jenny and Estrella here helped me get you up on the bank."

Jenny dropped down onto the grass beside her brother. She, too, was tear-streaked, but she was grinning as she gave him a hard hug. "You sure scared us, Justin. I can't believe we're all alive! And we've got Uncle Pete back, too!"

Uncle Pete's calm voice broke into her jubilation. "God certainly had His mighty hand around us today, kids! Let's stop and thank Him now."

The sudden snap of a breaking branch brought Justin's bowed head up with a jerk. His heart sank as three armed men quickly surrounded the little group under the tree.

Chapter Thirteen

HOMEWARD BOUND

Unlike the band of guerrillas that had held them hostage, these men were neatly dressed in complete camouflage uniforms. But their guns looked as well kept as those of the guerrillas, and they obviously knew how to use them.

Their dark eyes were cold and watchful as Uncle Pete and the girls slowly rose to their feet, their arms in the air. Justin, covered up by three jackets but dressed only in his boxer shorts, decided to stay where he was.

One of the men barked a question in Spanish, and Justin saw that Estrella looked both angry and afraid as she reluctantly answered. *Here we go again!* he thought wearily.

But just at that moment an impatient, familiar voice snapped an order in Spanish, and the three soldiers' cold frowns turned to smiles. Justin dropped his arms with a sigh of relief as Marine Lieutenant Steve Cardoza, looking as tough and competent as ever, stepped into the clearing.

"Steve!" Jenny was already running toward the broad shouldered Marine. Glancing sharply around the group, Steve looked relieved to see that they were all there. He eyed Estrella with surprise, but made no comment.

Jenny threw her arms around him with her usual enthusiasm. "We thought something had happened to you!"

Uncle Pete, too, stepped forward, drying mud crinkling on his bare chest and pants as he said, "Glad to see you made it through safely."

"And am I ever glad to see *you* all made it!" Steve said with a grin as he rumpled Jenny's hair. A small bandage ran across one side of his forehead where the guerrilla had struck him, but he was looking very fit again, and not at all as though he had hiked most of the night.

His expression was suddenly serious as he turned to stare out over the steep bank. "At first, I thought we were too late!"

"What *took* you so long?" Jenny demanded. "You should have been back *hours* ago!"

Steve dropped to the grass beside Justin and asked, "Are you okay, kid?"

When Justin nodded, he turned back to Jenny. "Well, it wasn't as easy to get help as I'd hoped. It took me several hours to find my way out to the main road in the dark. I finally located my jeep and started for Bogotá. I stopped in the nearest village and managed to wake up a store owner long enough to use his telephone. I called Mr. Bascom and asked him to get the chief of police out of bed."

He looked disgusted as he continued, "The chief of police wasn't very happy about being yanked out of bed in the middle of the night. It was dawn by the time I got to Bogotá, and the men I'd asked for still hadn't shown up."

He motioned to the soldiers, who now stood at ease, looking friendly and pleased. "I finally managed to get together a troop from the Colombian army and started back here, but when I reached the campsite and saw . . ."

He looked grim for a moment, then cleared his throat. "Well, for a moment, I didn't think I'd need any of them. Then I saw the tracks leading into the woods and realized that the guerrillas, at least, had escaped. I sent most of my men after them, hoping they'd taken you with them.

"I sent this party to check downstream. Then I saw fresh footprints running down this way along the cliff top—two sets of them fairly small."

He grinned at the two girls. "I figured that at least you two must be alive, so I headed down this way as fast as I could. And, of course, you know the rest." After a pause, he added, "Okay, now tell me *your* story."

Justin, Jenny, and Estrella all began to speak at the same time. In the end they let Uncle Pete explain what had happened since Steve escaped. Steve looked with respect at Estrella as Uncle Pete told of how she had rescued them. When Uncle Pete finished, Steve stood up.

"Well, now that we have you all safe and sound, let's get back to town. I imagine you could all use a good meal and some warm clothes, and some of you could sure use a bath!" He smiled at Justin and Uncle Pete.

Estrella and Jenny politely turned away as Justin stood up and awkwardly pulled on his mud-encrusted jeans and tennis shoes. He was stiff and sore all over and very thirsty, but the scenery no longer whirled around him when he moved. The mud that still caked his hair and face crackled with every movement, and large pieces of dry mud flaked off his jeans.

As the two girls turned around, Jenny giggled. Justin scowled at her. "What's so funny?"

Jenny's gold-brown eyes danced. "You should see yourself, Justin!" She broke into giggles. "You look like . . . like the Abominable Mudman!"

The sudden relief from the tension of the last two days was too much. Estrella started giggling, too, and Jenny was now holding her sides with helpless laughter. Uncle Pete's hearty "Ha, ha!" rang out from behind Justin, and even Steve and the soldiers were grinning broadly.

Justin looked down at the heavy, gray crust that covered even where Uncle Pete had tried to wipe him dry. He *did* look funny, he thought. The girl's giggles were contagious, and the dried mud crinkled around his mouth as he broke into a grin.

Steve interrupted the relieved laughter. "If you can walk, Justin, let's get started. It's a long walk back to the road, even if we cut across from here."

Justin cautiously took a few steps, wincing as his bruised body protested. He was sore, but he could walk. As he followed Steve away from the bank, Justin turned for one last look.

There was no sign now of the bubbling stream, nor of the evergreen forest that had carpeted the mountain valley an hour ago. A tranquil, gray-brown lake now stretched from bank to bank. Only the drift of an occasional piece of debris, and the whistling pop of an enormous air bubble coming to the surface, showed that the *lahar* was still settling.

They took the hike back to the road very slowly. Once there, Steve left the three soldiers with the army transport truck to wait for the rest of the soldiers. It was late afternoon before Justin joined the others in the lounge of the embassy guest house. A long, hot shower had washed away much of the stiffness, and with a very large meal under his belt, he felt much better.

The twins had just attempted another call to their parents when Steve walked in. To Justin's disappointment, there was still no answer at his home—not even the answering machine. His parents should be back from their camping trip by now!

Steve sat down and stretched out his legs. He, too, looked refreshed, his hair still wet from a recent shower. "That troop of soldiers just reported in. There's no sign of the guerrillas—they got completely away!"

"Good!" Estrella suddenly spoke up. Steve looked at her in surprise, and she said simply, "Well, they *were* kind to me. They were the only family I had."

Walking over to stare out the window, she added sadly, "Even if it *was* only because I could be of use to them."

"Well, I don't think it will make much difference," Uncle Pete put in. "With all our American families pulled out of the country and security tripled at the office, I don't think they'll bother Triton again."

He shook his head. "I'm afraid it may be a long time before we'll be sending married engineers and their families back to Colombia. Perhaps one day there will be true peace with the guerrillas."

"Well, it's all over for you three, anyway," Steve commented. "You are free to fly home anytime."

Jenny, curled up on the sofa beside Uncle Pete, looked over at Estrella, who still stood at the window. The long, shining curtain of hair hid her expression, but the slim shoulders drooped.

Jenny asked softly, "What about Estrella? What's going to happen to her?"

"Yeah, they can't put her in prison like those other guerrillas, can they?" Justin added anxiously. "She saved our lives!"

"No, of course they won't put her in prison," Steve assured them. "For one thing, she is only a child. And as you said, she is responsible for freeing the three of you."

"But where will she live?" Jenny asked. "Her family is gone."

"I think I may have a solution to that," Uncle Pete said. "I've got a missionary friend here in Bogotá . . ."

Justin grinned at his sister. He was beginning to think Uncle Pete had friends tucked away in every corner of the world.

"I called him," Uncle Pete continued, "and he thinks he may know of a home for her."

The sharp *ding-dong!* of the front doorbell rang through the building. Uncle Pete stood up. "That may be him now."

He hurried out of the room, and Steve went with him to unlock the door. The twins walked over to join Estrella at the window. Like all windows they had seen in Colombia, this one was heavily barred. The window looked down onto the street that ran in front of the guest house. Through the slats of the venetian blinds, they could see a car pulled up at the front steps.

Estrella turned from the window, and the three children looked shyly at each other. So much had happened since the last time they had sat there that they didn't know what to say.

Justin broke the silence. "We haven't thanked you for saving our lives, Estrella. I was wrong about you. You really were our friend all the time. You could have been killed coming back for us like that."

"I had to do it," Estrella answered simply. "It was my fault that you were in danger."

Looking at Justin, she added, "You were right about Carlos. He never did really care about me. None of them did! They just thought I'd be useful to them."

Her head drooped. "At least they gave me schooling and a place to sleep. I don't know what I will do *now.*"

Justin and Jenny were saved from answering by their uncle's booming call. "Kids, come on down here! I've got some folks here for you to meet."

The twins started for the door. Estrella hung back until Jenny grabbed her by the hand and pulled her after them. "Come on, Estrella! He means you, too!"

Justin and Jenny hurried down the wide staircase, Estrella following reluctantly behind. Justin heard his uncle's deep voice above a chatter of voices in the receiving room. Pausing in the doorway, he saw his uncle talking among a lively group of people. There was a short, bearded man, whom Justin guessed was Uncle Pete's missionary friend, and a Colombian couple perhaps a few years older than the twins' parents.

Silence fell abruptly as the four adults caught sight of the children. Justin eyed the visitors as they rose to their feet. The Colombian man was tall and thin, with curly, dark hair and a kind face. His wife was slightly plump. Something in her expression reminded Justin of his mother, and he liked her at once.

Uncle Pete stepped forward. "Kids, this is my friend, George Elinger. He is a missionary here in Bogotá. These are his friends . . ."

But he never got to finish his introduction. Justin suddenly realized that Estrella hadn't followed the twins into the room. She stood frozen in the doorway, her blue eyes wide and unbelieving as she stared at the Colombian couple.

"Doña Rosa?" Her voice was hardly above a whisper.

The Colombian lady turned toward the doorway with a jerk, astonishment on her plump face. Her dark eyes widened as she exclaimed, "Estrellita (Es-tray-yee-tu)!"

Estrella was moving now. Uncle Pete and Mr. Elinger looked at each other in bewilderment as she ran across the room and threw herself into the plump lady's arms. The tall, thin man moved close, and the room erupted into a babble of laughing and crying and Spanish chatter.

As Mr. Elinger moved away to join the excited group, Uncle Pete continued his introduction to the only two who were listening. "This is Mr. and Mrs. Gutierrez, friends of Mr. Elinger. They work with the street children here in Bogotá.

"They have no children of their own, but have a house full of teenage girls they have adopted."

He eyed his grinning niece and nephew sharply. "Why do I get the impression you know more about our visitors than I do?"

Just then, Estrella pulled the plump, dark-haired lady across the room to where the three Parkers were standing.

"This is Doña Rosa," she said unnecessarily. "Don Eduardo is her husband. You remember them, the ones I told you about? They took me in and wanted me to be their own daughter. They didn't know it was *me* they had been asked to come here to visit. But they want me to be their daughter—even though I once ran away from them!"

She shook her head in amazement. "How did you find them? *I* didn't even know where they had gone!"

Justin shrugged, still hardly able to believe this new surprise himself. "We didn't! I guess God must have found them for you."

Doña Rosa obviously didn't understand a word of what was being said, but she was smiling broadly. Before Justin could move, she stepped forward and kissed him heartily on both cheeks. Then she kissed Jenny, bursting into a chatter of Spanish.

Estrella laughed at their astonished expressions. "She is thanking you for finding me—the Colombian way!"

It was a long time before all the chatter died away. But at last, Mr. Elinger and the Gutierrezes stepped out into the big entryway. Estrella hesitated as Doña Rosa waved a hand and called to her in Spanish.

Turning to the twins, she explained, "They want me to go with them tonight."

She added uncertainly, "I would like to see my new home, but I do not wish to leave you, my friends. Do you mind?"

"Of course not!" Justin assured.

Jenny added, "You go ahead, Estrella. You've probably got lots to talk about. We *will* see you again, won't we?"

"I will not let you go without saying good-bye," Estrella promised. After a quick hug, she was gone.

The guest house seemed strangely quiet with Estrella gone. "I sure wish Mom and Dad would answer the phone!" Justin told Jenny for the third time as he looked with little interest through an outdated *Popular Mechanics* magazine.

Neither paid any attention to the sound of footsteps in the hall outside the lounge. A moment later, Steve poked his head around the door and announced, "Some people here to see you, kids!"

The door swung open, and the twins jumped to their feet, the magazine falling unnoticed to the floor. "Mom! Dad!" they yelled together.

It was several minutes before Justin or Jenny even noticed Mr. Bascom standing patiently by the door. Mr. Parker was finally able to explain. "We got home from our camping trip last night and called the embassy here right away. We were . . . well, to put it mildly, we were upset when we heard you were missing. We caught the first flight to Bogotá."

He paused, and Mrs. Parker went on. "Mr. Bascom had given us his number to call when we arrived. By the time we got here, he had heard from Steve that you were all safe. We called him from the airport, and he picked us up and brought us here."

A short time later, Justin and Jenny were squeezed in between their parents on the sofa. Mrs. Parker gasped in horror as they poured out the adventures of the last two weeks; Uncle Pete occasionally added a comment in his deep voice. Already, the fear and anger and hurt of the last hours were fading into exciting memories.

It was very late before any of the Parkers got to sleep that night, but they were all up and at the airport early the next morning. Mr. Bascom had booked them on the first flight back to Seattle, with a brief stop at Miami. This time, Justin appreciated the feeling of security as he watched the soldiers make their rounds of the airport and search through every inch of their bags.

Estrella and her new parents arrived at the airport just in time to see them off. Her delicate features were alive with happiness as she told the twins, "I love my new home and Mamá Rosa and Papá Eduardo. Remember that I told you they were moving to find a new job? It was then that they met this man, George Elinger. He was helping the *gamines,* the street children. Now they work with him."

She added with a smile, "There are four other girls living with us. They are very nice. Now I have sisters! But I will not forget that you two were my first true friends. You have taught me much. This time I will listen when Doña Rosa talks to me about God and forgiveness."

Turning to Justin, she said shyly, "Thank you for finding out about my father. Steve told me that it was your idea. Now I can remember him with love."

"Justin! Jenny!" the twins' father called out, motioning impatiently. The loudspeaker had ordered the passengers to pass through the final checkpoint. Estrella threw her arms around Justin and Jenny and hugged them fiercely.

"I'll never forget you—never!" she said passionately. She turned without another word and was gone.

The final call came to board Flight 908 for Miami. Picking up his briefcase as the line of passengers began filing down the long, narrow corridor that connected the waiting area to the Avianca 747, Uncle Pete looked down at the twins.

"Well, kids, our trip is about over. I guess the rest of this summer is going to seem pretty quiet."

"I'm not so sure about that," Mr. Parker interrupted as he handed over their tickets. "I've got some plans of my own!"

He grinned down at his son and daughter. "Remember that I told you we'd finished that Boeing project earlier than I expected? Well, I think it's time for a real family vacation. I've had an invitation to visit a Native-American friend of mine on a reservation in Montana. Are you interested?"

The sudden excitement on their faces was all the answer he needed. He turned to his brother as they filed onto the big plane.

"Speaking of that friend of mine, do you think you'd have time for a brief stop in Montana, too? There are some strange things going on out there with that mineral prospecting operation I told you about. . . ."

Justin's ears pricked up immediately. As he slung his handbag into the overhead rack and found a seat beside his father, he had a sudden feeling that his summer adventures weren't yet over.

Jenny was sandwiched between Uncle Pete and Mrs. Parker across the aisle. She was busily chattering to her mother as though she hadn't seen her in months. As the big jet lifted from the runway, Mr. Parker looked down at his son.

"You've gone through some frightening times in the last couple of weeks, Justin," he commented. His blue-green eyes that were so like Justin's twinkled as he continued. "Smugglers. Drug dealers. Guerrillas. I'll bet you kind of wish now that you'd settled for that dull summer vacation you were expecting."

"It *was* pretty scary sometimes," Justin admitted. "But I'm glad I came."

He thought of Estrella, her blue eyes sparkling with happiness as he had last seen her; of the Quechua boy in the Bolivian highlands who had become their friend; of a young pilot who had learned to pray instead of hate. They had all touched his life, and he and Jenny had touched theirs, and now nothing would ever be the same.

He shook his head vigorously. "Yeah, I'm glad I came. I wouldn't have missed these last two weeks for anything!"